ABOUT ISLAND PRESS

Island Press is the only nonprofit organization in the United States whose principal purpose is the publication of books on environmental issues and natural resource management. We provide solutions-oriented information to professionals, public officials, business and community leaders, and concerned citizens who are shaping responses to environmental problems.

In 2003, Island Press celebrates its nineteenth anniversary as the leading provider of timely and practical books that take a multidisciplinary approach to critical environmental concerns. Our growing list of titles reflects our commitment to bringing the best of an expanding body of literature to the environmental community throughout North America and the world.

Support for Island Press is provided by The Nathan Cummings Foundation, Geraldine R. Dodge Foundation, Doris Duke Charitable Foundation, Educational Foundation of America, The Charles Engelhard Foundation, The Ford Foundation, The George Gund Foundation, The Vira I. Heinz Endowment, The William and Flora Hewlett Foundation, Henry Luce Foundation, The John D. and Catherine T. MacArthur Foundation, The Andrew W. Mellon Foundation, The Moriah Fund, The Curtis and Edith Munson Foundation, National Fish and Wildlife Foundation, The New-Land Foundation, Oak Foundation, The Overbrook Foundation, The David and Lucile Packard Foundation, The Pew Charitable Trusts, The Rockefeller Foundation, The Winslow Foundation, and other generous donors.

The opinions expressed in this book are those of the author and do not necessarily reflect the views of these foundations.

THE NATIONAL WILDLIFE REFUGES

Coordinating a Conservation System through Law

ROBERT L. FISCHMAN

ISLAND PRESS

WASHINGTON · COVELO · LONDON

ISLAND PRESS is a trademark of The Center for Resource Economics.

Library of Congress Cataloging-in-Publication Data
Fischman, Robert, 1962–
    The national wildlife refuges : coordinating a conservation system
  through law / Robert L. Fischman.
     p.   cm.
    Includes bibliographical references (p.).
    ISBN 1-55963-990-3 (hardcover : alk. paper) — ISBN 1-55963-991-1 (pbk. : alk. paper)
     1. Widlife refuges—United States.   2. Public lands—United States—Management.
   3. Conservation of natural resources—United States.   I. Title.
   QL84.2.F55 2003
   333.95'16'0973—dc21   2003006688

British Cataloguing-in-Publication Data available

Printed on recycled, acid-free paper ♻

Book design: Teresa Bonner
Manufactured in the United States of America
09 08 07 06 05 04 03 10 9 8 7 6 5 4 3 2 1

I dedicate this book to my parents, Noah and Barbara Fischman.

CONTENTS

PREFACE AND ACKNOWLEDGMENTS

The National Wildlife Refuge System has been the unappreciated, quiet, middle child in the family of federal public lands. Neither the oldest nor the youngest, the largest nor the smallest, the most protected nor the least restricted, the Refuge System has languished at the periphery of public consciousness and legal scrutiny of public lands. With a few exceptions, such as the Arctic National Wildlife Refuge, which plays a prominent role in the public debate over the balance between energy development and wilderness protection, the refuges have sidestepped the dramatic controversies that have dogged other land systems: logging and road-building in the national forests, grazing intensity and fees on Bureau of Land Management lands, and snowmobile and personal watercraft use in national parks.

Unlike the National Park System, the Refuge System holds few of the signal icons of our natural heritage. It lacks the mammoth scale of the Bureau of Land Management System. No popular mascot like Smokey Bear represents the Refuge System. The refuges receive smaller appropriations per acre managed than any other federal public land system.

Yet, in its unobtrusive way, the Refuge System offers important lessons for those willing to explore the array of principles and forces that guide its operation. I have written this book to aid readers in that exploration. My aim is to engage a broad audience of resource managers, policy-makers, environmental activists, conservation biologists, refuge users, students, scholars, and public land lawyers.

The refuges contain a wider variety of ecosystem types than any of the other federal land systems and constitute a network of property for the maintenance and restoration of biological diversity. With some 550 national wildlife refuges covering 95 million acres of habitat as diverse as the North American continent has to offer, the Refuge System deserves a book-length, critical treatment of its resource management regime. After all, the refuges are the United States' principal reserves for nature protection.

Therefore, one important purpose of this book is to provide readers with a comprehensive explanation of the special legal authorities and administrative policies that govern management of the national wildlife refuges. Readers with an interest in local refuge activities or National Wildlife Refuge System policy will find a reference source in these pages. This book is a practical description and analysis of the new law of Refuge System management.

The law governing conservation of the National Wildlife Refuge System has undergone dramatic change in the past five years. Once subject only to the most vague of congressional mandates, the System now finds itself struggling to implement a comprehensive statute containing use preferences, binding substantive management criteria, and planning requirements. The 1997 National Wildlife Refuge System Improvement Act is the most recent comprehensive congressional charter, or "organic" legislation, for a public land system. Enacted with remarkably strong bipartisan support in Congress, the Improvement Act reveals congressional consensus on a broad array of ubiquitous public land management issues. It is the latest installment in the organic legislation narrative of steadily rising expectations and statutory detail.

This book offers an extended analysis of the 1997 Refuge Improvement Act, the first major new statute governing a system of federal public lands enacted since the 1970s. The Improvement Act introduces new statutory tools to achieve the Refuge System's conservation mission. These new tools include substantive management criteria to preserve ecological integrity, to respond to external threats to refuge environments, and to fulfill a conservation trust. This book also parses the Fish and Wildlife Service's implementing policies and regulations that translate the congressional mandates into operational instructions. Anyone seeking to influence or practice refuge management may use this book as a guide to the process and standards.

Along the way, I hope to convince readers that the Refuge System is an important model for sustainable resource management in other public lands systems. Readers not involved with refuges, but nonetheless concerned about ecological protection, will find a critical analysis of a conservation model that is increasingly prevalent around the world. This book illustrates how the Refuge System's "dominant use" regime can support sustainable development in a variety of settings. The recent evolution of conservation law in the Refuge System parallels larger trends in public land management and ecological protection. It is the broad applicability of the System's resource management principles rather than its special claim to unique status that makes the refuges most worthy of close scrutiny. Like the other public land systems, the refuges grapple with fragmented ownership and control of resources, local economic interests that benefit from activities that degrade the environment, and uncertain measures of ecological health. Like the other public land agencies, the Fish and Wildlife Service mediates between the aspirations of law and implementation on the ground. The Refuge System's ecological management criteria, the conflicts between primary and subsidiary uses, and the tension between site-specific standards and uniform national goals all offer important lessons for environmental governance generally.

This book explains the role and limitations of organic legislation as a tool for organizing a disparate collection of reserves into a larger system. Moreover, it reveals the underlying dynamic tensions that shape public land systems, with special emphasis on the rivalry between the executive and legislative branches and on the conflicts between national goals and local use preferences. I situate my analysis of and proposals relating to the National Wildlife Refuge System within a broader discussion relevant to a policy audience. The challenges of congressional management of agencies, legislative design, and presidential leadership cut across many areas of public affairs. I emphasize those aspects of history, legislation, regulation, and implementation that hold the greatest potential for cross fertilizing resource management of other public land systems. In this respect, I am less concerned about unique or peculiar features of the Refuge System and more interested in its attributes that hold lessons germane to land conservation in general.

References and Citations

Because this book serves as both a reference source and a readable analysis of conservation management in the Refuge System, I have included citations but compromised on their frequency and detail. The parenthetical references are brief. However, they are sufficient to permit readers seeking more information to find the relevant materials.

When discussing primary materials, such as statutes and regulations, I have been especially careful to guide readers to the legal sources. Three statutes are so central to this book that I have included their full text in appendix B. I provide complete citations to all other statutes in the text and exclude them from the References Cited section. I also provide complete citations to regulations and other materials found in the *Federal Register*. Where complete citations to primary sources are short, such as for the *Congressional Record* or the U.S. Fish and Wildlife Service *Manual*, I use them for the parenthetical references in the text. All other parenthetical citations refer to the sources described in References Cited.

Acknowledgments

Several institutions supported my research for this book. First and fore-most, Indiana University School of Law–Bloomington provided an intel-lectually nurturing environment, sabbatical leave, a fellowship, and reg-ular summer research grants for my work. It continues to be my academic home and a stimulating setting in which to consider legal, policy, and en-vironmental ideas. In particular, I thank my colleagues and deans Fred Aman, John Applegate, and Lauren Robel for their decisions and advice supporting my writing. Sharon Nejfelt provided excellent secretarial services.

Dean Anthony Kronman generously facilitated my work in 2001, when I spent my sabbatical as a senior research scholar at the Yale Law School. My 2000 visit to Vermont Law School would not have happened with-out the encouragement of Professors Celia Campbell-Mohn, Patrick Par-enteau, Karin Sheldon, and Stephanie Willbanks. They, and the staff of the Environmental Law Center (especially Tepin Johnson), were enor-mously welcoming and helpful to my study of the Refuge System.

The dedicated professionals at the U.S. Fish and Wildlife Service strive to practice stewardship under increasingly difficult conditions. We are all indebted to them for their countless unsung efforts in conserving national wildlife refuges. In addition to several Service and Interior Department officials who wish to remain anonymous, Dan Ashe and Sean Furniss were particularly helpful and unstinting in sharing their time and experience with me. I also owe thanks to Thomas Hawkins and Barbara Wyman.

Several experts from around the country reviewed portions of my work and graciously offered constructive comments. I owe particular thanks to Professors Dale Goble, Robert Keiter, and John Leshy for their critical perspectives. Veteran natural resource law attorneys Michael McCloskey and Jerome Muys took time from their busy schedules to recall the legal developments of the 1960s. Cheryl Oakes, the librarian and archivist for the Forest History Society, tracked down for me many key documents in the evolution of the term "organic" legislation. William Reffalt generously shared his historical research.

Some of the coverage in this book duplicates the topics I discuss in an article published in the *Ecology Law Quarterly* (Fischman 2002). I am grateful to that journal and the University of California for publishing my work and permitting me to reproduce portions of it in this book. The ar-ticle includes some greater detail and more legal references for the ma-terial covered in chapters 3 through 10 of this book. I have written this book to be less academic and more practical for an audience that may not have legal training. In addition to the broader coverage, this book contains more step-by-step information on planning and procedures that afford the public opportunities to participate in refuge management.

Students played important roles in the development of this book. My research assistants could not have served with greater alacrity, intelligence, and precision. They kept me motivated and on track. Law students Brent Bolin, Sasha Engle, Matt Gernand, Elizabeth Holgate, Jeffrey Hyman, Brandon Marx, Ben Mills, Kara Reagan, and Jason Smith offered invaluable research help. An Indiana University School of Public and Environmental Affairs student, Eloise Canfield, helped spark my interest in the 1997 Refuge Improvement Act with an excellent seminar paper. Linda Merola and Matt Wilshire, editors of the *Ecology Law Quarterly*, suggested many improvements to the article from which several chapters of this book derive.

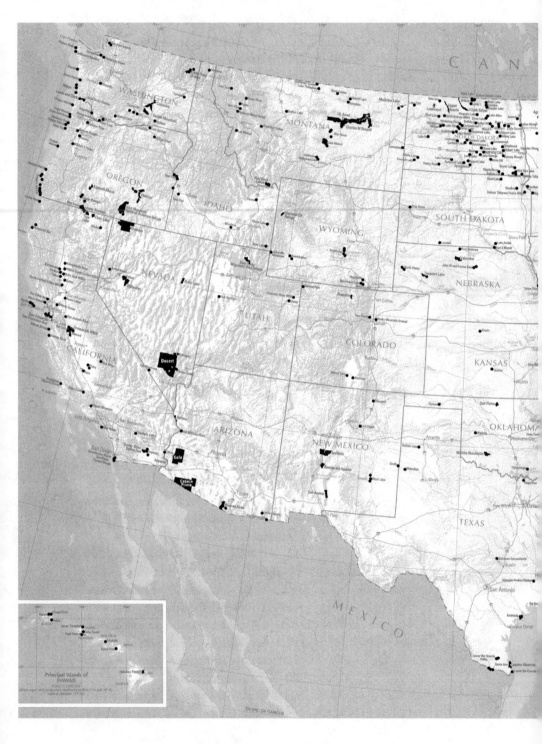

National Wildlife Refuge System (Western Half of the Contiguous States).
Source: National Atlas of the United States of America.

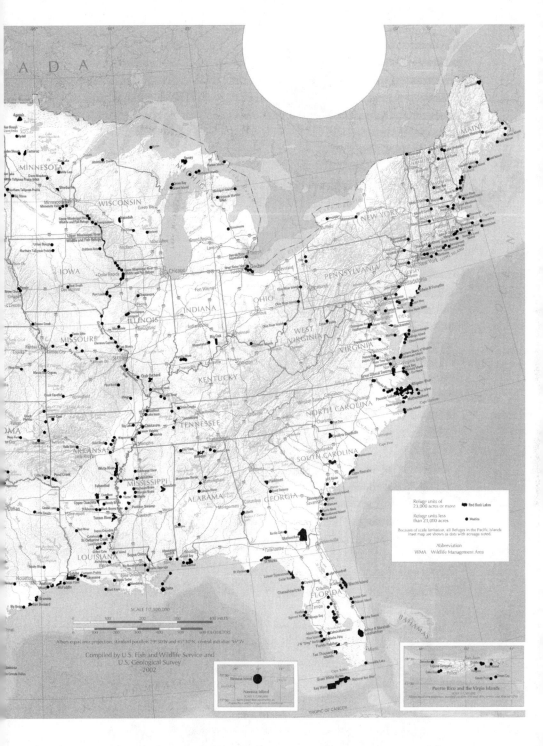

National Wildlife Refuge System (Eastern Hàlf of the Contiguous States and Caribbean). Source: National Atlas of the United States of America.

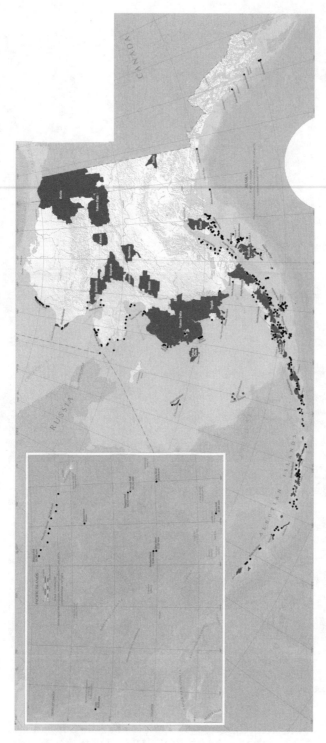

National Wildlife Refuge System (Alaska and Pacific Ocean Units). Source: National Atlas of the United States of America.

1 | *Introduction*

Imagine a network of federal lands and waters designed to sustain healthy ecosystems. Resource managers, taking advantage of appropriate opportunities, would restore degraded habitat and enhance the diversity of wildlife. The network would comprise hundreds of individual units, administered in a coordinated fashion to achieve large-scale goals such as supporting migratory animals and maintaining regional variations in biodiversity. It would facilitate connections between habitats to allow species to escape disturbance and disease, and to adapt to climate change. Such a system would serve as a refuge for animals and plants, especially those imperiled by activities on private lands. However, it would permit a wide range of other uses that do not interfere with the central conservation mission of the system. These compatible uses would build a form of sustainable development that allows people to prosper and enjoy the public lands without impairing living resources for future generations. This is the aspiration for the National Wildlife Refuge System.

Now, consider the condition of the actual national wildlife refuges. They are created under a hodgepodge of statutes, presidential orders, or administration actions that often establish location-specific variations on a nature protection theme. These public lands are either acquired or reserved from the existing public estate. The refuges are a jumble of sizes, shapes, and types. The bulk of the 95 million acre Refuge System comprises approximately 550 named national wildlife refuges. However, 50 coordination areas and thousands of waterfowl production areas also contribute to the System. The refuges range from the immense 19.3 million acre Arctic National Wildlife Refuge to small, acre-sized units near urban areas on the Atlantic coast. Every state has at least one national wildliferefuge.

The U.S. Fish and Wildlife Service (FWS, or Service) manages the refuges under austere budgets and nearly constant pressure for economic development, and with little political clout. Sometimes the FWS shares refuge control with states, other federal agencies, mineral rights holders, and landowners who have ceded only conservation easements to the federal government. Most refuges are far from an uncontaminated, pristine wilderness condition. Prior, adjacent, and upstream uses shape the circumstances and limit the conservation potential of individual refuges. Incompatible activities persist within the refuges themselves.

This book discusses the law that governs management of the national wildlife refuges. Along with each refuge's peculiar history, context, and physical characteristics, the law determines how well the FWS can close the gap between current circumstance and idealized aspiration. In an effort to improve coordination and conservation across the hundreds of refuges, Congress enacted the 1997 Refuge Improvement Act. The statute is the most recent legislative charter seeking to sew together public land units into a coherent, organized system of nature protection. This type of law, called organic legislation, has come to play a central role in American conservation. The 1997 Refuge Improvement Act, analyzed in part two of this book, sets out a comprehensive set of rules for resolving disputes and administering refuges. Specifically, the 1997 statute

1. defines a conservation mission for the Refuge System;
2. establishes a hierarchy of refuge use priorities;
3. requires comprehensive conservation plans for each refuge unit; and
4. binds the Service to a number of substantive criteria to ensure that the cumulative effects of refuge management decisions will not impair the System mission.

Not since the 1970s had Congress so thoroughly addressed the mission and management of a public land system. In doing so, Congress restocked the legislative toolbox for organic legislation. Accounting for advancements in science, the Improvement Act emphasizes the importance of conservation biology. For instance, one of the innovative, substantive management criteria requires the Service to ensure that refuges maintain "biological integrity, diversity, and environmental health" (1997 Improvement Act, § 5(a)(4)(B)).

The 1997 law frames a model for nature protection at a time when governments around the world are searching for better approaches to conservation. Dominant conservation use management through organic legislation to achieve sustainable development is the method by which the Refuge System seeks to pull together its disparate units into something more than the sum of its parts. Sustainable development, famously defined by the 1987 Brundtland Commission report as "meeting the needs of the present without compromising the ability of future generations to meet their own needs" (World Commission on Environment and Development 1987, 8), requires the maintenance of working ecosystems. The Refuge System's compatibility principle recognizes this fundamental dependence in limiting uses to those that do not impair the fulfillment of the System mission. That mission is to sustain a network of lands and waters for the conservation of plants, animals, and habitat, for the "benefit of present and future generations of Americans" (1997 Improvement Act, § 4). The compatibility principle invites a wide range of uses for refuges, subject to the limitation that they do not tear the sustaining fabric of nature.

The effectiveness of the Refuge System's compatibility criterion will determine how useful it might be to other governmental efforts (including local efforts to control private land use) in promoting sustainable development. Late in its tenure, the Clinton administration attempted to apply this compatibility approach to sustainable development in revising the core planning regulations for national forests. The Clinton regulations established nonimpairment of ecological sustainability as a fundamental, bottom line for national forest management. The relative ease with which the subsequent Bush administration brushed aside those regulations underscores the importance of the congressional commitment to compatibility in the Improvement Act. The Refuge System, meanwhile, continues to gain experience applying the compatibility principle, which is a polestar for international conservation programs, such as the Biosphere Reserve System.

Of all the federal public land systems, the National Wildlife Refuge System provides particularly revealing insights into the challenges and opportunities of conservation law. One reason for this is that the Refuge System occupies the middle of the permissible uses continuum of the federal public land systems. The law governing refuge management permits a wide range of activities, subject to the condition that they are compatible with the dominant use of conservation. So, for instance, recreation, oil and gas development, and grazing generally may occur in the Refuge System only to the extent that they are compatible with the health of animal and plant populations. This contrasts with multiple use management, which does not favor one type of use over another, and exclusive use management, which permits no other use but a single purpose.

The trend in public land management is away from the extremes of multiple and exclusive use regimes and toward more complex systems with hierarchies of dominant and subservient uses. Overseas, reforms in national public land laws have, for example, split the New Zealand multiple use forest lands into two dominant use regimes, one for commercial forestry and one for conservation. Nature preserve management in the developing world increasingly invites local communities to engage in compatible commercial activities, such as ecotourism and renewable resource extraction.

In the United States, exclusive use systems, whether military reservations or preservation enclaves, increasingly invite secondary, compatible uses. Multiple use systems, whether public forest lands or rangelands, increasingly condition each possible use on its ability to meet certain substantive criteria. In other words, public land management systems are becoming more like the National Wildlife Refuge System. Therefore, a better understanding of the history and law of the Refuge System will help guide us through the pitfalls and potential of future reform for other lands.

The Forces Shaping Refuge Management

Law is the principal tool we employ to resolve conflicts over land use. A legal examination of the national wildlife refuges uncovers the dynamic forces that shape our decisions about resource management. Legal developments highlight the constant presence of three important tensions that influence public resource management.

First, in the rivalry between the president and Congress, the executive branch has played the leadership role in the sphere of refuge management. Though the Constitution places power over public property in Congress, the presidents regularly pioneered key innovations in public land law, at least as early as Jefferson's Louisiana Purchase. The national wildlife refuges, more than any other system of public lands with the sole exception of the national monuments, bear the imprint of strong executive action. Repeatedly, legislation has merely endorsed and elaborated on prior executive initiatives. Examples abound, from the initial establishment of early wildlife conservation areas; through the creation of the FWS, the development of the compatibility standard, and the delineation of the hierarchy of dominant uses; to the recent inclusion of plant conservation in the mission of the System.

Second, the resolution of refuge management disputes reflects the ongoing effort to balance the conservation impetus behind the Refuge System with the desire to satisfy local interests in using public lands. This tension is particularly evident in attempts to reconcile recreation with wildlife protection. For example, the hunting community has always been an important constituency of the Refuge System, especially after the 1934 Duck Stamp Act compelled hunters to contribute to a fund for purchasing refuge lands. From the steady erosion of the old "inviolate sanctuary" limitation on hunting, to the more recent delineation of preferred uses on refuges, hunters have exerted their influence to prevent the Refuge System's brand of conservation from merging with the Park Service philosophy, which bans hunting in most national parks. Hunters have largely succeeded in this effort. In contrast, conflicts between conservation and other forms of recreation, such as the use of motorboats and recreational vehicles, have not been resolved so decisively. The tension between conservation goals and other refuge uses continues to spur conflict, now mediated through the discourse of compatibility and funding. Providing local people with decent livelihoods while sustaining the natural integrity that undergirds ecological services and economic goods is the same central challenge faced by sustainable development.

Third, the refuge law manifests a continual struggle to counteract the centrifugal, divergent push of unit establishment mandates with the centripetal, coordinating pull of systemic management. Organic legislation struggles to provide a coherent focus for disparate refuges to make the Refuge System greater than the sum of its parts. This tension is particularly acute for dominant use public land systems, such as the national wildlife refuges or the national parks. Each dominant use system comprises a collection of units created with their own, often individually tailored, legal charters. In 1966, Congress consolidated refuges into a conservation system closed to all uses except those found to be compatible with establishment purposes. However, the 1966 law failed to provide sufficient legal mechanisms to meet modern standards of conservation and coordination. The difference between the 1966 statute and the 1997 Improvement Act highlights the intervening development of public land law's concept of organic legislation. This book uncovers the evolution and meaning of organic legislation as a means of exploring the form and substance of the new refuge resource management regime. A close examination of national wildlife refuge law cautions that organic legislation is no panacea for public land systems with divergent individual unit establishment mandates. Continued leadership from the executive branch is required for the Refuge System to fulfill its promise as a conservation network restoring and maintaining ecological integrity.

Road Map to This Book

Though dedicated students of refuge management may read this book cover to cover, I expect that many readers will skip to the particular chapters addressing their interests. Therefore, I provide this road map to aid readers in understanding how their selected chapters fit into the book as a whole. Over the span of three parts, this book proceeds from more general, conceptual discussions to more applied, detailed topics. Part one of the book introduces and examines public land law and the Refuge System. Part two consists of a close analysis of the 1997 Refuge Improvement Act and its implementing policies. Part three covers specific issues that apply only to certain refuges.

Part One

Part one of the book lays the foundation essential for understanding the 1997 Refuge Improvement Act and refuge management. Chapter 2 begins with a primer of public land law and a comparison of the major public land systems. This establishes the context for a detailed description of the crazy-quilt Refuge System, with its diverse classification of units and management mandates. Chapter 3 describes the legal history of the Refuge System. Supplemented with the chronology of Refuge System development in appendix A, this chapter shows how the key management practices evolved through administrative innovation, executive fiat, and congressional compromise. Today, starting from scratch, no sensible designer would create a nature protection system resembling refuge administration. Like the taxonomy of the refuges themselves, the management mandates of the Service can be best understood as the gradual accretion of decisions over time. Appendix B supplements the legal history by providing the text of the key statutes that remain important to contemporary Refuge System management.

Chapter 4 explores a question at the heart of modern public land law: what is an "organic" act? The evolution in meaning of "organic act," one of the few specialized terms in the resource management field of environmental law, highlights the changing expectations of lawyers and the public toward conservation. When Congress explicitly justified its 1997 enactment of the Improvement Act on the need for Refuge System organic legislation, it implicitly affirmed the trends, discussed in this chapter, toward greater statutory detail and stricter mandates in resource management. The hallmarks of modern organic legislation, which I find to be purpose statements, designated uses, comprehensive planning, substantive management criteria, and public participation, provide a framework for part two's analysis of the 1997 Act. These five dimensions of systemic mandates also offer indicia for comparing the Refuge System's dominant use regime with other public land systems.

Part Two

Part two of this book, containing chapters five through nine, focuses on the key statute that has transformed the Refuge System from a backwater into a leading edge of conservation and sustainable development law. Viewing the 1997 Improvement Act as a paragon of organic legislation allows us to see its key features and to understand it as a manifestation of larger trends in public land law. The 1997 Improvement Act displays the hallmarks of modern organic legislation and updates our expectations of what Congress will specify in a public land system management charter. Appendix B includes the full text of the 1997 Act. The five chapters in part two correspond to the five hallmarks of organic legislation discussed in chapter 4. They analyze both the statutory provisions as well as the subsequent FWS policies designed to implement the new legislation.

Chapter 5 deals with the 1997 Act's purpose statement. The 1997 definition of the conservation mission of the System will help sew together a collection of land units created over a century under dozens of different authorities. The purpose of conservation both consolidates the existing strengths of the Refuge System and broadens the extent of ecological protection by including plants for their own sake. The Refuge System's updated purpose reflects the larger trend in resource management toward ecosystem sustainability. This chapter deals with several key elements of the conservation purpose, including the inclusion of plants, the role of science, and the meaning of "healthy populations."

Chapter 6 discusses the designated uses hallmark of organic legislation. In creating a tiered preference system, the Improvement Act manifests the vitality of the dominant use regime in modern conservation management. But, by placing individual refuge purposes at the apex of the dominant use hierarchy, Congress limited the ability of the 1997 Act to serve as a unifying force to manage refuges as a single, large system. The designated uses also display the continued influence of hunters and anglers in the unique subdominant category of wildlife-dependent uses.

Chapter 7 sketches the comprehensive planning provisions of the Improvement Act. Comprehensive planning comes late to the Refuge System, and it opens important new avenues for public participation and conservation strategies. However, the Improvement Act does not plow new ground in the planning hallmark. Instead, it mostly consolidates existing practices as required by other public land systems.

In addition to the standards for management established in the comprehensive conservation plans, there are also statutory criteria that bind agency administration of refuge resources. A substantive management criterion is a mandate to meet a statutory objective. The objective operates to limit resource management discretion. A specific management action, even if consistent with a plan, may still run afoul of the Improvement Act if it violates a substantive management criterion. Therefore, along with the planning mandate that will apply them, the substantive management criteria will effect the greatest changes in Refuge System administration. Chapter 8 analyzes the five key criteria establishing the minimum standards the Service must meet in performing refuge management: use compatibility; biological integrity, diversity, and environmental health maintenance; water rights acquisition; biological monitoring; and conservation stewardship. Although these criteria help shape plans, they apply to refuge activities irrespective of the actual plans. The criteria are also important because they will be footholds for litigation over management of the System. Given the tradition of judicial deference to the proprietary discretion of federal land management agencies, these substantive standards are crucial in spurring courts to review federal resource management decisions.

The Service implements the 1997 Improvement Act's substantive criteria through revisions to the FWS *Manual*. The most innovative conservation guidelines to emerge from the Improvement Act have been the Service's policy implementing both the compatibility and the biological integrity, diversity, and environmental health criteria. In particular, the policy provisions prohibiting habitat fragmentation and requiring managers to respond to external threats to refuges now stand at the forefront of protective public land administration.

The compatibility standard is a codification of the principle that has long guided dominant use in the System. However, the Improvement Act now requires refuge managers to provide written documentation that approved uses are compatible with refuge goals. Also, the Service must now periodically reevaluate compatibility determinations and explain them in the context of each refuge comprehensive conservation plan.

The most stunning substantive management criterion in the 1997 Act is the requirement to ensure maintenance of biological integrity, diversity, and environmental health. This is far and away the most ecologically informed organic mandate for any U.S. public land system. Along with the System purpose and compatibility standard, this criterion puts the power of law behind the ideas of conservation biology. The mandate for biological integrity, diversity, and environmental health is the strongest counterweight to the pervasive preference for wildlife-dependent recreation in the Improvement Act.

The duty to acquire water rights is the only affirmative mandate of its kind in U.S. organic legislation. Upstream water use outside of the refuge boundaries exacerbates the difficulties many refuges encounter in maintaining adequate water levels in lakes and flows in rivers. Therefore, this provision supports the Service's commitment to abate external threats.

The biological monitoring criterion provides a statutory requirement for the essential feedback component of adaptive management. Monitoring will generate data to help determine compatibility and revise comprehensive plans.

Finally, the affirmative conservation stewardship criterion looks to the future, when the System will face problems not specifically addressed in the current law. Although it may first be used as a shield by the Service to defend protective actions, it may ultimately be wielded as a sword to advance the Service's restoration mission, and the substantive management criterion to maintain biological integrity, diversity, and environmental health. This has been the implementation history of the analogous affirmative conservation mandate in the Endangered Species Act (Ruhl 1995).

Chapter 9 deals with the fifth hallmark of organic legislation, public participation, which is weakly advanced by the Improvement Act. The chapter provides a guide to Service decision-making processes, and marks the places where citizens can most effectively participate and influence the Service. It highlights the processes by which the Service develops its policies, comprehensive conservation plans, compatibility determinations, and step-down management plans. Though citizen suits and notice and comment procedures for adopting policy are important aspects of current refuge law, they are not (with the exception of rulemaking for compatibility) recognized or required by the act. The Service's notice and comment approach to revising the *Manual* is a significant implementation improvement. However, to engage the public more actively, the Service will have to move further beyond the required terms of the Improvement Act and experiment with innovative administrative tools to facilitate avenues of collaboration and appeal.

Part Three

Though its provisions are central to refuge management, the Improvement Act does not apply where it conflicts with individual refuge purposes. The supremacy of the individual units tends to resist well-intentioned efforts to put the System on track for comprehensive reform. Part three of this book, containing chapters 10 through 12, examines the specialized laws and documents that create somewhat different management regimes for different refuges.

Chapter 10 describes the purposes set out in the various sources that create individual Refuge System units and authorize acquisition of land. These so-called establishment purposes for refuges range from narrow missions, such as providing habitat for a single species, to broad goals, such as sustaining waterfowl migrations. The diverse management mandates of individual refuge units create the preeminent challenge for organic, systemic legislation.

Sources of establishment purposes include statutes, presidential orders, and administrative materials (collectively, "establishment documents" or "establishment instruments"). Establishment documents vary considerably in their degree of specificity. Although many refuges were established by committee, administrative, or executive directive, Congress has, nonetheless, shown remarkable deference to the purposes in the establishment documents. Statutes attempting to provide comprehensive authority and management requirements for the Refuge System explicitly limit their application to circumstances where they do not conflict with the particular purposes established for individual refuges. Though this is also the case for the National Park System, the other major federal public land system in which establishment mandates are important, it is more surprising for the Refuge System. Whereas all of the establishment mandates limiting the operation of the systemic, organic mandate in the National Park System are themselves statutes, the establishment mandates for many units of the Refuge System derive from nonlegislative sources, such as public land orders. Even though establishment mandates do not figure prominently in the national forests and Bureau of Land Management (BLM) lands, special unit designations containing specialized purposes do exist and are increasing.

Chapter 11 discusses the special rules governing refuge resource management in Alaska. The chapter begins with a discussion of subsistence uses, which occur only in Alaskan refuges. It then describes the ways in which the law loosens normal Service control over refuges for certain corporate lands selected under the Alaska Native Claims Settlement Act of 1971. Finally, the chapter covers the contentious debate over the Arctic National Wildlife Refuge, which has unique statutory provisions requiring congressional action before oil and gas may be developed. Though in a category by itself, the struggle over Arctic refuge management illustrates the conflicts between commodity production on the one hand, and wilderness and wildlife protection on the other.

Outside of Alaska, federal law limits refuge oil and gas development to special circumstances. Chapter 12 discusses the two types of petroleum production in refuges. First, some refuges overlie federal oil and gas reserves and are thus subject to the federal government's leasing program for fuel minerals. Generally, drilling of federally owned oil under refuges occurs only if a lease predates reservation of the refuge or if it is necessary to protect the federal property interest in a hydrocarbon pool that another driller is draining. Second, acquired refuges sometimes overlie privately owned oil and gas deposits. A different set of legal and management issues arises in this "split estate" setting.

Conclusion

Finally, chapter 13 of this book concludes with some observations about how well Refuge System law resolves the three historic tensions and achieves modern conservation goals. It begins with an evaluation of the 1997 Improvement Act's response to the persistence of incompatible refuge uses. The chapter then considers the System as a model for future public land conservation and sustainable development. The appendices at the end of the book provide a portable reference of acronyms and abbreviations, Refuge System history, key statutory provisions, and the units composing the Refuge System.

Though the Improvement Act and the Service's new *Manual* policies look great on paper, serious hurdles to successful implementation remain. The decades-old problems of underfunding, jurisdictional limitations, and local economic pressures continue to stymie reform of the System. The courts will generally remain deferential to Service decisions. In particular, the substantive meaning of compatibility, conservation, and maintenance of biological integrity, diversity, and environmental health will continue to resist searching judicial scrutiny. But there are strong new footholds for litigation, namely the objectively verifiable duties to make written determinations of compatibility and to monitor the status and trends of wildlife and plants. Still, the fate of coordinated conservation management through organic legislation now rests with the FWS and the Interior Department.

PART ONE

Understanding Refuge Resource Management

2 | *What Is the National Wildlife Refuge System?*

Public land law and its relationship to on-the-ground resource management constitute a distinct branch of environmental and administrative policy. This chapter begins by placing refuge management in the larger framework of public land law. Though the National Wildlife Refuge System shares its basic legal foundations with other public lands, there are a few key differences that distinguish the Refuge System's dominant use regime for protecting nature. After comparing the refuges with other public lands, this chapter surveys the hodgepodge of units that compose the Refuge System. The peculiar characteristics of the Refuge System help explain the circumstances that give rise to the special challenges of refuge management and the legal response to those challenges.

Public Land Systems in the United States

The myriad public land systems in the United States all operate under the same basic constitutional and administrative framework. Though the U.S. Constitution does not mention administrative agencies, it does allocate basic governmental responsibilities among the three branches of government. The administrative framework under which agencies operate, though ultimately constrained by the Constitution's separation of powers, is primarily constructed from twentieth-century statutes, such as the Administrative Procedure Act. This section first reviews the basic legal regime that governs all public land systems. It then describes the statutory and administrative variations that distinguish the public land systems from each other.

The Basic Legal Regime

All states retain judge-made, common law to resolve private disputes over environmental harm, such as "toxic torts," which can occur when people or organizations act negligently to expose victims to injury from contaminants. Nonetheless, federal statutes and the agency decisions that implement those statutes dominate the field of environmental law. The law governing the behavior of agencies is called administrative law. Therefore, environmental law, with its complex legislation and alphabet soup of implementing agencies, overlaps substantially with and has contributed significantly to the development of federal administrative law. Because agencies manage refuges, parks, forests, and other national property, public land law sits squarely within this mainstream of environmental law. Any comprehensive study of resource management on the public lands must consider the guiding role of statutes written by Congress, regulations promulgated by agencies, and the policies and institutional practices that agencies employ.

The U.S. Constitution, the root source of all federal power, gives to Congress the power to "dispose of and make all needful rules and regulations respecting the territory or other property belonging to the United States" (U.S. Constitution art. IV, § 3). This is why legislation serves as such an important touchstone for enunciating management standards for public land. The Supreme Court has consistently interpreted this congressional power so broadly as to reach regulation of private property uses that threaten to frustrate legitimate public land management goals, including wildlife protection. In this important respect, federal authority on the public lands goes beyond the rights of an ordinary, private proprietor (*Kleppe v. New Mexico* 1976). Federal authority also preempts conflicting state law. In the absence of conflict, state law generally applies concurrently with federal law on federal public lands.

Land management agencies, such as the Fish and Wildlife Service (FWS) and the National Park Service, derive most of their management authority from statutes in which Congress delegates to the agency some power to make rules and implement policy. In this way, Congress can avoid getting tangled in the detail and expertise required to apply general principles, such as maintaining healthy populations of wildlife, to particular situations and places. Agencies can more quickly adapt to changing circumstances through informal actions and can cultivate expertise through specialization much more effectively than can legislatures.

However, with general executive powers vested in his office by the Constitution (U.S. Constitution art. II, § 1), the president also exerts control over public property. Indeed, many property-management decisions of the federal government are more executive, oriented toward the day-to-day operation of government, than legislative, oriented toward broadly applicable, binding rules on society. Therefore, the president and the appointees to whom he delegates power also influence agency practice. Beginning as early as President Jefferson's bold negotiation of the treaty with France to purchase Louisiana Territory, the executive branch has frequently pioneered innovation in public land law. Congress has generally endorsed these executive prerogatives, despite questions about their constitutionality.

The third branch of government, the courts, also exerts its influence over public land management, primarily through judicial review of agency action. Though this influence is far less pervasive than legislative and executive control, it nonetheless helps shape decisions. Under the Administrative Procedure Act (APA), citizens who are adversely affected by an agency action may go to a federal court to have a judge review the legality of the action (APA § 702). Though an action may be illegal because it is unconstitutional, most APA suits challenge actions as being contrary to some underlying legislation, such as a public land statute. In this way, the APA serves as a bridge to bring judicial review to the numerous resource management statutes that do not explicitly provide for citizen suits.

Constitutional principles of "standing" that limit courts to a reactive role of simply responding to a particular dispute require that a citizen bringing a suit demonstrate concrete injury caused by the agency action. The injury must be something more than a generalized harm shared by everyone, such as squandered tax revenue. An economic injury to a property right, an aesthetic injury to recreational practice, or an environmental injury to a used resource may all serve as bases for standing. In addition, the APA limits standing to people whose injuries are within the "zone of interests" Congress sought to protect in the underlying statute. Regardless of the extent of the zone, people subject to agency enforcement actions may always appeal administrative sanctions to the courts.

In addition to reviewing violations of public land legislation, courts may also adjudicate claims that agencies violated the general procedures of the APA itself. Among these APA requirements is the prescription that agencies maintain contemporaneous administrative records that document the factors considered in making decisions (*Citizens to Preserve Overton Park v. Volpe* 1971). Other important cross-cutting procedural laws, such as the National Environmental Policy Act, require the agency to consider certain factors, such as environmental impacts and alternatives, in particular ways, such as through an environmental impact statement.

In public land law, courts almost always defer to agency determinations when the agency record displays a reasonable consideration of facts and arguments. Challenges to agency decisions typically succeed only where the agency acted in an arbitrary or capricious manner, which would include an agency decision contrary to a clear legal standard (APA § 706). Challengers to agency action have a heavy burden to persuade a court to invalidate an agency decision. Agency expertise, tradition, and the APA all tilt the playing field in favor of the agency. Readers interested in affecting public land management should strive to achieve their aims at the agency level. Once an agency has issued a final decision, judicial or legislative fixes are difficult to obtain. Though successful litigation overturning an agency decision can receive wide recognition and have far-reaching effects, it is the notable exception proving the rule that agencies can generally rely on judicial deference to win lawsuits.

With the exception of claims that the government took private property without providing just compensation, as required under the Fifth Amendment to the Constitution, judicial relief for suits against agencies takes the form of an injunction. If a court finds that the agency violated some law, it will typically enjoin the agency from carrying out the challenged action and remand the decision back to the agency. A remand requires the agency to drop its decision or start a new process to reaffirm or modify its decision in a way that cures the defect found by the court. Though rare in practice, the APA also authorizes courts to review agency inaction. When courts find that an agency is violating some law by not acting when it should, they can issue injunctions affirmatively ordering action.

Generally, the original policy of the federal government toward public lands was disposal. Disposal policy seeks to transfer resources out of federal ownership through sales, grants, and rewards. Disposal provided federal revenue and offered incentives for activities such as homesteading, mining, and railroad construction. Lands ceded by the Thirteen Colonies (beginning with New York in 1781) and acquired by the new federal government from European empires and Indian tribes were held by the United States for surveying, orderly development, and future growth. Management of this public domain was purely custodial until the late nineteenth century, when the federal government began to withdraw many parcels from the land disposal laws and reserve them for a particular purpose involving long-term federal retention. The federal public estate today includes both these withdrawn and reserved lands as well as property the United States has more recently acquired (or, reacquired) from states and private owners. Today, the federal government owns approximately 700 million acres of the 2.3 billion acres of land in the United States. Since 1781, the federal government has disposed of almost 1.3 billion acres of public lands.

Nonetheless, many real property resources, including timber, range, and especially minerals, remain subject to disposal under public land law, even on reserved lands, such as wildlife refuges. In general, mining law allows disposal by lease or by fee ownership (depending on the mineral) unless a statute or executive order explicitly withdraws a parcel or system of public land from the domain of mining law. Other real property resources on federal land typically are subject to disposal under law governing the system in which they are located. Therefore, the National Wildlife Refuge System Improvement Act governs timber harvesting, grazing, and utilization of rights of way in refuges.

The Variety of Public Land Systems

The federal public land management regimes range along a continuum defined by the extreme poles of unfettered multiple use and single-purpose exclusive use. Within this continuum, the National Wildlife Refuge System stands out in the center as a particularly important application of law to achieve a dominant purpose: nature protection. Often spotlighted with the somewhat smaller National Park System as a prototypical dominant use regime of public land management, the Refuge System has been and continues to be shaped by the same forces that have remade public land management and conservation law during the past four decades.

These forces have tended to compress land management regimes toward the dominant use center of the continuum. Even land systems previously associated with the ends of the continuum, such as multiple use Bureau of Land Management (BLM) grazing lands and exclusive use military reservations, are converging toward the dominant use middle. Few exclusive use areas today fail to promote at least the ecological values associated with restricted access; even bombing ranges manage wildlife habitat for conservation. For instance, the navy manages for conservation more than half of the controversial 22,000-acre Vieques bombing range. In addition to providing protection for endangered species, the navy boasts expending "significant resources" to research and develop databases for animals and plants. On May 1, 2001, the navy transferred 3,100 of these acres to the FWS to manage as a national wildlife refuge. The air force also invests in a conservation program that covers all its military bases. Even the Energy Department's highly protected sites devoted to nuclear engineering permit some grazing and public access. Indeed, the FWS cooperates in managing the Hanford Reach National Monument on Department of Energy lands.

At the other extreme, multiple use areas increasingly constrain the types and extent of permitted activities through substantive management conditions, such as the prevention of permanent impairment (on BLM lands) or the maintenance of biological diversity (on national forest lands), and through zoning in comprehensive plans (in both multiple use systems). Therefore, a better understanding of the dominant use Refuge System, which occupies the increasingly popular middle of the spectrum, helps identify the trends that are continually reshaping all public land management.

Ultimately, though, Refuge System law belies the notion that a single spectrum from multiple to exclusive use can fully characterize dominant use regimes. The multitiered hierarchy of purposes and uses, established through piecemeal additions to the Refuge System as well as through detailed organic legislation, represents the accretion of mandates and political compromises that become more specific and intertwined over time. Also, the rise of performance standards in management mandates, such as requirements to acquire water rights, monitor wildlife, and maintain biological diversity, complicates any effort to map public land law regimes on a linear scale. Even the National Forest System, a classic multiple use regime, originated with a statutory and administrative framework that set priority uses: "to improve and protect" forests, "to secure favorable conditions of water flows, and to furnish a continuous supply of timber" (1897 Organic Act, ch. 2, § 1, *codified at* 16 U.S.C. § 475). Nonetheless, multiple, dominant, and exclusive use remain common and helpful labels to generalize the coarse differences among public land systems.

MULTIPLE USE SYSTEMS

The multiple use federal public lands, constituting the national forests and the BLM lands, are by far the largest systems. The National Forest System comprises 191 million acres in 155 national forests and 20 national grasslands. The national forests were reserved from the public domain beginning in 1891 and were acquired, particularly in the eastern half of the country, beginning in 1911. The U.S. Forest Service of the Department of Agriculture has managed this system since 1905 under organic legislation that originated in an 1897 statute and received a substantial overhaul in the 1976 National Forest Management Act.

The BLM lands are the remains of the original public domain that were not privatized under the homesteading or mining laws, that were not granted to states or railroads, and that were not reserved for some other public land system. The Bureau of Land Management of the Department of the Interior has managed this system since 1946. But the BLM did not receive organic legislation calling for permanent federal retention and comprehensive management of the system until the 1976 Federal Land Policy and Management Act. The BLM manages 262 million acres of surface estate and an additional 700 million acres of subsurface minerals under the 1976 law. The BLM administers its lands through state offices, which divide their jurisdictions into districts.

DOMINANT USE SYSTEMS, INCLUDING THE REFUGE SYSTEM

The dominant use systems of federal public lands are the national parks and the national wildlife refuges. The National Park System comprises 83 million acres in 369 units. The national parks were reserved from the public domain beginning with Yellowstone in 1872 and today consist of acquired as well as reserved lands. The National Park Service of the Department of the Interior has managed this system since it was created under organic legislation of 1916, substantially revised in 1978.

Though I will describe the Refuge System in much greater detail in the next section, it is interesting to note the basic facts about the refuges here. The Refuge System comprises 95 million acres in nearly 550 national wildlife refuges. Like the national parks, the refuges are a mix of acquired and reserved lands. The U.S. Fish and Wildlife Service of the Department of the Interior has managed most of the refuges since it was created by executive order in 1940. Congress did not consolidate the refuges into a single system until the 1996 Refuge Administration Act, which was substantially revised and expanded by the 1997 Improvement Act.

Although most statutory references to the manager of the Refuge System refer to "the Secretary" (of the Interior), I often use "the Fish and Wildlife Service" interchangeably to indicate the decision maker because the Service is the line agency actively administering the System. As Michael Bean and Melanie Rowland note, however, the System consolidated by Congress in 1966 included game ranges established for both wildlife conservation and livestock grazing purposes (Bean and Rowland 1997, 289). These units were jointly managed by the FWS and the BLM until 1976 when Congress, in reaction to an attempt by the Interior Department to designate the BLM as the sole manager for three game ranges, required all System units to be "administered by the Secretary through the (FWS)" (Pub. L. No. 94-223, *codified at* 16 U.S.C. § 668dd). This amendment to the Refuge Administration Act also declares that all units within the System shall remain in the System except under certain limited circumstances (Larsen 1975).

Exclusive Use Systems

Because the exclusive use systems of public lands are so narrowly focused on a particular mission, they are not generally included in discussions of public land law. Nonetheless, the federal government owns substantial acreage in three exclusive use systems. The Department of the Interior holds 55 million acres in trust for over 500 American Indian tribes in approximately 300 Indian reservations. The fiduciary duty of the federal government should constrain management for the exclusive purpose of benefiting the tribes. Unfortunately, the squalid history of conflicts of interest and negligence continues to mar Indian land management.

The other two principal exclusive use systems serve national security goals. The Department of Defense manages 27 million acres of military reservations, and the Department of Energy manages 2.4 million acres of nuclear engineering sites. In many cases, the severe restrictions on public access to these lands have preserved important wildlife habitat. On the other hand, secrecy enshrouding management of these lands has led to instances of appalling degradation and a collection of the most severely contaminated sites in the country.

Overlay Systems

In addition to these principal public lands systems, the federal government also overlays conservation designations on some of its lands. These "overlay" systems do not alter which agency or land system governs designated units. But the overlay systems do place special management requirements on the agencies in administering the overlay lands. The three most important overlay systems, which are managed by multiple agencies under whose jurisdiction the lands fall, consist of the wilderness areas, the national monuments, and the wild and scenic rivers. So, the Brigantine Wilderness Area in the Edwin B. Forsythe National Wildlife Refuge is part of the overlay National Wilderness Preservation System. But it is also part of the Refuge System and remains managed by the FWS under Refuge System legislation except where the more specific provisions of the Wilderness Act conflict.

Parts of the 106 million acres of wilderness fall within all four principal multiple and dominant use agencies. Managed under the preservationist terms of the 1964 Wilderness Act, the 630 wilderness areas typically exclude roads, buildings, and motor vehicles. Similarly, national monuments, designated by the president under the 1906 Antiquities Act, are designed to preserve historic, archaeological, and "other objects" of "scientific interest" situated on public lands (1906 Antiquities Act, ch. 3060, § 2, *codified at* 16 U.S.C. § 431). Though limited in size to the "smallest area compatible with proper care and management" of the resource (id.), monuments can be millions of acres in area to protect large ecological resources encompassing whole landscapes. There are now approximately 100 national monuments encompassing 80 million acres (Squillace 2003).

The National Wild and Scenic Rivers Act of 1968 authorized the creation of a network of free-flowing rivers, classified as wild, scenic, or recreational, depending on their degree of development. Public land agencies must prepare management plans and take actions "to protect and enhance the values" for which the river segment was designated (16 U.S.C. § 1281(a)). Although part of a protective overlay system where they fall on federal lands, stretches of wild and scenic rivers may pass through private lands, where they constrain only activities requiring federal approval. The primary protective mechanism of the act limits activities of federal agencies (especially the licensing of hydropower dams) that would have "a direct and adverse effect on the values" for which the segment was designated (16 U.S.C. § 1278). This system currently consists of 160 segments of river totaling 11,300 miles.

The Crazy-Quilt Refuge System

The National Wildlife Refuge System is a tangle of land units with widely varying sizes, purposes, origins, ecosystems, climates, levels of development and use, and degrees of federal ownership and Service control. This is due to the "opportunistic" growth (Leopold et al. 1968, W-1) of wildlife refuges, migratory bird refuges, waterfowl production areas (WPAs), game ranges, wildlife management areas, and other land unit categories into the System. Units were created in response to crises, personal preferences of high-ranking officials (and legislators), funding availability, social program priorities, donations, and, of course, wildlife needs. The retrospective task of bringing coherence to this conglomeration requires historical context, flexible interpretation, and a modicum of imagination.

Despite the diverse authorities and origins of the individual wildlife refuges, all share a general purpose of animal conservation. Beginning in

1940 with a presidential proclamation renaming scores of refuges, there has been an ongoing effort to consolidate the refuge unit types into fewer categories (Presidential Proclamation No. 2,416, 54 Stat. 2,717 [July 25, 1940]). Beginning in the 1960s, important systemwide legislation provided central principles around which refuge management would coalesce. Appendix A of this book contains a chronology summarizing key events that shaped today's System. Chapter 3 fleshes out the development of the Refuge System in detail.

This section of the chapter begins by describing the taxonomy of the System, which is the untidy method by which the Service names unit types and categorizes them for management purposes. The Refuge System's tortuous history has given rise to a collection of units that defy logical organization. This results in bewilderingly different categorizations for similar refuges. For instance, a prairie pothole acquired through the Farm Service Agency (FSA) may be an FSA unit refuge or a WPA, depending on its location. Similarly, a "wildlife management area" (WMA) may be a national wildlife refuge or a coordination area, depending on whether it is administered through a cooperative agreement. Reorganizing the Refuge System so that unit names and categories more accurately describe their management is a perennial topic of interest for reformers.

Next, this section surveys the diversity of landscapes in and uses of the refuges. Though it is difficult to generalize about the attributes of such a far-flung and varied System, its sheer size makes it a significant conservation network. Of all the conservation land categories in the United States, only the overlay system of wilderness areas, consisting of 106 million acres, is larger than the Refuge System. The 83 million acre National Park System, the 44 million acre BLM collection of conservation lands, now called the National Landscape Conservation System, and even the 13 million acre system of nonpublic preserves managed by The Nature Conservancy are all smaller. The Refuge System has the potential to be the preeminent ecological protection network in the nation. The rest of this book focuses on those aspects of the System that explain the ways in which the refuges serve that mission and the respects in which they fall short.

The Taxonomy of the Refuge System

Most land managed by the FWS is part of the Refuge System. The taxonomy of the System is illustrated in figure 2.1. The approximately 95 million acres of the System comprise 92 million acres of national wildlife refuges, three million acres of WPAs, and 0.3 million acres of coordination areas (U.S. FWS 2002a).

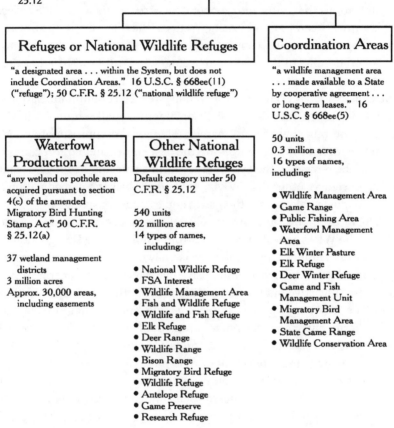

National Wildlife Refuge System

"various categories of areas that are administered . . . for the conservation of fish and wildlife, including species that are threatened with extinction, all lands, waters, and interests therein administered . . . as wildlife refuges, areas for the protection and conservation of fish and wildlife that are threatened with extinction, wildlife ranges, game ranges, wildlife management areas, or waterfowl production areas." 16 U.S.C. § 668dd(a) as interpreted by 50 C.F.R. § 25.12

Refuges or National Wildlife Refuges

"a designated area . . . within the System, but does not include Coordination Areas." 16 U.S.C. § 668ee(11) ("refuge"); 50 C.F.R. § 25.12 ("national wildlife refuge")

Coordination Areas

"a wildlife management area . . . made available to a State by cooperative agreement . . . or long-term leases." 16 U.S.C. § 668ee(5)

50 units
0.3 million acres
16 types of names, including:

- Wildlife Management Area
- Game Range
- Public Fishing Area
- Waterfowl Management Area
- Elk Winter Pasture
- Elk Refuge
- Deer Winter Refuge
- Game and Fish Management Unit
- Migratory Bird Management Area
- State Game Range
- Wildlife Conservation Area

Waterfowl Production Areas

"any wetland or pothole area acquired pursuant to section 4(c) of the amended Migratory Bird Hunting Stamp Act" 50 C.F.R. § 25.12(a)

37 wetland management districts
3 million acres
Approx. 30,000 areas, including easements

Other National Wildlife Refuges

Default category under 50 C.F.R. § 25.12

540 units
92 million acres
14 types of names, including:

- National Wildlife Refuge
- FSA Interest
- Wildlife Management Area
- Fish and Wildlife Refuge
- Wildlife and Fish Refuge
- Elk Refuge
- Deer Range
- Wildlife Range
- Bison Range
- Migratory Bird Refuge
- Wildlife Refuge
- Antelope Refuge
- Game Preserve
- Research Refuge

FIGURE 2.1. The Taxonomy of the National Wildlife Refuge System

The Refuge System contains two major categories of units: coordination areas and refuges. Coordination areas are federally owned lands managed by states under cooperative agreements with or long-term leases from the FWS. Though these 50 coordination areas are part of the System, they are excluded from key statutory requirements of the 1997 Improvement Act, such as comprehensive planning and the substantive criterion of compatibility for all uses, which apply only to refuges (16 U.S.C.

§§ 668dd(d)(3), (e); U.S. FWS Manual 602 FW 1.6(F); 603 FW 2.6(E)). Older statutory requirements, such as the compatibility criterion for approval of recreational uses, continue to apply to coordination areas, as lands within the System. Though defined by statute and regulation to be managed by states (16 U.S.C. § 668ee(5); 50 C.F.R. § 25.12), the FWS Realty database notes that coordination areas may be managed by cities and organizations that enter into cooperative agreements with the Service. This gap between law and practice reflects the difficulty of flexibly responding to conservation opportunities within the antiquated taxonomy.

All other units of the System are refuges, regardless of whether that term is included in their names. So, Bull Mountain Game Range, Falls of the Ohio National Wildlife Conservation Area, Hart Mountain National Antelope Refuge, and National Bison Range are all national wildlife refuges, despite their formal names. Though the approximately 550 named national wildlife refuges are the best known and largest component of the refuges in the System, they form a category defined by what it is not: refuges other than WPAs. Appendix C lists the named national wildlife refuges, along with their sizes and establishment dates.

The most important affirmatively defined category of refuges is the WPA. The WPAs are often excluded from studies of the Refuge System because of their unwieldy numbers, relatively narrow focus on increasing bird populations, and lack of intensive management. In general, WPAs have less restrictive public use conditions than other refuges in the System. The WPA may be a fee simple interest owned outright by the federal government or an easement to conserve resources on privately owned land. Nearly 95 percent of the WPAs protect the northern prairie wetlands ("potholes") that are critical waterfowl habitat.

The WPA is a category so confusing that even the FWS fails to get it right. Though WPAs are supposed to be limited to "any wetland or pothole area acquired pursuant to section 4(c) of the amended Migratory Bird Hunting Stamp Act" (50 C.F.R. § 25.12(a)), some WPAs are acquired under other programs, such as the Emergency Wetlands Resources Act, or through Farm Service Agency transfers.

Also confusing are the numbers of WPAs reported by the FWS. Though the Service often cites the nearly 3,000 WPA units owned outright by the United States, there are approximately ten times that number of WPA areas if one counts all the conservation easements that the FWS holds over private lands. The Service groups the WPAs, which are relatively isolated, small wetlands or prairie potholes, into 37 "wetland management districts." To qualify as a WPA, the property must be within one of 193 counties with acquisition targets. Most of these counties are located in eight north-central states: Iowa, Minnesota, Michigan, Montana, Nebraska, North Dakota, South Dakota, and Wisconsin. However, other states, such as Idaho and Maine, have acquisition targets and, therefore, wetland management districts. Wetland management districts also acquire wetland and grassland easements to enhance habitat for migratory birds.

WPAs are often acquired by the Department of Agriculture. After a Department of Agriculture reorganization in 1994, the Farm Service Agency (FSA) succeeded the Farmers Home Administration as the principal federal lender to farmers. When the FSA acquires properties with waterfowl production values through foreclosure or bankruptcy, it may transfer them to the FWS. If these properties are located in a qualifying county, they generally become WPAs. If they are outside of a WPA county, then the FWS categorizes them as FSA interests. With the exception of the FSA interests, refuges that are not WPAs are the named national wildlife refuge units (listed in appendix C) that constitute the core identity of the System.

What FWS property is excluded from the System? As I explore in the discussion of the 1966 Refuge Administration Act in chapter 3, most fish hatcheries and administrative holdings are not part of the System. However, some fish hatcheries may be part of the System because they happen to occur within a System unit. For instance, the Hagerman National Fish Hatchery is part of the Hagerman Coordination Area in Idaho, and the Ouray National Fish Hatchery is located on the Ouray National Wildlife Refuge in Utah.

On some units of the Refuge System, the Service shares management control. For instance, the National Aeronautics and Space Administration cooperatively manages Merritt Island National Wildlife Refuge (which includes the Kennedy Space Center) with the Service (16 U.S.C. § 459j-4). Also, the Bureau of Reclamation administers the agricultural leases, subject to Service control, in the Tule Lake, Lower Klamath, Upper Klamath, and Clear Lake refuges (*Klamath Forest Alliance v. Babbitt* 1998). Other cooperating agencies include the Tennessee Valley Authority and the Department of Defense. In 1976, the Game Range Act ended joint management with the BLM of four large refuges and placed them under the exclusive control of the Service (Pub. L. No. 94-223, § a(1)). This 1976 law now limits the ability of the president to transfer control of any refuge from the Service (id, § a(3)).

As a general matter, the Refuge System lacks control of the airspace above and the minerals below the surface of the refuge. The Federal Aviation Administration generally controls aeronautical activity, but the Department of Defense manages overflights of military aircraft on many refuges. As I discuss in chapter 3, these overflights have been an ongoing source of conflict arising from their adverse effects on wildlife. Chapter 12 describes oil and gas development in refuges.

Finally, many refuges, such as the Klamath Basin refuges in Oregon and California, the Deer Flat in Idaho, and the Upper Mississippi River in Minnesota, Illinois, Iowa, and Wisconsin, are located along rivers or lakes that are managed by the Bureau of Reclamation or the U.S. Army Corps of Engineers for flood control, irrigation, or other purposes. These refuges often are subject to water level variations or water deliveries that are outside of Service control and can frustrate conservation purposes.

The Refuge System also contains special overlays of preservation zoning. The Refuge System includes over 20 million acres of wilderness areas, mostly in Alaska, on 65 refuges. This amounts to approximately 20 percent of both the Refuge System and the total wilderness area acreage in the United States. The wilderness areas range in size from an eight million acre unit in the Arctic National Wildlife Refuge in Alaska to a tiny six-acre unit in the Pelican Island National Wildlife Refuge in Florida.

The Alaskan refuges also contain most of the System's river segments protected under the Wild and Scenic Rivers Act. Some 1,400 river miles of the 10,815 miles of wild and scenic rivers in the United States occur in refuges. The System's wild and scenic rivers range from the 285 mile Ivishak River in the Arctic National Wildlife Refuge to a five-mile segment of the Niobrara River flowing through Nebraska's Fort Niobrara National Wildlife Refuge.

The National Park Service manages most national monuments. But recent executive orders have broadened the monument management agencies to include the BLM and the FWS. In 2000, President Clinton established the 195,000 acre Hanford Reach National Monument. The FWS manages nearly 165,000 acres of this monument, which is the only one in the Refuge System.

The Resources of the Refuge System

It is not simply the large size and numerous units that make the Refuge System extraordinary. More important to the significance of the System are its broad reach and diverse landscapes. These attributes, in turn, generate a great deal of public use of and interest in the refuges. They also make the System a key network for protecting representative ecosystems and sustaining migrating animals, such as ducks and caribou. A map of the System is located on pages xvi–xviii.

As with the National Park System, the bulk of the Refuge System lands and its largest units occur in Alaska. Though only four percent of refuge units are located in Alaska, they constitute 85 percent of the System's acreage. The Arctic National Wildlife Refuge tops the list of giant refuges with 19.3 million acres. Yukon Flats National Wildlife Refuge runs a close second with 19.2 million acres. The 3.6 million acre Alaska Maritime National Wildlife Refuge has the largest sweep, containing a string of islands that would stretch from California to Florida if superimposed on the lower 48 states. Nonetheless, there are some very large refuges outside of Alaska, including Desert (1.6 million acres) in Nevada, Charles M. Russell (910,000 acres) in Montana, Cabeza Prieta (860,000 acres) in Arizona, Okefenokee (390,000 acres) in Georgia and Florida, Hart Mountain (270,000 acres) in Oregon, Alligator River (160,000 acres) in North Carolina, and Aransas (110,000 acres) in Texas. Several refuges containing important habitat are under 100 acres in size. The smallest, Mille Lacs in Minnesota, logs in at only 0.6 acre.

WPAs tend to be small, averaging 223 acres in size. The smallest, North Dakota's Medicine Lake WPA, is less than an acre. The largest, Montana's Kingsbury Lake WPA, is 3,700 acres.

Every state and several territories have at least one unit in the Refuge System. The spread of the System is evident in the location of the top three states in numbers of refuge units. North Dakota has 64, California has 38, and Florida has 29. The System's origins in wildlife conservation are evident in its habitats, which support more than 700 bird, 220 mammal, 250 reptile and amphibian, and 200 fish species. The four major bird migration corridors (flyways) across the United States—the Atlantic, Mississippi, Central, and Pacific—contain concentrations of hundreds of refuges. These flyway refuges provide breeding, feeding, and resting habitat for millions of birds each season. The WPAs protect thousands of prairie wetlands (potholes) in an area of the northern plains otherwise dominated by private agricultural land use.

Endangered and threatened species protection has triggered the acquisition of 56 refuges, including Crystal River in Florida for manatees, Oklahoma Bat Caves for bats, Hakalau Forest in Hawaii for indigenous birds, and Ash Meadows in Nevada for a variety of imperiled plants and fish. The System contains a total of 180 animal and 78 plant species listed under the Endangered Species Act.

An indication of the quality of Refuge System habitat comes from the many units recognized by international programs designed to protect ecosystems of global significance. The United Nations Educational, Scientific and Cultural Organization's Man and the Biosphere Program designates as "biosphere reserves" protected ecosystems that are managed to reconcile the conservation of biodiversity with sustainable use. Five units of the Refuge System occur in biosphere reserves: Blackbeard Island, Wolf Island, and Cape Romain National Wildlife Refuges fall within the Carolinian–South Atlantic Biosphere Reserve; Farrallon National Wildlife Refuge occurs in the Central California Coast Biosphere Reserve; and Alaska Maritime National Wildlife Refuge includes an Aleutian Islands Unit, which is in the Aleutian Islands Biosphere Reserve.

The 1971 Ramsar Convention provides criteria for the designation of "wetlands of international importance." Units of these extraordinary wetlands sites occur in 19 national wildlife refuges, including Izembek in Alaska, Edwin B. Forsythe in New Jersey, Okefenokee in Georgia and Florida, Ash Meadows in Nevada, Pelican Island in Florida, and Sand Lake in South Dakota. Similarly, the Western Hemisphere Shorebird Reserve Network designates areas providing essential habitat for migratory shorebirds. The Refuge System contains 20 of these designated areas.

Though the Refuge System is best known for its natural resources, it also contains significant cultural resources. Hundreds of sites within refuges are eligible for protection under the National Historic Preservation Act, and seven are National Historic Landmarks. Landmark sites include a shipwreck and its cargo in Iowa's DeSoto National Wildlife Refuge, archaeological remains of paleoindians in North Dakota's Lake Ilo National Wildlife Refuge, and petroglyphs in New Mexico's Sevilleta National Wildlife Refuge.

The Refuge System attracts 37 million visits annually, which is modest compared to 214 million visits for the National Forest System and 280 million visits for the National Park System. The visitation statistics reflect the relatively low public recognition of the refuges compared to the national forests and parks. Nonetheless, all but two percent of the System is open to the public for some form of recreation. As figure 6.1 illustrates, the Refuge System's chief priority use, after conservation (the primary use), is wildlife-dependent recreation.

Wildlife-dependent recreation includes hunting, fishing, wildlife observation and photography, and environmental education and interpretation. Hunting occurs on 290 refuges and attracts two million visitors annually. Though most hunters target waterfowl, refuges also offer big game (especially in Alaska), upland bird, and small mammal hunting. Fishing occurs on 260 refuges and attracts six million visitors annually. This includes both fresh- and saltwater fishing. Wildlife observation and photography bring in 16 million visitors annually to the Refuge System. The Refuge System contains 230 field stations offering environmental education programs. Because wildlife refuges are better distributed around the country than other public land systems, they can educate a great many people close to home. A refuge is within an hour's drive of every major U.S. city (U.S. FWS 2002b).

Nonwildlife-dependent recreation also occurs on refuges. The most prevalent of these activities are boating, picnicking, horseback riding, swimming, and camping. Also common are waterskiing, recreational trapping, and off-road vehicle use, which (along with motorboating) give rise to widespread conflicts with the ecological protection mission of the System (U.S. GAO 1989).

Additional conflicts arise from military and economic uses of refuges. The military uses of refuges, especially air exercises, generally fall outside the jurisdiction of the Service. The principal economic uses are rights-of-way for roads, pipelines and other utilities, and agriculture. However, logging, commercial fishing, commercial trapping, and mining also occur on some refuges. Chapter 12 discusses the special challenges of oil and gas development in the Refuge System.

Conflicts among users, or between users and the conservation mission of the System, fuel the development of new law. As the next chapter illustrates, rising concern over use conflicts led directly to key legislation and litigation. Certainly, the path-breaking 1997 Improvement Act emerged from an outbreak of concern about the ability of the Service to manage the refuges under existing authority in a manner that would achieve the System's comprehensive conservation potential.

3 | The History of the National Wildlife Refuge System

Rather than springing forth fully conceived, the National Wildlife Refuge System has grown through fits and starts. Refuge System law likewise emerged gradually over time to form today's management framework for conservation. Perhaps the most important message of the periodic attempts at reform is the steady growth of and enduring support for the only major federal public land system reserved principally for the benefit of wildlife. Today's high extinction rates and loss of biological diversity are acutely modern concerns; however, the challenges they present have precedent in the development of the Refuge System. The history of the System is worth examining as an example of how legal tools for achieving conservation goals evolve toward greater complexity and control of discretion.

Much of the comprehensive legislation concerning the Refuge System has a pretend quality to it. In 1956 when Congress "established" the Fish and Wildlife Service (FWS), in 1966 when it "designated" a National Wildlife Refuge System, and again in 1997 when it legislated a mission for the System, Congress merely endorsed executive branch innovations implemented years earlier. Statutory endorsement of executive innovation does bolster reforms and prevent subsequent administrations from revoking policies. However, the convoluted history of refuge establishment, the timid character of the Service, and the dim public awareness outside of the hunting community all contribute to congressional neglect of the Refuge

System. Moreover, Congress has consistently failed to reconcile its respect for individual refuge purposes with a desire to create an integrated system in which each unit contributes to a broad national goal. Compared to the other major public land systems, the Refuge System has suffered especially austere appropriations for management, lax oversight, and slow progress in modernizing organic legislation. Despite these disadvantages, the strong tradition of executive branch leadership on and power over refuges provides a basis for the U.S. FWS to take bold initiatives toward ambitious systemic management.

The law of the Refuge System has developed largely through accretion. With some notable exceptions, few statutes revoke or substantially modify older laws. The notable exceptions include the increase in the proportion of refuge lands acquired under the Duck Stamp Act that are open to hunting and the repeal of the Refuge Recreation Act's fiscal criterion as applied to wildlife-dependent recreation. All of the laws discussed in this chapter, even the old ones, remain in force unless specifically noted otherwise.

This chapter begins with the early history of the refuges, from their initial establishment, and follows their growth in numbers and importance. It traces the key developments that shaped refuge management and ultimately influenced the newest public land system charter, the 1997 Refuge Improvement Act. Separate sections describe the most significant statutes, beginning with the first serious attempt at legislative control of Refuge System management, the 1962 Refuge Recreation Act. The chapter then analyzes the 1966 Refuge Administration Act, a consolidation of and charter for the System that extended the compatibility criterion to all uses on refuges. The next important statute, the 1980 Alaska National Interest Lands Conservation Act (ANILCA), nearly doubled the size of the System. More importantly, ANILCA included mandates for comprehensive planning and purpose preferences that paved the way for the 1997 Refuge Improvement Act. The chapter then proceeds to review the controversies that swirled around incompatible refuge uses and generated pressure for reform of the 1966 framework legislation. Finally, this chapter concludes with President Clinton's 1996 effort to advance refuge management reform through an executive order. The 1996 order is the last significant legal development to occur before enactment of the 1997 Improvement Act, which I cover thoroughly in part two of the book. Appendix A contains a chronology of significant events in the development of the Refuge System.

Early History

As with the National Park System, the Refuge System's roots lie in the withdrawal of certain parcels of public domain with natural significance from resource disposition laws and reservation of those parcels for conservation purposes. However, compared to the Park System, whose origin dates to the congressional reservation of Yellowstone in 1872, the Refuge System has been shaped more by executive action.

Benjamin Harrison's 1892 order protecting Afognak Island, Alaska, as a "forest and fish culture reservation" is probably the first presidential proclamation withdrawing public domain for wildlife conservation (Proclamation No. 39). Afognak Island is now part of Kodiak National Wildlife Refuge. However, Harrison's order actually created a forest reserve under an 1891 act (sometimes called the General Revision Act), which authorized the president to set aside from occupation and sale public lands covered with timber (Ch. 561, 26 Stat. 1,095, 1,103). Though the Afognak reservation provided for protection of sea lions and sea otters, it appears to have been motivated primarily by the need to sustain commercial harvests of marine mammals. It did not succeed in spurring any significant conservation program. Harrison does, however, deserve credit for at least recognizing the need to regulate harvests and for testing presidential power to rein in commercial excess. Nonetheless, his more significant accomplishment in public land history was his use of delegated congressional authority under the 1891 law to reserve the first forest areas that would become the National Forest System.

In 1901, William McKinley issued a presidential proclamation (Proclamation No. 5) establishing the Wichita Forest Reserve, which is now the Wichita Mountains Wildlife Refuge, under the same 1891 forest reserve law. However, the proclamation makes no reference to wildlife conservation. Nonetheless, national concern about wildlife protection was rising. The 1900 killing of the last wild passenger pigeon marked a symbolic transition. The demise of the vast, roaming flocks of the pigeon, once the most abundant bird in the world, dramatized the plight of migratory birds in particular (Wilcove 1999, 27–30).

The Lacey Act of 1900, which bolstered state conservation efforts by making interstate transportation of animals killed in violation of state law a federal crime, began congressional involvement in the Progressive Era wildlife conservation project (Bean and Rowland 1997, 15–16). Representative John F. Lacey of Iowa, after whom this landmark statute is named, was also instrumental in enacting the 1905 legislation transferring management of the National Forest System to the Department of Agriculture's Forest Service and the 1906 legislation giving the president authority to reserve lands as national monuments (Hays 1959, 43, 189, 196).

But it is Theodore Roosevelt who personifies best the ascendancy of this political movement. He viewed the conservation imperative as a moral issue as well as a necessary condition for sustaining national prosperity (Morris 2001, 516–518). Roosevelt had long expressed concern for the viability of birds targeted by plume hunters for the fashion and costume industry. In Florida's Indian River drainage, where Pelican Island is located, the plume hunters were decimating egrets, ibises, roseate spoonbills, and other birds with colorful feathers (Cutright 1985, 223).

Theodore Roosevelt's legendary, charismatic expansiveness established the strong association between the Refuge System and executive power. Congress, in 2000 legislation (Pub. L. No. 106-408), properly traced the birth of the Refuge System to President Roosevelt's March 14, 1903, proclamation reserving Pelican Island as a "preserve and breeding ground for native birds." The proclamation gave the Department of Agriculture's Division of Biological Survey, a predecessor agency to the FWS, management authority. The Pelican Island proclamation differed from the previous executive reservations in citing no statute authority.

A popular anecdote about Roosevelt's establishment of Pelican Island refuge reflects his audacious style and the precedent-setting origins of the Refuge System (Morris 2001, 487, 519; Cutright 1985, 223). According to Charles F. Wilkinson, Roosevelt asked the Justice Department about presidential power to establish the Pelican Island Reservation:

> A few days later, a government lawyer, sallow, squinty-eyed, pursed-lipped—a classic lawyer—came to the White House. He solemnly intoned, "I cannot find a law that will allow you to do this, Mr. President."
>
> "But," replied T.R., now rising to his full height, "is there a law that will prevent it?" The lawyer, now frowning, replied that no, there was not. T.R. responded, "Very well, I so declare it." (Wilkinson 1996)

Between 1903 and 1909, Roosevelt decreed a total of 52 bird and 4 big game reserves where none had existed before. Soon Congress, prompted by Roosevelt, jumped on the bandwagon and reserved land that would become wildlife refuges, beginning with the Wichita Mountain Forest and Game Preserve in 1905, the National Bison Range in 1908, and the National Elk Refuge in 1912. Congress also endorsed Roosevelt's executive reservations in 1906. The Refuge System grew with remarkable speed during its first decade, primarily driven by the executive branch.

Both the boundaries and the purposes of early refuges bear the distinctive signature of the president. In contrast, although the executive branch primarily drew the boundaries of the National Forest System, Congress has set the uniform mandates for management of national forest units since 1897 (Act of June 4, 1897, 30 Stat. 35). National parks are established and given mandates by statute. Even statutes that establish individual refuges or impose systemwide requirements often merely endorse or slightly modify earlier executive actions. Examples include 1905 legislation for the Wichita Mountains Wildlife Refuge (ch. 137, 33 Stat. 614) and ANILCA provisions, including those for the Alaska Maritime National Wildlife Refuge (Pub. L. No. 96-487, § 302). Executive and administrative documents establishing wildlife refuges outnumber statutes by almost six to one. Although some units of the National Park System, such as national monuments, originate as executive actions, the vast majority of park units were authorized by Congress.

Haphazard at first, the growth of the Refuge System evolved to focus on particular geographic regions and broad national needs with the Migratory Bird Treaty Act of 1918 (Ch. 128, *codified at* 16 U.S.C. §§ 703–711). In addition to establishing the first significant, preemptive, federal restrictions on hunting, the act implemented new treaty obligations to sustain populations of certain birds. Fulfilling the treaty commitments has been an important impetus for the creation of refuges ever since. Today, more refuges are designed to support a national network maintaining migratory bird habitat than for any other purpose. This is one reason why so many refuges are clustered along the major north–south migratory flyways in the lower 48 states. Other important wildlife conservation treaties signed by the United States that support the designation and management of refuges include the 1940 Western Hemisphere Convention on Nature Protection and Wild-Life Preservation and the 1971 Ramsar Convention on Wetlands of International Importance. Although President Clinton signed the Biodiversity Convention negotiated at the 1992 Rio Earth Summit, the Senate has failed to ratify it.

The Migratory Bird Conservation Act (MBCA) of 1929 is a significant landmark in the growth of the Refuge System because it authorized, contingent on the permission of the state in which the property is located, ongoing purchase of lands to serve as avian refuges (Ch. 257, 45 Stat. 1,222, *codified at* 16 U.S.C. §§ 715–715r). It also provided the first multirefuge, uniform purpose statement. Though Congress had approved the use of federal funds to purchase land for wildlife conservation as early as 1909 on an ad hoc basis (Reed and Drabelle 1984, 8), the MBCA established a general, standing rationale for acquiring refuges to serve as "inviolate sanctuaries" for migratory birds. Beyond that basic purpose, however, the 1929 Act contained no management mandates for refuge administration. And, in subsequent years, beginning with the 1949 Migratory Bird Hunting Stamp Act (ch. 421 § 2), Congress progressively whittled away at the *Waterfowl* hunting restrictions in the "inviolate sanctuaries."

However, then—as now—authorization of government spending did not guarantee actual appropriations. Funds to purchase refuges in the early years of the Great Depression were scarce (Reed and Drabelle 1984, 9). After a precipitous decline in waterfowl populations in the early 1930s, Congress enacted the Migratory Bird Hunting Stamp Act of 1934 (Pub. L. No. 73-124, ch. 71, *codified at* 16 U.S.C. §§ 718–718(h)). This legislation created a dedicated fund for acquiring waterfowl conservation refuges from the sales of federal stamps that all waterfowl hunters would be required to affix to their state hunting licenses. The law, therefore, is commonly called the Duck Stamp Act. Ninety percent of the Duck Stamp fund revenues were earmarked for acquisition of habitat and the remainder for refuge management.

Since 1934, the federal government has collected more than $500 million from duck stamp sales (U.S. FWS 2001a, IX-4). Periodic congressional appropriations and loans (later forgiven) have bolstered the fund's stamp income. Along with the Land and Water Conservation Fund Act of 1964 (Pub. L. No. 88-578, *codified at* 16 U.S.C. §§ 460l-4–460l-11), which collects receipts from a motorboat fuels tax and payments for federal offshore oil and gas leases, the Duck Stamp Act funding mechanism remains the major source of money for purchasing expansions to the Refuge System (Bean and Rowland 1997, 284; Fink 1994, 17).

With assured acquisition funding, the growth of the Refuge System accelerated after 1934, as illustrated in figure 3.1. Although reservation of public domain would remain an important source of refuges, particularly in Alaska, land acquisition would be the dominant engine of growth in the number of refuges after 1934 (U.S. FWS 2002a). Thus, the most prevalent purpose for refuges is to contribute to the conservation of "the continental migratory waterfowl population" (Leopold et al. 1968, W-1).

On the other hand, from the perspective of area, the relative importance of acquisition is very low. After the establishment of the huge refuges in Alaska in 1980, the proportion of reserved public domain grew to 97 percent of the Refuge System (Reed and Drabelle 1984, 22). Even

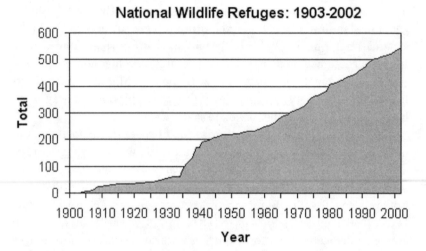

This graph shows the growth in the number of national widlife refuges over the past century. The period immediatley following the enactment of the Migratory Bird Hunting Stamp Act of 1934 witnessed the greatest sustained rate of refuge establishment. Since the 1960s, the rate of refuge creation has remained fairly steady at about seven per year. The graph does not include waterfowl production areas.

FIGURE 3.1. The Number of National Wildlife Refuges: 1903–2002

prior to 1980, 82 percent of the System's acreage had been reserved from public domain (U.S. FWS 1976, II-38).

The bewildering taxonomic diversity of units in the Refuge System owes much to acquisition funding mechanisms. Many of the units purchased with Duck Stamp Act monies were named migratory bird refuges. After a 1958 amendment to the Duck Stamp Act, the FWS began acquiring waterfowl production areas, typically small wetlands or prairie potholes, which are exempt from the "inviolate sanctuary" mandate of the MBCA (Pub. L. No. 85-585, *codified at* 16 U.S.C. § 718d(c)). Refuges reserved or transferred from existing public lands might be designated any of a wide variety of names (e.g., wildlife refuge, game range, wildlife and fish refuge, migratory waterfowl refuge, migratory bird refuge) depending on the source (e.g., Congress, the president, the secretary of the interior) and the particular purpose of the establishment. In addition, the Department of the Interior has long accepted donations for refuge lands (U.S. FWS 1976, II-38). Chapter 10 discusses in detail the range of establishment methods.

As hunters contributed cumulatively greater sums through the mandatory duck stamp, they also gained stronger statutory handles to assert their interests in hunting on the refuges. A steady erosion of the "inviolate sanctuary" standard of the MBCA now allows the secretary to make regulations allowing hunting of migratory game birds on up to 40 percent of an area established under the MBCA (16 U.S.C. §§ 668dd (d)(1)(a) (enacted as part of the 1966 National Wildlife Refuge System Administration Act, Pub. L. No. 89-669, § 4)). Congress had already expanded hunting in refuges established under the MBCA authorization on up to 25 percent of the area in 1949 (Act of Aug. 12, 1949, ch. 421, § 2, 63 Stat. 600). Increases in hunting potential on MBCA refuges came as trade-offs for increases in duck stamp prices (Fink 1994, 27; Gergely et al. 2000, 108). Even the current 40 percent standard may be exceeded to an unlimited extent where the secretary finds that it would be "beneficial to the species" (Fish and Wildlife Improvement Act of 1978, Pub. L. No. 95-616, § 6, *codified at* 16 U.S.C. § 668dd(d)(1)(A)). Hunting of other kinds of animals is not specially restricted on these refuges. The political influence wielded by hunters would continue to play a key role in shaping the 1997 Improvement Act.

The Great Depression also established a constituency among local governments to support commodity uses of refuges that generate revenue. The Refuge Revenue Sharing Act of 1935 (ch. 261, 401, 49 Stat. 383, *codified at* 16 U.S.C. § 715s) transferred to local counties 25 percent of all revenue from the sale of "timber, hay, grass, or other spontaneous products of the soil" and from an assortment of other money-making, commodity-based activities. This law endures as an incentive for local interests to exert political pressure to maintain refuge revenue-generating activities.

Another New Deal innovation, expedited presidential reorganizations of government departments, created a new agency to manage refuges. In 1940, President Franklin Roosevelt established the U.S. FWS and placed it in the Department of the Interior, where it remains today (Reorganization Plan No. 3, April 2, 1940, 54 Stat. 1,231, 1,232). The Service was a merger of the Bureau of Fisheries with the Bureau of Biological Survey. Roosevelt had transferred these two parent bureaus from the Departments of Commerce and Agriculture, respectively, to the Interior Department a year earlier (Reorganization Plan No. 2 of 1939, 53 Stat. 1,431, 1,433).

The FWS, though, can trace its origins to the U.S. Fish Commission created by Congress in 1871 to study a decline in fish and recommend remedies (U.S. FWS 2000a, 4). The origins of the Biological Survey date back to the 1880s (Worster 1994, 262). Until the 1939 reorganization, the Department of Agriculture's Bureau of Biological Survey managed most of the wildlife refuges, including all of the ones principally created for bird conservation. Therefore, prior to 1939, refuges were closer institutional cousins to the national forests than to Interior Department lands such as national parks. This helps explain why the Bureau of Biological Survey, under the leadership of C. Hart Merriam and in following years, had a strong economic orientation (Worster 1994, 262–263).

Finally, in 1956, Congress enacted what is sometimes called the organic act for the FWS (Worster 1994, 262–263). The Fish and Wildlife Act of 1956 (Pub. L. No. 1024, *codified as amended* 16 U.S.C. § 742a) purported to "establish" the FWS even though the Service had been in existence for 16 years. The only provision in the 1956 Act dealing with refuges requires the Service to "take such steps as may be required for the development, management, advancement, conservation, and protection of wildlife resources through research, acquisition of refuge lands, development of existing facilities, and other means" (§ 7(a)(5)). This represents a much broader grant of authority to acquire refuges than had been provided by prior legislation (Reed and Drabelle 1984, 22). After 1956, Congress gave carte blanche to the executive branch to acquire refuges not just for migratory birds but for any wildlife. The Refuge System database shows 166 refuges that include at least some lands acquired under the 1956 Act. Other legislation with broad purposes for refuge designation had limited geographic application. For instance, the Lea Act of 1948 (66 Stat. 238, *codified at* 16 U.S.C. §§ 695–695c) authorized the acquisition and development of management areas for wildlife generally but only in California.

Although subsequent reorganizations would reshape the FWS, they would not significantly modify its land management responsibilities. The most significant change would be transfer of the Bureau of Commercial Fisheries from the FWS to the Commerce Department's National Oceanic and Atmospheric Administration in 1970. Commentators have noted that the Service has been largely ineffective in fulfilling its conservation responsibilities in part because of its "roving parentage," self-conflicting mandates, unstable budget base, and insecure legislative foundation (Clarke and McCool 1996, 111–112; U.S. House 1975, 29–44). Like the U.S. Environmental Protection Agency three decades later, the Service would struggle to establish a coherent institutional identity out of the disparate agencies from which the president and Congress pieced it together.

The 1962 Refuge Recreation Act

The 1962 Refuge Recreation Act (Pub. L. No. 87-714, *codified at* 16 U.S.C. §§ 460k–460k-4) marked the beginning of the modern trend, culminating in the 1997 Refuge Improvement Act, to provide the Service with systemic management guidance. Appendix B contains the text of the Refuge Recreation Act. Prior to 1962, the "inviolate sanctuary" provision of the MBCA of 1929 applied to many refuges and provided a basis for restricting or encouraging certain activities, but it did not apply systemwide and did not set out practical criteria for implementing the term. Congress had issued specific management mandates for individual refuges prior to 1962 but had never put forward a comprehensive vision for how the FWS should administer the System.

In the early 1960s, growing recreational pressures spurred Congress to enact systemwide legislation. By 1960, the Refuge System was hosting 11 million visitor days annually, more than double the number in 1954 (U.S. GAO 1989, 9). By way of comparison, the System today hosts 37 million visitor days annually. The Recreation Act mandated that public recreation use be permitted in a refuge "only to the extent that is practicable and not inconsistent with . . . the primary objectives for which each particular area is established" (§ 1). This restriction on refuge use is significant as the first codified, systemic statutory provision to employ a criterion of consistency to determine management. Compatibility (a more prevalent term for consistency) with establishment objectives would become the touchstone for refuge management over the next 40 years. The 1962 Recreation Act also highlighted the fiscal constraints on the ability to manage recreational uses in a way that ensures conservation. This gap between what can be done and what the Service can afford to do emphasizes the importance of appropriations in public land management.

As with most refuge legislation, the 1962 consistency standard borrowed from existing Service practice. As early as 1960, the Service had incorporated the standard into its management regulations (25 Fed. Reg. 8,397, 8,413). The Service and its predecessor, the Biological Survey, likely employed some version of the consistency standard to evaluate proposed refuge uses since the early days of the System. Congress had employed consistency language in refuge appropriations at least as early as 1945 (U.S. House 1961, 57). And noncongressional establishment documents employed the compatibility standard to limit uses on refuges as early as 1936 (Executive Order No. 7,509 Establishing the Fort Peck Game Range, 1 Fed. Reg. 2,149–2,150 [1936]). The ultimate origins of the standard, however, are even older. As part of a 1910 seal conservation statute, Congress allowed the killing of seals in the Pribilof Islands whenever the secretaries of commerce and labor find that it "is not inconsistent" with the preservation of the herd (Ch. 183, 36 Stat. 326).

In the 1962 Recreation Act, Congress applied the consistency standard only to the primary purposes of each refuge. This narrowed the potentially broad application of a standard that could demand compatibility with all the goals or objectives of a refuge. To ensure that the FWS followed the congressional directive, the statute outright prohibits "those forms of recreation that are not directly related to the primary purposes" of the refuge until the secretary of the interior determines

a. that such recreational use will not interfere with the primary purposes for which the areas were established, and
b. that funds are available for the development, operation, and maintenance of these permitted forms of recreation (§ 1).

This limitation on the secretary's (and hence the Service's) delegated proprietary discretion is unusual for the early 1960s. At the time, Congress required no other land management agency to make determinations before allowing recreation use. Although noninterference or consistency, two terms that are used interchangeably in the legislative history and statute, are not difficult thresholds to surmount, they nonetheless starkly contrast with the prevailing public land management mandates at the time, such as the Multiple-Use, Sustained-Yield Act of 1960 (Pub. L. No. 86-517, *codified at* 16 U.S.C. §§ 528–531), which breathe discretion at every pore (*Strickland v. Morton* 1975).

The second required determination in the Recreation Act is extraordinary even today, when most public land mandates contain more detailed criteria for determining what uses may be permitted. The fiscal criterion requires that funds be available to develop, operate, and maintain the forms of recreation. It is a rare congressional recognition of the practical difficulties public land agencies generally, and the FWS in particular, have in accommodating public demands for recreation. These agencies constantly struggle to obtain appropriations to maintain adequate, safe, and (today) environmentally sound recreational operations (Clarke and McCool 1996, 53, 107–125). As of 1981, the General Accounting Office (GAO) reported an unfunded $650 million backlog for refuge development and rehabilitation (U.S. GAO 1981, 22). In 1996, the Service estimated a total maintenance backlog of $440 million to provide effective wildlife management and meet public use needs (U.S. House 1996, 1). By 2000, Congress was concerned enough about the backlog to require the Service to report on long-term plans to address priority operation, maintenance, and construction needs in the System (Pub. L. No. 106-408).

Conditioning recreational use on adequate funding is a clever way to create a constituency for operational appropriations, which often take a backseat to the more glamorous appropriations for new acquisitions and facilities. A group wishing to open up a refuge to a certain type of recreation (e.g., snowmobiling) would have to lobby Congress to appropriate funds for the attendant administrative costs. Conditioning recreation on an administrative finding of adequate funds also gives the Service, generally a timid agency (Clarke and McCool 1996, 107–125), a statutory scapegoat to better justify administratively sensible but unpopular decisions. Steven L. Yaffee has shown how this strategy of congressionally imposed prohibitive policy works. In implementing its endangered species program, the Service favored clear, prohibitive guidelines because they give unambiguous direction and allow the Service to deflect criticism by maintaining that its hands are tied by a statute (Yaffee 1982, 149–150). Moreover, the fiscal criterion relieves some of the pressure on the agency to divert funds from conservation to recreation. The legislative history of the Recreation Act indicates that the FWS had been diverting funds in this manner (U.S. Senate 1962).

Unfortunately, the Recreation Act does not define what constitutes an adequate level of funding for the purposes of satisfying the fiscal criterion. This flaw probably accounts for the relative obscurity of this standard in refuge management. The fiscal criterion is not widely discussed or implemented. However, the fiscal criterion still applies today to limit non-wildlife-dependent recreation in the System. The Service and citizens should stir this dormant provision into action.

Moreover, the fiscal criterion is an early predecessor of a statutory tool used in pollution control. The "hammer provision," most prominently employed in the 1984 amendments to the Resource Conservation and Recovery Act (RCRA) (Pub. L. No. 94-580, §1, as amended by Pub. L. No. 98-616), is widely viewed as an innovation of pollution control law. A hammer provision operates by providing a draconian (prohibitive) rule that will take effect on a particular date unless the agency has promulgated a substitute regulation. For instance, the 1984 RCRA amendments would have virtually banned the land disposal of any hazardous waste for which the Environmental Protection Agency (EPA) had not promulgated a treatment standard by specified dates (42 U.S.C. § 6942). The fiscal criterion in the Recreation Act is an overlooked antecedent tool for shifting the political dynamic of interest group lobbying (whether of hazardous waste generators regulated under RCRA or snowmobilers seeking to ride in refuges) from avoidance, delay, and budgetary austerity, to prompt appropriation of the necessary funds to make and implement determinations.

The Recreation Act also contains an unusual acquisition provision authorizing the secretary to obtain limited areas of land for recreational development adjacent to refuges to avoid adverse effects upon fish and wildlife (§ 2). In this poorly drafted section, it is ambiguous whether the provision is an expansion or just a clarification of the 1956 wildlife conservation purposes acquisition authorization (Pub. L. No. 1024, § 7(a)(5)). As always, though, acquisition is limited by available appropriations, and Duck Stamp funds may not be used to purchase these recreational areas. However, the idea of grafting a recreational area onto a refuge established primarily for wildlife protection illustrates well the difficulty of applying the consistency management standard. Because many refuges have expanded piecemeal through several separate acquisitions or reservations (or transfers or donations) it may be inaccurate to speak of a primary purpose for the refuge as a whole. Instead, different areas within a single refuge may have been established for different purposes. This historical reality adds an additional layer of complexity to the management of the Refuge System.

Finally, the Recreation Act authorizes the secretary to cooperate with a wide variety of entities, to accept donations, to establish reasonable fees, and to issue permits for public use (§ 4). Before this legislative authorization, the secretary already had discretion to engage in these activities. Agencies routinely cooperate in their day-to-day operations within their delegated authority, and the Interior Department had long accepted donations to the System. As early as 1912, the Department accepted land donated by the Izaak Walton League for the National Elk Refuge (Reed and Drabelle 1984, 21). Nonetheless, exhortations to cooperate and coordinate are a staple of public land law, and in this respect the Refuge System is typical. The establishment of fees and permit programs likewise was already a long-established authority of federal land management agencies. The principle that general proprietary responsibility to administer public lands includes the establishment of binding rules had been widely accepted at least since the Supreme Court's landmark *Grimaud* decision in 1911 (*United States v. Grimaud*).

The Recreation Act set key precedents for the Refuge System specifically and environmental law generally. The act established the first systemwide limitations on refuge management. It also codified the compatibility principle that has come to be the touchstone of dominant use management. In both these ways, the Recreation Act helped sow the seeds of the imminent growth of organic legislation. Finally, the fiscal criterion in the act hints at a path not taken in resource management law but one that subsequently emerged as an important route for congressional control of the EPA in pollution control law.

The 1966 Refuge Administration Act

The 1966 Refuge Administration Act took the next step toward a comprehensive, organic statute for the Refuge System. Indeed, the 1997 Refuge Improvement Act is codified as amendments to the 1966 law (16 U.S.C. §§ 668dd, 668ee). The 1966 Act consolidated the land units managed by the Service into a Refuge System and provided a comprehensive management mandate applicable to all uses, not just recreation. It also extended the applicability of the compatibility standard. Appendix B contains the text of the Refuge Administration Act.

Congress enacted the 1966 Refuge Administration Act as part of a bill whose purpose was "to provide a program for the conservation, protection, restoration, and propagation of selected species of native fish and wildlife . . . threatened with extinction, and to consolidate, restate, and modify the present authorities relating to administration . . . of the National Wildlife Refuge System" (Pub. L. No. 89-669, § 1(a)). This legislation is commonly divided into the Endangered Species Preservation Act of 1966, which authorized the secretary of the interior to acquire land and to review certain programs to conserve species at risk of extinction, and the National Wildlife Refuge System Administration Act of 1966. Though the Service often shortens the name of this key statute to the NWRSAA, I will use the more easily recognizable terms "Refuge Administration Act" or "1966 Act."

The partnering of the Refuge Administration Act with an endangered species conservation measure emphasizes that the refuge reform features in the law were animated in large part by extinction concerns. Today, the connection between refuges and endangered species continues to be strong. Approximately 260 species listed under the Endangered Species Act (ESA) occur on refuges, and the ESA acquisition authority has added 56 refuges to the System.

The extinction concern in the 1966 legislation was part of a more general trend in the mid-1960s to begin managing public lands for preservation purposes. The trend is important for the Refuge System both because it is instructive about the milieu in which Congress enacted the

Refuge Administration Act and because other preservation statutes of the era directly shape management of refuges. Just two years before the 1966 Act, Congress enacted the Wilderness Act, which created a new system of public lands that would be managed to minimize the traces of development (Pub. L. No. 88-577, *codified at* 16 U.S.C. §§ 1131–1136). Two years after the 1966 Act, another statute emerged from the preservation movement: the National Wild and Scenic Rivers Act (Pub. L. No. 90-542, *codified at* 16 U.S.C. §§ 1271–1287). Like a wilderness area, a designated wild and scenic river is managed by the agencies responsible for the units on which it occurs. As discussed in chapter 2, the Refuge System includes both wilderness areas and wild and scenic rivers.

In this spirit of preservation, the 1966 Refuge Administration Act consolidated the wildlife refuges and was the first statute to refer to them as a National Wildlife Refuge System. The following subsection discusses this formative provision of the Act. The Refuge Administration Act also provided the first comprehensive management mandate for the Refuge System, borrowing the compatibility (or, "not inconsistent with") principle from the 1962 Refuge Recreation Act. The second subsection addresses this management mandate.

Consolidation of Units

Congress, in 1966, designated as the National Wildlife Refuge System "all lands, waters, and interests therein administered by the Secretary as wildlife refuges, areas for the protection and conservation of fish and wildlife that are threatened with extinction, wildlife ranges, game ranges, wildlife management areas, or waterfowl production areas" (§ 4(a)). This constitutive phrase remains important because it has never been amended or repealed. Although the 1997 Improvement Act substantially revises the management and administration of the System, it does not alter this definition of the System. The only prior legislation grouping refuges for management purposes was the 1962 Recreation Act, which applied to "national wildlife refuges, game ranges, national fish hatcheries, and other conservation areas administered by the Secretary . . . for fish and wildlife purposes" (§ 1). These two descriptions of the land base to which legislation applies both include catch-all phrases and lists of unit types.

The catch-all phrase in the 1966 statute refers to areas created to stop species' slides to extinction. In contrast, the 1962 catch-all language refers much more broadly to other conservation areas designated for fish and wildlife purposes. There is no indication in the legislative history that this difference in coverage is intentional. Furthermore, although the 1966 statute lists more categories of FWS administered units, it does not list national fish hatcheries, a unit category included in the 1962 statute. All of the units listed in the 1966 statute and absent from the 1962 statute's list would fall under the 1962 catch-all description. On the other hand, only those national hatcheries propagating fish threatened with extinction could plausibly be considered part of the Refuge System under the 1966 definition. Congress could reasonably have intended to exclude hatcheries (and administrative sites) from the scope of the Refuge System because they are operated as production (or administration) facilities rather than as natural ecosystems. This limitation on the scope of the System is widely accepted within the Service.

However, it is important to note that the 1962 Recreation Act, which applies to all "conservation areas administered by the Secretary of the Interior for fish and wildlife purposes," still requires a compatibility determination for each recreational use at hatcheries, regardless of whether they are part of the Refuge System (§ 1). More broadly, the continuing operation of the Recreation Act raises the question of whether "other conservation areas administered by the Secretary for fish and wildlife purposes" but outside of the jurisdiction of the Service, such as Bureau of Land Management (BLM) national conservation areas and national monuments, or national park units, might be subject to the recreational compatibility determination requirement. Though a literal reading of the statute would indicate that they are, the Interior Department has never applied the Recreation Act to non-FWS lands.

Another concern is whether Congress in 1966 might have intended to exclude from the System coordination areas that were not established for species threatened with extinction. The absence of coordination areas in the 1966 Act's list of specific unit types is significant because the Service began to call areas cooperatively managed with agreements "coordination areas" at least as early as 1959 (U.S. FWS 1959). But, other than a Department of Agriculture submission referring to the bill as "redefining" the Refuge System, there is nothing in the legislative history to suggest that Congress meant to consolidate anything less than all of the land management units of the FWS into a system (U.S. Senate 1966). On the other hand, the 1966 statute was part of a larger bill whose underlying theme is the protection of species threatened with extinction, whereas most coordination areas are managed for nonendangered game.

The Service resolves this ambiguity in scope by expansively interpreting the 1966 statute to define the System to include "other areas for the protection and conservation of fish and wildlife including those that are threatened with extinction" (50 C.F.R. 25.12). The FWS regulations call on the director of the FWS to determine, for those areas not specifically listed in the law but that are nevertheless managed by the Service, whether they are managed "for the protection and conservation of fish and wildlife" (65 Fed. Reg. 62,461 [2000]). If so, such areas are included in the System. This broader phrase used in the regulatory definition originates in the 1966 statute's introductory language preceding the list of lands included in the System:

> For the purpose of consolidating the authorities relating to the various categories of areas that are administered by the Secretary . . . for the conservation of fish and wildlife, including species that are threatened with extinction. (§ 4(a))

It is a stretch for the Service to interpret the statutory phrase introducing the purpose of consolidating units into a system as an element in the list of what constitutes the System. Nonetheless, it is an uncontroversial interpretation that ensures complete coverage of all of the significant land areas managed by the Service in the Refuge System. When the FWS expanded the scope of its regulatory definition of the Refuge System in 1976 from language that mirrored the 1966 statute ("areas for the protection and conservation of fish and wildlife that are threatened with extinction" (50 C.F.R. 25.1 [1975])) to the current regulatory definition, it did not highlight the expansion (40 Fed. Reg. 12,270 [proposed rule] [1975]; 41 Fed. Reg. 9,166 [1976] [final rule]). The promulgation of the final rule did not indicate any comment or controversy about the change, which was part of an effort the Service characterized as a reorganization and revision of the regulations.

This confusing and legally tenuous definition of the Refuge System reflects the difficulty of managing the crazy quilt of units together in an integrated system that is more than the sum of its parts. As I will explore in greater detail in chapter 10, the disparate origins of refuge units exacerbate the uncertainties about and the crosscurrents in the definition of the Refuge System.

Comprehensive Management Mandate

Compatibility is the key concept, borrowed from the 1962 Recreation Act, that Congress applied to limit the FWS's discretion in managing uses of the Refuge System. The 1966 Refuge Administration Act constructs a legal framework for refuge administration that is quite modern for its time. This modern structure, adopted subsequently in the Clean Air and

Clean Water Acts, as well as in the 1982 amendments to the ESA, first imposes a number of restrictions but then provides a regulatory (often a permit) program to allow otherwise prohibited acts. This approach makes the prohibitory section of a statute primarily important in determining the scope of activities that will be subject to agency regulation. So, for instance, the ban on discharges of pollutants in the Clean Water Act is principally important not so much for actually prohibiting discharge, but for defining what activities will be subject to regulation under the Clean Water Act. The regulatory section of a modern environmental law then establishes the terms under which the activity will be allowed. In the Clean Water Act example, the regulatory section describes the conditions under which permits may be granted.

The Service calls its application of this approach the "closed until open" policy (65 Fed. Reg. 62,460 [2000]; 50 C.F.R. § 25.21). The FWS may open areas of refuges to compatible uses by regulation, individual permit, or public notice (50 C.F.R. § 25.21).

The prohibitory section of the 1966 Refuge Administration Act, therefore, defines the scope of activities requiring explicit permission from the Service to occur legally on refuges. It bans in any unit of the System:

1. disturbing, injuring, cutting, burning, removing, destroying, or possessing any U.S. property, including natural growth,
2. taking or possessing any animals or animal parts, including nests and eggs, and
3. entry, use, or occupancy for any purpose. (Pub. L. No. 89-669, § 4(c))

The term "take" in the prohibition is further defined in the 1966 Act to mean "to pursue, hunt, shoot, capture, collect, kill, or attempt" to do any of these things (Pub. L. No. 89-669, § 5(b)). This definition, typical of wildlife laws of the time, does not include the term "harm." "Harm," part of the definition of "take" in the ESA, broadens the prohibition (Pub. L. No. 93-205, § 3 *codified at* 16 U.S.C. § 1532). The FWS has defined "harm" to include, under certain circumstances, "significant habitat modification or degradation where it actually kills or injures wildlife by significantly impairing essential behavioral patterns, including breeding, feeding or sheltering" (50 C.F.R. § 17.3). The Supreme Court upheld this definition in *Babbitt v. Sweet Home Chapter of Communities for a Great Oregon* (1995). The other broad definitional term present in the ESA's definition of "take" but absent in the Refuge Administration Act's definition is "harass." The absence of the term "harm" in the Refuge Administration Act's definition of "take" suggests that incidental significant habitat modification is not prohibited, even where it significantly impairs essential behavioral patterns of animals. Nonetheless, the overall scope of the Refuge Administration Act's prohibitions is broad. The prohibition on entry and use covers most activities that would directly harm wildlife, including habitat modification within a refuge. Of course, transboundary pollution coming from outside the refuge can harm species through air/water degradation without direct human entry or use. This sort of external threat to refuge resources (now addressed in Service policy under the 1997 Act) is beyond the scope of the 1966 Act.

The broad prohibitions of the 1966 Act are not applicable under any one of three exceptions. The first exception exempts persons authorized to manage areas in the System (Pub. L. No. 89-669, § 4(c)). The second exception is for express provisions of establishment documents (id.). This exception highlights the continual management problems created by the wide variation in the language and style of establishment documents. The 1966 Refuge Administration Act consolidates the refuges into a system for comprehensive management only to the extent that establishment documents and amendments, which number over 1,000, allow for common ground. Organic or comprehensive mandates for public land systems are limited in their effectiveness where the system units have individual mandates (Fischman 1997).

The third exception is for activities permitted under Service regulations. For those areas where establishment documents are silent, refuges may be managed by the Service to allow only those activities provided by regulation (Pub. L. No. 89-669, § 4(c)). That is why section 4(d) of the 1966 statute, authorizing regulation and imposing the compatibility criterion, is so important (Pub. L. No. 89-669, § 4(d)). Section 4(d) authorizes two kinds of regulations. The first (section 4(d)(1)) and more general kind of regulation permits the use of an area in the System for any purposes when the secretary "determines that such uses are compatible with the major purposes for which such areas were established." This constraint borrows from the 1962 Recreation Act delegation, which required that the secretary make determinations and also imposed a noninterference criterion. The determination component of the delegation may not have carried much weight in the 1960s, but after the Supreme Court's landmark *Overton Park* decision, agency determinations must be supported by an administrative record which reveals that the agency took into account the relevant factors (*Citizens to Preserve Overton Park v. Volpe* 1971). In the case of compatibility determinations, the relevant factors would be the effects of the proposed uses and the consequences of those effects on achieving the major purposes.

The compatibility criterion in section 4(d)(1), which authorizes general use regulations, differs in two respects from the compatibility criterion in the 1962 Recreation Act. First, the 1966 statute uses the term "compatible with" as opposed to "not interfere with." This difference is not significant. The 1962 statute itself employs the terms "compatible with" and "not inconsistent with" in a context which suggests that the "not interfere with" criterion is meant to include those two standards (Fink 1994, 28). The 1966 statute, though it abandons the "not interfere with" criterion, does use "not inconsistent with" in the provision authorizing the secretary to enter into contracts (§ 4(b)(1)). The legislative history of the 1966 statute does not compare the phrasing of its compatibility criterion with that of the 1962 law. Richard Fink shows that some commentators have conflicting interpretations about the comparative burdens imposed on the Service by the compatibility criteria under the two statutes (Fink 1994, 28). I will dispense with such hair-splitting and adopt the common practice of equating the meaning of the terms "not interfere with," "compatible with," "consistent with," and "not inconsistent with."

Second, the 1966 statute applies the compatibility criterion to "major" purposes of the establishment document(s) (Pub. L. No. 89-669, § 4(d)(1)). In contrast, the 1962 statute applies the criterion to the "primary" purposes or objectives (Pub. L. No. 87-714, § 1). Like the variation in the phrasing of the compatibility standard, this is a distinction without a difference. Nothing in the legislative history of the 1966 law suggests that Congress meant to change the scope of the purposes to which the compatibility criterion applies. As I discuss in chapter 8, however, the 1997 Act applies the compatibility criterion to an unmodified set of "purposes," which does alter the analysis by expanding the domain of goals against which proposed refuge activities are judged (16 U.S.C. § 668ee(1)).

The other, and more specific, kind of regulation authorized in section 4(d)(2) allows the Service to grant or permit easements. Although Congress mandated the same compatibility standard, employing the same phrase as the general authorization of regulations, it did broaden the scope of the purposes to which the compatibility criterion applies. Instead of major or primary purposes, easement regulations must be compatible with "the purposes" of the establishment document (Pub. L. No. 89-669, § 4(d)(2)). This suggests that the easement regulatory standard should be interpreted more strictly than the general standard: a wider range of subsidiary, secondary, or minor purposes are subject to protection against incompatible easements. Congress's establishment of a higher threshold for approving some uses (easements) than others foreshadows the important hierarchy of uses in the 1997 Improvement Act, and discussed in chapter 6.

In whatever form, the congressional mandate to test all regulatory decisions against the purposes set out in establishment documents to overcome the broad prohibitions in the Act highlights a core dilemma. As legislation seeks to consolidate and integrate into a single system all the diverse areas managed by the FWS, it also elevates the importance of the establishment documents by using their multifarious purposes as limits on agency regulation. This tension between the convergent pull of Refuge System legislation and the divergent push of individual refuge purposes continues to contribute to conflicts and inefficiencies in refuge management. It also led, in 1997, to an effort to impose a uniform System mission against which to measure the compatibility of uses.

Finally, there are other provisions of the 1966 Refuge Administration Act that explicitly confirm certain management practices generally implicit in proprietary discretion. Proprietary discretion is the latitude agencies of the federal government have to make routine management decisions for the protection of public property. The Act authorizes the secretary to enter into contracts for the provision of public accommodations when they are not inconsistent with the primary purpose of a refuge, to accept donations of funds, and to acquire lands by exchange under certain conditions (§ 4(b)). The Act also confirms the continued application of the 1962 Recreation Act and the federal mining laws, where they are consistent with establishment documents (§§ 4(h) and 4(c)). The explicit statement that mining laws continue to apply to System lands unless the lands are withdrawn (by establishment instruments) clarifies that the general prohibition on entry to refuge lands in section 4(c) likely does not prohibit prospecting, locating, and discovering minerals to secure mining rights on lands otherwise open to hardrock mining.

The 1966 Act limits the regulatory power of the secretary over fish and wildlife to lands within the System. Nonetheless, other statutes, such as the Migratory Bird Treaty Act and the ESA, provide independent regulatory power to the FWS to regulate animals on lands outside of the System. Moreover, Congress provided that regulations permitting hunting and fishing within the System shall be, "to the extent practicable, consistent with State fish and wildlife laws and regulations" (§ 4(c)). This consistency standard can lead to disagreements between states and the Service over how best to regulate hunting and fishing, where allowed on a refuge. Like most disputes with states over wildlife management, the Service generally prevails so long as it makes a minimal effort to articulate a good reason to deviate from state laws.

Because the 1966 Refuge Administration Act failed to set out clear objectives and substantive criteria for management, it never succeeded in protecting natural resources to the extent achieved by many of the other conservation statutes of the time. More than any other factor, the weaknesses of the Refuge Administration Act led to the management problems that created the need for the 1997 Improvement Act (Criss 1999, 16). A stronger organic act would not have allowed the Service to drift so far from the refuge goals. It would have provided a shield for the Service to use in resisting pressures for incompatible uses. Also, a stronger statute would have facilitated more effective judicial intervention. Nonetheless, the 1966 Act remains one of the foundation documents for modern organic legislation. Its framework influenced the structure of the 1997 Improvement Act. And, the 1966 Act's compatibility criterion continues to shape refuge management today.

The Alaska National Interest Lands Conservation Act of 1980

Like the 1962 Recreation Act, which established a management criterion that Congress extended more broadly in 1966, the 1980 Alaska National Interest Lands Conservation Act (ANILCA) (Pub. L. No. 96-487, 94 Stat. 2,371) employed new resource management tools that Congress would apply systemwide in 1997. The most important of these tools are the mandatory comprehensive refuge unit plan and the hierarchy of purposes.

Three attributes make Alaska significant for the System. First, the state is the location of the first executive withdrawal (for Afognak Island, parts of which are now in Kodiak National Wildlife Refuge) and congressional hunting prohibitions for wildlife conservation (in a series of statutes beginning in 1868). Second, Alaska contains unique, wild, and spectacular landscapes and animals. Most famous is the Arctic National Wildlife Refuge, often called America's Serengeti (Hohovek 2000). The Service describes this refuge, hosting a "rich pageant of wildlife," as "among the most complete, pristine, and undisturbed ecosystems on Earth" (U.S. FWS 2002f).

Third, and most importantly, Alaska contains, by far, the largest refuges and the greatest total refuge acreage. The Arctic National Wildlife Refuge is the System's largest, at 19.6 million acres. The 16 Alaska refuges add up to 77 million acres, or nearly 83 percent of the area of the System.

As Bradley Karkkainen has observed, the Alaska refuges "may come closer than any other category of federal lands to constituting genuine biodiversity reserves," in part because they are large enough to cover whole ecosystems (Karkkainen 1997, 36).

Due to these special characteristics, Alaska's relatively recent statehood, the unique aboriginal claims settlement regime, and the state's high proportion of federal public land, Alaska refuges are managed under special rules. The source of many of the rules is ANILCA. The special rules applicable in Alaska in some cases serve as models to promote improvements in administration throughout the entire System. These are the provisions I focus on in this section. Other special provisions, such as those dealing with subsistence activities on refuges, have little or no relevance to the rest of the Refuge System. These are the special provisions I address in chapter 11. Special rules, though often justified, may frustrate uniform policy and comprehensive management of the System.

ANILCA functioned in part as an establishment document, adding 53.7 million acres of land to the Refuge System in nine new refuges and in additions to six of the seven existing refuges (ANILCA §§ 302, 303; 16 U.S.C. § 668dd note). The significance of this portion of ANILCA, which tripled the size of the Refuge System, is the purposes it set out for both the new and the existing units. ANILCA established a hierarchy of purposes that foreshadows the approach of the 1997 Improvement Act. ANILCA subordinates purposes dealing with water quality, water quantity, interpretation, environmental education, and subsistence use to higher priority purposes dealing with conservation of animals and their habitat. ANILCA established this multitiered system of purposes by conditioning the subordinate ones with clauses such as "to the maximum extent practicable" and "in a manner consistent with [higher priority conservation purposes]" (ANILCA §§ 302, 303; 16 U.S.C. § 668dd note).

More significantly, from the perspective of systemic management, ANILCA required the Service to engage in comprehensive refuge unit planning. Although at least one establishment statute had required comprehensive planning at the time of ANILCA (Minnesota Valley National Wildlife Refuge, Pub. L. No. 94-466 [1976]), the Refuge System was the only major federal public land system without a comprehensive planning mandate in 1980. The System would remain unique in lacking a systemic unit planning mandate until 1997. The planning requirements for Alaska refuges established an important precedent and gave the Service valuable experience in modern public land planning. Indeed, the 1997 Refuge Improvement Act allows ANILCA provisions governing refuge management to prevail where they conflict with the more recent legislation (Pub. L. No. 105-57, § 9(b)).

For each Alaska refuge, ANILCA required a "comprehensive conservation plan" (§ 304(g)(1)). Like the Park Service general management plans (16 U.S.C. § 1a-7(b)) and the BLM resource management plans (43 U.S.C. § 1712), but unlike the Forest Service land and resource management plans (16 U.S.C. §§ 1604(f)(5), (g)), ANILCA comprehensive conservation plans do not need to be revised after a set period of time, nor do they need to be based on substantive planning regulations (ANILCA § 304(g)). Nonetheless, comprehensive conservation plans must describe a range of natural and cultural values of the refuge, areas suitable for use as administrative or visitor facilities, special access issues, and "significant problems which may adversely affect the populations and habitats of fish and wildlife" in the refuge (ANILCA § 304(g)(2)). Based on these descriptions, the plan must fulfill four substantive requirements:

1. designate areas within the refuge according to their respective resources and values;
2. specify programs for conserving fish and wildlife, and other special values, to be implemented within each area;
3. specify the uses within each area which may be compatible with the major purposes of the refuge; and
4. set forth those opportunities which will be provided (if compatible with refuge purposes) for fish and wildlife-oriented recreation, ecological research, environmental education, and interpretation. (ANILCA § 304(g)(3))

These four planning requirements are the only substantive statutory management mandates for the content of plans. Together, they offer a sketchy blueprint for zoning the refuges in a way that both forces the agency to look ahead at how it can achieve its goals and allows the public to anticipate future actions, opportunities, and conditions on refuges.

ANILCA also includes procedures that the Service must follow in promulgating comprehensive conservation plans. In preparing plans, the Service must consult with appropriate Alaskan state agencies and native corporations and hold hearings in the vicinity of local villages (§ 304(g)(4)). The interested public outside of Alaska also may get involved in planning by reviewing and commenting on proposed plans, which must be made available at each FWS regional office and announced through notices in the *Federal Register* (§ 304(g)(5)). Of course, National Environmental Policy Act environmental impact statement procedures, especially the evaluation of alternatives, apply to comprehensive conservation planning as well (42 U.S.C. §§ 4321-4345; 40 C.F.R. Part 1500).

The Service's planning experience with ANILCA became an important foundation for subsequent implementation of the 1997 Improvement Act, which requires comprehensive plans for all refuge units. Despite the gargantuan size of the Alaskan portion of the System, it served as a pilot effort to extend modern elements of organic legislation to refuges. The need for that extension became painfully clear in the 1980s and 1990s, when a series of reports and investigations focused attention on the widespread problem of incompatible uses in the Refuge System.

The Struggle with Incompatible Uses

The problem of incompatible uses occurring on refuges spurred reform as early as 1962, when Congress enacted the Recreation Act to limit recreational activities that threatened the ability of refuges to fulfill their purposes. In 1968, the secretary of the interior appointed Professor A. Starker Leopold to chair an advisory committee for the Refuge System. Thirty-four years earlier, President Franklin Roosevelt had appointed Leopold's father, Aldo Leopold, to an advisory committee that recommended an aggressive program to acquire lands for wildlife habitat. This recommendation bolstered support for the 1934 Duck Stamp Act. In 1963, A. Starker Leopold's committee on wildlife management in the national parks issued an influential report with recommendations on the long-term challenges for the National Park System.

The 1968 Leopold committee report was an important policy document describing long-range systemic goals for the Refuge System. It stated that a wildlife refuge "should be a 'wildlife display' in the most comprehensive sense" where the "full-spectrum of native wildlife may find . . . a home" (Leopold et al. 1968, W-3). The report repeated the recommendation by stating that the refuges "should be consciously developed as show places for all kinds of wildlife" (Leopold et al. 1968, W-16). Not surprisingly, this articulation of the goal for refuges resembles the influential recommendation of the 1963 Leopold report, that each national park "should represent a vignette of primitive America" (Leopold et al. 1963, 3).

The 1968 Leopold committee summarized its recommendations by "proposing to add a 'natural ecosystem' component to the program of refuge management" (Leopold et al. 1968, W-4). In this suggestion, the Leopold committee sought an overarching, guiding principle that would provide a uniform direction for System management, represent a reasonable accommodation of most establishment purposes, and push the

Service to respond to growing ecological concerns. The term "natural ecosystem," which the Leopold committee felt compelled to place within quotation marks, is now common resource management jargon. The FWS today adheres to a policy of ecosystem management for all of its programs (U.S. FWS 1999; 052 FW 1).

While surveying refuge management issues, the 1968 Leopold report identified a number of situations where uses were interfering with wildlife conservation. For instance, the report described the upland sagebrush areas of the Malheur refuge as "largely sterile of wildlife," possibly due to intensive grazing (Leopold et al. 1968, W-9–W-10). The report also discussed the pressures of recreation on the Refuge System and recommended that the Service develop master plans for refuges that outline the limits of recreational use to avoid disturbing wildlife values (id., W-15). The report expressed particular concern that refuges in highly populated regions in the East and Midwest might succumb to pressure to allow incompatible levels of recreation (id., W-14–W-15). The Leopold report observed that once a nonwildlife-related recreational activity becomes established at a refuge, it is difficult to terminate (id., W-15). This concern remains evident today, where proximity to urban areas leads to pressure for park-like amenities, such as picnic grounds, campsites, and boat ramps (Olsen 1989, A21; U.S. House 1989, 96).

In 1976, the Service prepared a comprehensive environmental impact statement for its proposed management plan for the System over the following ten years. In response to the physical and fiscal limitations of the System, the plan would realign priorities to emphasize conservation and curtail (or reduce the rate of increase of) secondary benefits, such as recreation (U.S. FWS 1976, I-3, I-8). Noting that operational funds and staff had not kept pace with the tripling of visitation levels and the doubling of area of the System from 1957 to 1975, the Service stated:

> Public demands on System facilities have increased considerably beyond the capacity to provide services. Efforts are being made to reduce the demand to conform with legislative intent, existing facilities, enforcement and management capabilities. To achieve this balance will necessitate the shifting of funds and manpower to those basic management activities that will sustain the integrity of the refuge resources. This equilibrium should be achieved by 1985. (U.S. FWS 1976, I-8)

Nonetheless, the description of the proposed management activities contains no specific examples of incompatible uses or procedures to eliminate them, other than some general guidelines in the mitigation chapter (U.S. FWS 1976, chap. IV).

Unfortunately, the Service failed to meet its target date of 1985. Refuge managers, the GAO, and environmental groups continued to warn of threats to resources caused by activities on refuges (U.S. FWS 1983; U.S. GAO 1981; U.S. GAO 1984, 1989, 12). However, the Service did not make any of the bold changes needed to address many of the conflicts. A 1981 U.S. GAO report concluded that "local pressures to use refuge lands for such benefits as grazing, timber harvesting, and public recreation prevent refuge managers from effectively managing refuges primarily for wildlife" (U.S. GAO 1981, 28). As an example of incompatible uses, the report discusses the Cold Springs refuge where overgrazing and incompatible public use, such as off-road vehicle motoring and camping, destroyed wildlife habitat and adversely affected wildlife (id. at 29). That same report also criticized the Service for failing to update the *Refuge Manual*, which provided guidance and operating procedures for managers, since the early 1960s (id., at 23–24). A 1983 government-sponsored survey of refuge managers indicated that problems internal to the refuges played at least some role in resource degradation in 42 percent of all resource problems (U.S. FWS 1983).

Although the Service revised its *Refuge Manual* in 1986 to provide compatibility determination guidelines for refuge managers, incompatible uses continued to cause serious problems for refuge conservation (U.S. GAO 1989, 13). The guidelines required managers to follow five steps in reviewing uses: identification of proposed use, description of proposed use, assessment of the impacts of the use, consideration whether avoidance or minimization may make proposed incompatible use compatible, and final determination of compatibility and any conditions that may be placed on the use (id.). A 1989 GAO report concluded that "[r]efuge managers have considerable discretion in implementing these guidelines and in making approval decisions. Further, in many situations FWS does not require that the justification for compatibility decisions be documented" (id.). Nonetheless, judicial review of compatibility determinations under the 1962 and 1966 laws upheld FWS decisions in all but one dispute, involving boating and waterskiing in Ruby Lake National Wildlife Refuge (*Defenders of Wildlife v. Andrus* 1978). There were many unsuccessful court challenges to Service management of refuges during this period (Bean and Rowland 1997, 292–298; Tredennick 2000, 59–62).

The 1989 GAO report documented the failure of the Service to make headway against the proliferation of incompatible uses despite the continual warnings over the previous two decades. Because Service management of the Refuge System remained decentralized and because the Service lacked useful information about compatibility determinations for secondary uses, the GAO conducted a survey of all refuge managers, prepared 16 detailed studies, and evaluated FWS policy. The GAO findings revealed a shocking level of incompatible secondary use through both statistics and qualitative information. The survey found secondary uses occurring on 92 percent of refuges and harming conservation goals on 59 percent of refuges (U.S. GAO 1989, 16, 18). The FWS had approved many of the secondary uses under the 1986 *Refuge Manual* guidance. Among the most commonly occurring harmful secondary activities were mining, off-road vehicles, air boats, military exercises, waterskiing, power boats, rights-of-way, grazing, logging, hunting, and beach use (U.S. GAO 1989, 20–21).

Examples of refuges harmed by incompatible uses included the Des Lacs refuge in North Dakota, where the Service maintained high lake levels to allow recreational boating. The high water severely limited the ability of the Service to manage wetlands for the refuge's primary purpose, migratory bird production (U.S. GAO 1989, 22). Also, power boating and waterskiing on the lakes disrupted bird-nesting activities, cutting bird production in half. In responding to the GAO report, the FWS conceded that "Des Lacs is not an isolated case" (U.S. House 1989, 96).

Why was the Service allowing these incompatible uses to persist? The 1989 GAO report found that, in two-thirds of the situations, incompatible uses stemmed from two main causes (U.S. GAO 1989, 24). First, despite the compatibility guidance from the *Refuge Manual*, the Service allowed nonbiological factors to influence its approval of secondary uses (id., 24–27). Coupled with the absence of periodic reevaluation and documentation of compatibility decisions, the influence of political or economic interests supported uses that hampered the achievement of refuge purposes. For instance, in the Des Lacs refuge, local officials persuaded Service leadership to block attempts by refuge managers to adjust lake levels to enhance waterfowl production because of concerns related to local commerce in waterskiing, a golf course's need for water, and nearby aesthetic and property values (id., 26). Elected members of Congress exert even greater influence over Service decisions.

Furthermore, the GAO found that the Service lacked financial data on the costs of managing secondary recreational uses (id., 2). This finding suggested a violation of the 1962 Refuge Recreation Act requirement that the secretary determine that funds are available for the development, operation, and maintenance of any permitted secondary recreation uses

(§ 1). The GAO reported that the secretary "merely asserts that sufficient funds are available," without quantifying how much money actually might be spent on managing recreation (U.S. GAO 1989, 27). A number of refuge managers told the GAO that the costs of managing recreation "are high and draw a significant portion of limited refuge funding away from wildlife [conservation]" (id.).

The other main cause of harmful incompatible uses identified by the GAO was the limited jurisdiction of the FWS over many refuges. The following constraints on jurisdiction impeded the Service's ability to control secondary uses:

1. lack of ownership of subsurface mineral rights that limit the Service's control over mining;
2. Defense Department privileges that limit the Service's control over military air and ground exercises;
3. shared jurisdiction over navigable waters that limit the Service's control over boating, swimming, and beach use; and
4. easement components of refuges that limit the Service's control over farming and grazing. (Id., 28–29)

Where the Service does not have jurisdiction to control harmful uses, the GAO recommended that it acquire property rights to expand its jurisdictional reach, attempt to continue to work cooperatively with users, or remove the refuge from the System. However, removal should be used only as a last resort, according to the GAO (id., 33). These problems stemming from limited jurisdiction, like the other findings of the 1989 GAO report, had been raised by many of the earlier studies calling for reforms. For instance, the Leopold report found the divided jurisdiction, which weakens Service management of some refuges, to be "an unsatisfactory arrangement" (Leopold et al. 1968, W-12). The 1981 GAO report cited grazing management problems at the Charles M. Russell National Wildlife Refuge as illustrating an instance where shared management responsibilities with the BLM "thwarted" refuge objectives (U.S. GAO 1981, 29).

In part because it amplified so clearly the troubling conclusions from previous reports, the 1989 GAO report ignited a new wave of reform efforts to conserve refuge resources. After a congressional hearing to evaluate the findings of the 1989 GAO report, Congress considered a number of reform bills to strengthen the operational mandate of the Refuge System. These bills varied in their comprehensiveness, but many contained sections addressing refuge planning, compatibility determination standards, and the role of recreation (Tredennick 2000, 72–75). These topics ultimately found their way into an executive order and the 1997 Refuge Improvement Act.

Responding to the 1989 GAO report, the Service convened a Compatibility Task Group, which conducted its own study in 1990 that confirmed the GAO finding (Bean and Rowland 1997, 292; U.S. Senate 1994, 6). In 1992, frustrated by the lack of progress in reducing incompatible uses, a group of environmental organizations sued the secretary of the interior. The plaintiffs, which included the Wilderness Society, National Audubon Society, and Defenders of Wildlife, claimed that the Service was continuing to allow incompatible recreational and commercial uses on specified refuges. They also challenged the process by which the Service approved uses throughout the System (Tredennick 2000, 70–71; U.S. Senate 1994, 6–7). When the Clinton administration took office in 1993, it reached a settlement in the suit that called for written determinations of which uses in the System were compatible with the primary purposes of the refuges on which they were occurring and the availability of funds for managing recreational uses (U.S. House 1997a, 3). The settlement also committed the Service to "terminate or modify incompatible uses" (Bean and Rowland 1997, 292; U.S. Senate 1994, 7). Also in 1993, the Interior Department inspector general issued a report documenting Service failure to manage refuges "in a manner that would effectively enhance and protect the wildlife" (U.S. Senate 1997, 40). By 1997, when the House Resources Committee reported on the bill that would become the Refuge Improvement Act, the FWS had reviewed over 5,200 uses and found compatibility problems on 40 refuges.

President Clinton's 1996 Executive Order

In response to the management problems highlighted in the 1989 GAO report and the neglect by Congress, President Clinton issued an executive order in 1996 to reform administration of the Refuge System. In so doing, he followed in the tradition of strong executive leadership in shaping the Refuge System. The executive order allowed the Democratic president to blunt attempts in the Republican Congress to enact legislation that would have expanded and made more secure hunting in the Refuge System. Just as prior presidential actions had established the first refuges, created the FWS, and supported agency development of the compatibility criterion for refuge management, Executive Order 12,996 laid the groundwork for subsequent congressional action in 1997.

The executive order formulates three levels of mandates for the Refuge System that progressively provide more detail for systemic management:

the mission, guiding principles, and directives. The executive order sets out a broad ecological mission for the System "to preserve a national network of lands and waters for the conservation and management of fish, wildlife, and plant resources" (Executive Order No. 12,996, § 1). This mission reflects for the first time a concern for plants in and of themselves, not just in their role of providing animal habitat. This interest in plant conservation significantly broadens the purposes of the Refuge System. The ecological mission, characterized by President Clinton as the "dominant refuge goal," is the standard against which uses are compared to determine compatibility (Clinton 1997).

The midlevel guiding principles for management of the System add little to the initiatives the Service was already pursuing. The first principle lists the public uses that may constitute compatible wildlife-dependent recreation (Executive Order No. 12,996, § 2(a)). Because these uses are defined in the next level of mandates as priority public uses, this guiding principle is surplusage. The second guiding principle affirms the central ecological mission by mandating conservation and enhancement of the "quality and diversity of fish and wildlife habitat" (id., § 2(b)). The third principle is that partnerships with other federal agencies, state and tribal governments, businesses, and nongovernmental organizations make significant contributions to management of the System (id., § 2(c)). Finally, the fourth principle provides for public participation in acquisition and management decisions (id., § 2(d)).

The executive order's most detailed mandates are the directives to the secretary concerning use of the Refuge System, based on a hierarchy of purposes for the System. This approach of creating different tiers of purposes first appeared in the 1980 ANILCA establishment mandates. The executive order defines "priority general public uses" as compatible wildlife-dependent recreational activities involving hunting, fishing, wildlife observation and photography, and environmental education (id., § 3(a)). These priority uses enjoy a level of promotion that other uses do not. The directives provide expanded opportunities for, and enhanced attention in planning and management to, these priority uses, where compatible with the mission (id., § 3). Hunting, although a preferred use, is nonetheless subordinate to ecological conservation.

Although the executive order strengthened the System by articulating a mission and establishing a hierarchy of uses to aid management and planning, it failed to address directly the principal problems identified in the 1989 GAO report that led to the proliferation of harmful, incompatible uses in the System. The lack of written compatibility determinations, absence of periodic reexamination of permitted uses, and failure to collect data on the costs of managing recreation were all left unaddressed by the executive order. Also, unlike systemic legislation, the executive order is revocable at will by the president, cannot be the basis for judicial review (id., § 4), and does not carry the prestige of an organic statute to bolster agency power (Clarke and McCool 1996, 111).

For all of these reasons, the 1996 executive order set the stage for the most important statute Congress has passed for the Refuge System: the 1997 Improvement Act. As part two of this book will show, the approach taken and terms defined in the executive order powerfully influenced the content of the subsequent legislation. However, before examining the 1997 Act in detail, chapter 4 addresses the meaning of the term "organic" legislation. The term will provide a framework for exploring the key elements of the 1997 Act. The framework will highlight the most important features of the 1997 legislation and help relate the Improvement Act to other public land laws.

4 | *The Meaning of Organic Legislation*

The 1966 Refuge Administration Act consolidated a system "for the conservation of fish and wildlife" (Pub. L. No. 89-669, § 4(a)) and provided a framework for management that prohibited all uses unless they complied with management regulations authorized by the act. Yet the legislative history of the 1997 Improvement Act is replete with references to the lack of, and need for, organic legislation for the National Wildlife Refuge System. A typical example in the key committee report for the 1997 bill succinctly characterizes the special meaning ascribed to the term "organic act" in public land law. It states that "unlike the National Parks, National Forests and Bureau of Land Management (BLM) lands, the National Wildlife Refuge System remains the only major Federal public lands system without a true 'organic' act, a basic statute providing a mission for the System, policy direction, and management standards for all units of the System" (U.S. House 1997a, 3). Commentators now routinely make statements like "there was no organic act for the National Wildlife Refuge System until . . . 1997" (Peterson 2000, 194).

This chapter expounds on the development of the modern meaning of organic legislation. In doing so, it explains why legislators at the close of the twentieth century, looking back to the 1966 law, failed to see the systemic authority intended by their predecessors. The chapter's first section traces the evolution in the use of the term "organic" to describe certain legislation. It demonstrates a clear trend in public land law toward greater use of the term and increased statutory detail. The next section explains how the term is used today by identifying the key distinguishing features of modern organic legislation. These features, which I call hallmarks, provide a framework for analyzing the 1997 Improvement Act in the context of the larger issues of public land law.

This chapter's exploration of the meaning of organic legislation is designed both to reveal the overlooked historical origins as well as to probe the deep structure of comprehensive public land laws. In the context of the Refuge System, my exposition of organic legislation should strengthen legal interpretations that resolve ambiguities and conflicts in favor of the centripetal forces of coordinated, systemic management. My hallmarks of organic legislation may also be used as a menu for reform in addition to a guide for interpretation.

A better understanding of the meaning of organic legislation allows us to grasp more firmly the project of conservation lawmaking. "Organic act" is such a key term in public land law that an exploration of its meaning reveals important underlying assumptions about our system of federal natural resource administration. Identifying the underlying structure of organic legislation can help us forecast how the 1997 reforms might play out. When we compass the emergence of organic legislation in public land law generally, we more readily see the significance of the Improvement Act as something more than an attempt at Refuge System reform. Properly understood as the most recent development in organic lawmaking, the 1997 Act points toward new legal control techniques on public lands and likely revisions of other natural resource statutes.

"Organic act" rhetoric was an important part of the debate over the 1997 Act. Indeed, the legislative history of the Refuge System since 1960 is best understood as a search for ever more effective organic authority to bring coherence to the far-flung units managed by the FWS for a wide array of purposes. Thus, a review of refuge legislation provides an excellent guide for tracking the evolution of the "organic act" concept.

Evolution of the Term

The early legal meaning of "organic act" (or "organic law") was a statute conferring powers (defining and establishing the organization) of government (*Black's Law Dictionary* 1910; *Words and Phrases* 1972, 477–478). Most of the references to "organic act" in legal materials prior to 1970 refer to legislation organizing a municipality, territory, state, or nation. The term was also used occasionally to refer to a law granting powers to nongovernmental entities, such as joint-stock associations. The term "enabling act" was more frequently employed to refer to statutes establishing new states.

With the rise of administrative agencies in the late nineteenth and early twentieth centuries, the term "organic act" came also to be applied to laws that establish agencies or delegate power to executive departments. This usage retains the core meaning of the term, as organizing a political or public institution. Although not employed at the time of passage, the use of the term "organic act" to characterize the 1916 statute creating the National Park Service is an example of this application to agencies. In this sense, it is correct to characterize the 1956 Fish and Wildlife Act, a foundational delegation of legislative power to the Fish and Wildlife Service, as an organic act (Clarke and McCool 1996, 114; U.S. House 1975, 29–44). This is also how the term can be understood in the 1975 hearing on a proposal to create a Bureau of National Wildlife Refuges with the sole responsibility to manage refuges (U.S. House 1975, 6). When describing the creation of a new administrative or political entity, the term "creative act," or, less commonly, "organization act," may also be used.

However, in contemporary public land law, we use the term "organic act" in a substantially different sense. In addition to signifying the organization of an agency or political institution, we also use the term to refer to a charter for a network of public lands. This more recent, more specialized sense of "organic act" derives from the same root as that of the word "organize." The etymology of "organ" can be traced partly to organon, a Greek word for tool, and ergon, a Greek word for energy. "Organic" refers to something that constitutes or coordinates a system, the way organs work together to operate a body as a system. Likewise, in chemistry, the term "organic" refers to the compounds generally found in organized bodies (Safire 2001).

The 1916 "Act to Establish a National Park Service" (this is the formal title of the law passed by Congress at the time) is an organic act in the traditional sense of creating, and delegating authority to, a new agency. It is also an organic act in the contemporary, public land law sense because it establishes a comprehensive mandate for all national park units. Nonetheless, the names by which this statute are known vary. Standard references on the Park System refer to it variously as the National Parks Act (Ise 1979, 191–192) and the National Park Service Act (Runte 1987, 103). Even within the same treatise, it receives the various titles National Park Act and National Park System Act (Coggins and Glicksman 2002, §§ 2.03[2][a], 6.03[1]). The U.S. Code Popular Name Table now calls it the National Park Service Organic Act. It is, of course, all of these things.

For public land law, the 1916 National Park legislation is an important organic act not merely because it created the Park *Service,* but because it organized a Park *System.* Similarly, while the Federal Land Policy and Management Act (FLPMA), did not create the BLM, it is nonetheless the organic act for BLM lands because it organized them into a coherent system. And, of course, the 1897 statute establishing uniform management and administration of forest reserves (today's national forests) is the Ur-organic act in natural resources law even though it did not create an agency. This act granted forest reserve management authority to the secretary of the interior, who administered the reserves through the General Land Office until Congress transferred the lands to the Department of Agriculture in 1905. The analogy to organs working in concert to create bodily health captures the gist of Herbert Kaufman's observation in his classic study discussing the challenge of managing the expansive, decentralized National Forest System: "Unity does not demand uniformity, but it does require consistency and co-ordination" (Kaufman 1960, 80). Kaufman ultimately determined that the Forest Service achieved unity in restraining the "centrifugal tendencies" of the large organization (id., 203–207).

Although it is commonplace today to refer to the old national forest and national park statutes as organic acts, they were not known by those terms at the time they were enacted. Neither statute contains the term. Indeed, the 1897 Act did not have a title at all because it was a rider on a larger piece of legislation. Gifford Pinchot, the first Forest Service chief, ubiquitous conservation proponent of the Progressive Era, and participant in the negotiations over the legislation, described the act as the "Pettigrew Amendment to the Sundry Civil Act of June 4, 1897" (Pinchot 1972, 116). In his seminal 1956 book on forest policy, Samuel Trask Dana referred to the law as the "Forest Reserve Act of 1897" (Dana 1956, 107, 118). Some variation on Dana's terminology was common in references to the act until 1970 (Clawson and Held 1957; Gates 1978; Ise 1920; Kaufman 1960; Smith 1930).

The specialized meaning of "organic act," as something different from a statute creating an agency, is a usage that first appeared in the 1950s and grew with the modern era of environmental law in the 1960s. The use of the term "organic" to describe the 1916 law was rare until that time. The earliest reference to a public lands organic act that I have found appears in a 1931 memorandum by Horace M. Albright, director of the National Park Service. In discussing the preparation of park development plans, he cites the "organic law creating the Service" (Dilsaver 1994, 99). Director

Albright subsequently used the term "organic act" sporadically, but always in reference primarily to the mandates of the Service, not the system of park units (Albright and Cahn 1985, 286; Albright and Shenck 1999, 147).

Federal cases reported on the Westlaw electronic database of legal sources did not use "organic act" in the context of the creation of the National Park Service (let alone, System) until 1970. The Westlaw result may be as much a function of the lack of judicial challenges to the agency based on the 1916 law as it is a reflection of the use of the term "organic act." But a Westlaw search likewise failed to turn up any Forest Service cases before 1970 using the term "organic act." The Forest Service had been more heavily involved in litigation before 1970 than had the Park Service. Nonetheless, even the seminal cases establishing the proprietary management authority over national forests delegated in the 1897 statute, such as *United States v. Grimaud* (1911), did not employ the term "organic act" to refer to the 1897 statute. Other key, pre-1970 cases interpreting the 1897 law also failed to use the term "organic." Additional authoritative sources, such as a U.S. Attorney General Opinion, referred to the "act of June 4, 1897" (1964).

The Forest Service itself, in setting forth the basic regulations implementing the 1897 statute, did not use the term "organic act" in either its original national forest management manual or its first set of regulations. The original manual, the 1905 "Use Book," employs the term "Act of June 4, 1897." The initial 1936 regulations "relating to the protection, occupancy, use and administration of the national forests" adopt the term "Act of Congress of 1897" (1 Fed. Reg. 1090).

The term "organic act" first began to creep into Forest Service use in the 1950s and 1960s. In 1953 congressional testimony, Forest Service chief Richard E. McArdle used the phrase "organic act for the national forests of the East" to characterize a 1911 statute that authorized the acquisition of eastern lands (U.S. House 1953, 211). However, in the very same testimony he referred to the 1897 statute as the "Act of June 4, 1897." Much more significantly, the 1958 edition of the *Forest Service Manual,* the key operational document for the national forests, refers to the 1897 law as the "organic administration act." The periodic publication of the Department of Agriculture compiling the principal laws relating to the national forests followed suit in 1964 and began referring to the "Administration Act of 1897" (as prior editions had called it) as the "Organic Administration Act of 1897."

In the 1960s, as the modern era of environmental law dawned, the specialized public land law meaning of "organic act" began to appear sporadically in the scholarly literature. The first reference to the 1897 law as an organic act that I have found in a journal occurred in Michael McCloskey's 1966 article on the Wilderness Act. The reference occurs in his discussion of the rights of ingress and egress to inholdings "under the Forest Service's organic act of June 4, 1897" (McCloskey 1966, 313). Just five years earlier, when McCloskey published his analysis of the 1960 Multiple Use–Sustained Yield Act and its relationship to the 1897 act, he did not use the term "organic." Instead, he used the older term in stating that the Pettigrew rider to the appropriations bill "thus became what is known as the '1897 act'" (McCloskey 1961, 58).

By 1970, the modern meaning of "organic" had come into widespread use. That year witnessed the first reported federal court opinion to use the term to refer to the 1897 and 1916 acts. Oddly enough, the case was destined to emerge as a signal test of environmental group standing to challenge agency action. The court of appeals decision on the dispute over development of the Mineral King area in California referred to the 1897 legislation for forests as the "Organic Administration Act" and the 1916 law as the "Organic Act of the National Park Service" (*Sierra Club v. Hickel* 1970).

Also in 1970, the Public Land Law Review Commission issued its landmark report, which employed the term "organic" to refer to the 1897 statute (PLLRC 1970, 93, 151). The Commission, which Congress chartered in 1964 (Pub. L. No. 88-106), contracted with Shepard's Citations, Inc., to produce an exhaustive compilation of public land laws. That compilation fails to call either the "Forest Reserve Act of 1897" or the National Park Service Act "organic." The Commission published the compilation in 1968, just two years before the final Commission report using "organic" in its modern sense (PLLRC 1968, 218, 349). Also, no hint of the coming change in the use of the term "organic" is revealed in a 1967 symposium engaging many of the people and issues involved in the Commission's work (*Natural Resources Journal* 1967).

Part of the significance of the usage of "organic" is rhetorical. Characterizing a statute as organic may strengthen an agency's image of having a distinctive, important mission from Congress. The Public Land Law Review Commission's legal chief and assistant general counsel, Jerome C. Muys, recalls that the Commission did not itself coin the term "organic" legislation to refer to the 1897 and 1916 laws. Instead, Muys remembers that material the Commission received from the agencies, especially the Forest Service, had used the term. He speculates that the Forest Service may have first used the term in its modern sense to distinguish itself as a prestigious agency with a strong mandate, as compared to the BLM. This interpretation, which is consistent with the recollection of Michael McCloskey and with the evidence already discussed here from the Department of Agriculture, makes sense in light of one of the chief recommendations of the Commission to Congress: subsume the Forest Service within a new Department of Natural Resources (PLLRC 1970, 281–286). The merger of the Forest Service with other resource management agencies would have all but destroyed the institution, with its storied history. At the time of the deliberations of the Public Land Law Review Commission, the Forest Service was already in a defensive mode from the passage of the 1964 Wilderness Act. The congressional wilderness overlays on Forest Service land represented the "antithesis of some conceptions of multiple use management and in a sense the act expressed a lack of faith in the ability of the Forest Service to implement the multiple use requirement" (Huffman 1978, 277). The Forest Service sought to portray itself as more than just another resource management bureau. An organic act bolsters the foundation for something more substantial and may have helped the Forest Service resist the merger. Echos of this strategy are evident in the context of the 1997 Improvement Act debates, where describing the desire for an assortment of statutory improvements as the need for a fundamental organic act may have made the case for legislation more compelling.

In addition to its rhetorical value, however, the specialized meaning of "organic act" as a comprehensive, organizing, unifying framework for a public land system provides a sharp contrast to establishment legislation, which addresses just a specific parcel of land. Though there is at least one modern instance in which Congress did not follow this usage convention, on the whole it captures the terminology that has evolved over the past 35 years. By the time Congress enacted the National Forest Management Act and the Federal Land Policy Management Act in 1976, the term "organic" was a normal part of the discourse over the management strictures for the system of national forests and BLM lands, respectively.

One modern instance of aberrant usage occurs in part of the National Park Mining Regulation Act of 1976. A section of the act refers both to the purposes of the National Park System and to the "individual organic Acts for the various areas of the National Park System" (Pub. L. No. 94-429, § 2). Though this use of the term might correspond to the early "creative" meaning (acts that create individual park units), by 1976 Congress should have referred instead to the "individual establishment Acts." The overwhelming consensus is to reserve the term "organic" only for systemic legislation applicable to all units of the Park System (*Denver University Law Review* 1997).

Modern judges also sometimes get the terminology wrong. In *Sierra Club v. U.S. Forest Service*, Judge McKay refers repeatedly to the "Norbeck Organic Act" as the statute establishing a wildlife preserve managed by the Forest Service (*Sierra Club v. U.S. Forest Service* 2001). However, the 1920 statute does not use the term "organic." Instead it refers to the "creation" of a reserve (Ch. 247, 41 Stat. 986). It is an establishment statute.

Although many statutes address systemic concerns on public lands, some do so more comprehensively than others. All might be considered forms of organic legislation. But which truly deserve the title "organic act"? The 1962 Recreation Act could not be characterized as organic because, though it applied systemwide, it dealt with just one aspect of management—recreational use. The 1966 Act might properly be called an organic act because it consolidated the refuges into a system and provided a broad management framework. But why then, in light of the 1966 Act, did the legislative history of the 1997 Improvement Act call for a Refuge System organic act? Answering this question illustrates another facet of the significance of the meaning of organic legislation.

As the 1970 Public Land Law Review Commission Report observed, the 1966 Act did provide a (conservation) goal for administering the System. The 1966 Administration Act dealt comprehensively with all refuge uses. Indeed, the Public Land Law Review Commission contrasted the Forest Service and BLM lands, which suffered from an "absence of statutory goals," with the Refuge System, Park System, and Wilderness System, which each had "a clearly defined primary purpose" (PLLRC 1970, 42). Because the 1966 Refuge Administration Act provided more congressional guidance than either the 1916 Park System or the 1897 Forest System legislation, it is inconsistent today to call the 1897 law an organic act but deny the moniker to the 1966 Act.

It was only more recently that refuge advocates voiced frustration with the act's lack of affirmative guidance for management and a precisely defined mission. As the level of statutory detail in public land law increased throughout the 1970s, expectations for what Congress should provide in organic legislation rose as well (Fischman 1997). The broad guidance that left land managers with wide latitude, contained in such landmark, systemwide statutes as the 1960 Multiple-Use, Sustained-Yield Act for national forests (Pub. L. No. 86-517, *codified at* 16 U.S.C. §§ 528–531) and the 1966 Refuge Administration Act, no longer provided sufficient congressional direction after the environmental law revolution of the late

1960s and early 1970s. This explains the demands in the 1990s for a Refuge System organic act. For instance, a 1994 Senate committee report on proposed Refuge System organic legislation stated that:

> The absence of an articulated mission and purposes of the System is seen by many as limiting the ability of the USFWS to manage the System in a cohesive fashion and places the System at a disadvantage in the competition for funds with agencies having a clear legislative mandate. (U.S. Senate 1994, 4)

The meaning of the term "organic act" continued to evolve even after it became associated with systemic management of public lands. Over the past three decades, environmental legislation grew in complexity and strengthened the role of judicial oversight. In tandem with these developments, our expectations of the minimum standards for an act that would effectively organize a public land system likewise grew. We can better understand broader trends in public land law by tracing how our standards for characterizing a statute as "organic" have risen over time.

The Hallmarks of Modern Organic Legislation

By the late 1990s, although Congress had fortified the 1897 and 1916 laws, the Refuge System lagged in the greater statutory detail associated with contemporary organic legislation. I sort this statutory detail into five basic categories that now serve as hallmarks for legislation deserving the title "organic act": (1) purpose statements, (2) designated uses, (3) comprehensive planning, (4) substantive management criteria, and (5) public participation. Although not every major public lands act possesses each of these attributes, these hallmarks do characterize modern public land organic law and they are helpful criteria in separating limited or piecemeal alterations from comprehensive reform.

Legislation possessing most or all of these hallmarks can accurately be considered organic. The five hallmarks are the essential table of elements from which Congress synthesizes modern public land statutes. The hallmarks also identify topics for reform of laws lacking effectiveness in key areas. Though most organic acts display the five hallmarks, the authority contained in an organic act is by no means the *exclusive* authority or mandate for management of a public land system. The untidy realities of public land law require managers to navigate "an almost impenetrable maze of arguably relevant legislation . . . [generating] considerable confusion" (*California Coastal Comm'n v. Granite Rock Co.* 1987, 606 [Powell, J. concurring and dissenting]).

The articulation of a systemic purpose remains the sine qua non of organic legislation. An organic act must generate a purpose to guide land management across an array of individual units to create a coordinated system. Otherwise, each unit proceeds in its own direction, in response to its own local circumstance. Unless a collection of public land units can align to become more than the sum of its parts, it cannot be considered a system. Without a mission, conservation systems generally suffer from the same maladies as the pre-1997 Refuge System:

> Management continuity to meet the long-term needs of wildlife [is] frequently sacrificed or subordinated . . . to the demands of the local public. Lack of a congressional mandate in the form of system purposes is, in the bureaucratic world, akin to lack of identity. (U.S. Senate 1992a, 24)

Systemic purposes, however, usually must be defined in the most general of terms for them to speak to the diverse circumstances of far-flung lands. A conservation purpose for the Refuge System, for instance, must be applicable both to the Alaska Maritime National Wildlife Refuge, which extends over a thousand miles to encompass 2,400 islands, and to Mason Neck National Wildlife Refuge, a bicycle ride away from Washington, D.C. Also, because Congress revisits organic legislation infrequently, purpose statements must be written somewhat vaguely to avoid locking in particular ecological understandings that may soon be superseded.

Nonetheless, most post-1970 organic acts, concerned with orchestrating individual land units into harmonious public land systems, contain missions with defined terms. A defined mission is particularly useful in resolving conflicts and ambiguities in establishment authorities. Although an organic act rarely contains all of the delegations of power to a land management agency, the systemic purpose serves as the interpretive pilot to guide implementation of other relevant laws.

To relate broad purposes to real management decisions, organic legislation typically designates particular uses to be prohibited, preferred, encouraged, or merely tolerated. The designated uses in an organic act often are the strongest indicators of the cultural values reflected in the system. In contrast to performance standards, which look objectively to effects of activities to decide what to allow, designated uses concentrate on the categories or types of the activities themselves. For instance, Refuge System legislation designates hunting as a use that receives special encouragement, in part because a hunting tax funds the purchase of many refuges and refuge expansions. This is a judgment based on concerns for tax fairness and the leadership role that hunters have played in the American conservation movement. It is not principally based on the effects of hunting on the land, waters, and wildlife of the refuges.

Though we often describe public land systems based on their designated use regimes (i.e., multiple use, dominant use, exclusive use), no modern organic legislation permits a use solely on the basis of the qualitative attributes of the use. Substantive management criteria demand that a use in a permitted category not exceed a particular effect level. For instance, the BLM must avoid "unnecessary or undue degradation" in allowing the multiple uses to occur on its lands (43 U.S.C. § 1732(b)). However, organic legislation sometimes prohibits an activity outright, based on its type without regard to its effect. The category of new roads and buildings in wilderness areas is an example of this (16 U.S.C. § 1133(c)).

Comprehensive planning is a key element in any organic act because it ensures that individual management decisions are made not haphazardly but rather to promote some greater goal namely, the system mission. It provides a framework within which individual unit administrators may make management decisions and segregate particular uses to appropriate zones. Planning facilitates the evaluation of cumulative effects from a projected series of small actions authorized over the term of the plan (Loomis 1993, 363). Uniform, systemwide rules that govern planning exert a coordinating force on the diverse array of activities that may occur on land units. The comprehensive plan translates the general mission statements and broadly permissive designation of uses into prescriptions for a particular area over a particular time. It is the link between the systemic mandate and the local project.

The rise of substantive management criteria is an almost entirely new development of modern organic legislation. More than any other hallmark, the appearance of substantive management criteria characterizes the reforms of the 1970s. Substantive management criteria represent a reversal of the proprietary tradition, which relied on the "expert" judgment and location-specific experience of a unit administrator. Unlike designated uses (or best technology standards in pollution control), substantive management criteria shift the discourse over conflicts away from judgments about the worthiness of an activity and toward measurable benchmarks of environmental consequences (e.g., whether the activity would exceed the threshold criterion of "unnecessary or undue degradation" of lands). In this way, substantive management criteria (like ambient standards in pollution control) are closely aligned with the utilitarian view that outcomes matter more than intentions. The rise of substantive management criteria with the use of the term "organic" legislation belies the cynical claims of Professors Fairfax and Popper that "our tools for thinking about public resources have not changed much in a century" (Fairfax 2000, 105; Popper 1988).

The statutory use of environmental criteria to condition land managers' discretion has changed the nature of public land law. Though we still distinguish among public lands systems by categorizing them as multiple or dominant use, substantive management criteria have joined the designated uses as a signature feature of organic acts. The Forest Service's diversity mandate, the BLM's no undue degradation criterion, and the National Park Service's unimpaired standard reveal as much about these agencies' land management programs as do the terms "multiple" or "dominant" use. As I explore in chapter 8, the 1997 mandate to maintain biological integrity, diversity, and environmental health is a distinctive milestone characterizing the Refuge System brand of conservation.

The final hallmark of modern organic legislation is public participation. Public participation requirements transformed administrative law in the 1970s (Stewart 1975). Natural resources law did not escape this transformation, which contributed to the revision of systemic legislation. Public land management agencies today must provide stakeholders opportunities to contribute to decisions about individual projects, comprehensive plans, and systemwide policies. For instance, the National Environmental Policy Act provides citizens avenues to contribute to and comment on mandated environmental impact analyses for agency proposals for action. Though the organic acts themselves generally contain few directly applicable provisions relating to appeals, information disclosure, advisory committee activity, and judicial review, these avenues for public participation are all maintained through administrative law statutes and judicial doctrines. Much of this hallmark is folded into organic acts by reference to these other statutes and doctrines.

A deeper understanding of organic acts may aid in the application of lessons from natural resources law to pollution control law. An important criticism of the Environmental Protection Agency's (EPA's) piecemeal pollution control authorities is that they are myopic to the distant long term: they fixate on the specific, close-up problems but lack clear vision for integrated environmental quality improvement. In response, critics often propose more comprehensive, coordinated management, through an "integrating" statute for the EPA (Davies and Mazurek 1998; *Environmental Law* 1992; National Academy of Public Administration 1995; Stephens 2002; Sussman 1996). Another way to think about these proposals is to consider what an organic act for a system of pollution control might look like. Rather than orchestrating a tangle of unit establishment mandates, an EPA organic act would have to integrate a tangle of medium-, pollutant-, sector-, and (sometimes) place-specific pollution control mandates.

The disaggregation of elements that constitute an organic act provides a basis for evaluating the new Refuge Improvement Act. Organic legislation performs a set of tasks to coordinate the disparate units of a public land system so that they cohere rather than fragment. In its ideal form, an organic act makes public land units more than the sum of their parts, just as the human body is more than just a wet bag of organs. This is a particular challenge for the Refuge System because of the diverse array of unit establishment mandates. The next five chapters, which constitute part two of this book, analyze how the 1997 Improvement Act manifests the five hallmarks of organic legislation. I will address each hallmark in the same order as described in the preceding text, which moves from more general provisions to ones that require greater detail and more specific procedures for implementation.

PART TWO

The National Wildlife Refuge System Improvement Act of 1997

5 | *Purpose Statements*

It is important to remember that refuges have two sets of purposes: the comprehensive purpose of the National Wildlife Refuge System and the specific purposes for which individual refuges were established. Almost all of the Improvement Act's legislative history acknowledges the dual nature of the System mission. A major challenge for the Improvement Act is to provide a unity of purpose for the System while preserving the individual establishment mandates for the refuge units. Though the act's set of objectives for the System is as detailed as any organic legislation, it also strengthens somewhat the divergent force of individual refuge purposes. The retention and strengthening of individual refuge purposes, discussed in chapter 10, will limit the ability of the act to achieve comprehensive reform of the administration of the national wildlife refuges. This chapter focuses on the broader, comprehensive purposes of the Refuge System.

Prior to enactment of the 1997 Improvement Act, Congress had provided little guidance to the Fish and Wildlife Service (FWS) on the purposes for consolidating refuges into a system. Conservation has always been the common theme of establishment mandates for the individual units. However, conservation encompasses a range of concerns from ecosystem preservation, to endangered species recovery, to sustaining game populations for hunting, to optimum yield economic development. Thus, the mere mention of "conservation," without a definition, in the purpose and findings section of prior legislation, such as that for the 1966 Refuge Administration Act, accomplished little in the way of unifying the hodgepodge of refuges.

Specifying a systemic purpose, or mission, is a prerequisite to aligning and coordinating unit management for a larger goal. A mission statement must be detailed enough to serve as the ultimate test for management plan adequacy and, ultimately, implementation success. (Of course, substantive management criteria provide more specific objectives for actual performance assessment.) On the other hand, the mission must be sufficiently general to provide relevant direction to a wide range of refuge types. The diversity of units, the same characteristic of the System that creates the need for a coordinating mission, also limits the degree to which a mission statement can provide detailed answers to management dilemmas, such as regulation of lake levels and impoundments.

The Improvement Act's legislative history asserts that "refuges have not always been managed as a national system because of the lack of an overall mission for the System" (U.S. House 1997a, 3). This concern had been raised as early as 1968 in the Leopold committee report discussed in chapter 3. Indeed, the House report accompanying the 1997 Act explains that an important problem, which surfaced in hearings and evaluations, was that refuges were managed more as a collection of disparate units than as a true system. Congress sought to "remedy this shortcoming by establishing an over-arching mission statement . . . to guide overall management of the System and to supplement the purposes for which individual refuges have been established" (id., 8). Appendix B contains the text of the 1997 Refuge Improvement Act.

Although an overall mission is a necessary condition for systemic management, it is not sufficient. While the 1997 Act does provide the first statutory mission for the System, it may not succeed in spurring systemic management. This is because the 1997 Act allows individual refuge purposes in establishment documents to override the mission statement where they conflict: "[I]f a conflict exists between the purposes of a refuge and the mission of the system, the conflict shall be resolved in a manner that first protects the purposes of the refuge, and, to the extent practicable, that also achieves the mission" (§ 5(a)(4)(D)). This may continue to support divergent management among the units.

The 1997 Refuge Improvement Act states: "The mission of the System is to administer a national network of lands and waters for the conservation, management, and where appropriate, restoration of the fish, wildlife, and plant resources and their habitats within the United States for the benefit of present and future generations of Americans" (§ 4). The Improvement Act defines "conservation" and "management" as synonymous. In this respect, "conservation" under the Improvement Act is different from "conservation" under the Endangered Species Act (ESA). Under the ESA, conservation requires restoration, at least to the extent of enhancing species populations and habitat so that the species is no longer on the brink of extinction (16 U.S.C. §§ 1532(3), 1536(a)(1)). In the Improvement Act, however, "conservation" requires restoration only under the discretionary circumstances where it is "appropriate." Both conservation and management mean "[1] to sustain and, where appropriate, restore and enhance, healthy populations of fish, wildlife, and plants utilizing . . . [2] methods and procedures associated with modern scientific resource programs" (§ 5(4)). This definition largely reiterates the language of the mission itself.

The remainder of this chapter explores the five key elements of this mission statement for conservation and its application in practice. The first section analyzes the meaning of the element of the mission requiring the Service "to sustain and, where appropriate, restore and enhance healthy populations." The second section discusses the expansion of the refuge mission to include plant conservation. The third section attempts to determine what the "methods and procedures associated with modern scientific resource programs" might be. The fourth section reviews issues associated with other aspects of the System mission: habitat conservation, the role of future benefits, and latitude for exercise of agency discretion. Finally, the fifth section highlights the importance of coordination in fulfilling the Improvement Act's mission.

Sustaining, Restoring, Enhancing Healthy Populations

This systemic mission of conservation has a desired goal of sustaining and, where appropriate, restoring and enhancing healthy populations of animals and plants. There are two alternative ways to interpret this language. One interpretation would understand "healthy" to describe only the quantitative threshold where population levels are sustainable. An alternative interpretation of the goal would include both quantitative characteristics (e.g., the number of individuals in a population) and qualitative attributes (e.g., the condition of health).

The legislative history interpreting the mission statement offers scant help in choosing between these definitions. However, the qualitative threats to refuge plants and animals from habitat alteration and contamination are an important theme of the reports of the 1980s and 1990s documenting the System's incompatible uses. The 1997 Act is, in large part, a response to those reports.

Additionally, the overall emphasis in the Improvement Act on nature protection further strengthens the case for the qualitative interpretation of "healthy." Although the FWS has long worked with population size management, the use of the term "healthy" in the definition of conservation is a new systemic mandate that directs the Service to examine more closely environmental quality concerns affecting refuges. This view is bolstered by the Act's substantive management criterion to ensure the maintenance of biological integrity, diversity, and environmental health (§ 5(a)(4)(B)). It is also the interpretation favored by the Service, which defines "environmental health" to mean "[a]biotic composition, structure, and functioning of the environment consistent with natural conditions, including the natural abiotic processes that shape the environment" (602 FW 1.6(I)). The Service has stated that its goals include both qualitative and quantitative components of a region's ecology (66 Fed. Reg. 3,812 [2001]).

The FWS has taken an important step in adopting the purpose of sustaining, restoring, and enhancing healthy populations through its performance review standards. As James Q. Wilson noted in his classic study of bureaucracy, measured outcomes tend to "drive out work that produces unmeasurable outcomes" (Wilson 1989, 161). The Service has established both the quantitative and the qualitative aspects of the mission as elements in its Government Performance and Results Act (GPRA) review. Quantitative goals include the GPRA plan to restore 600,000 acres and annually improve 3.2 million acres of habitat in the System (U.S. FWS 2000–2005, 35). The five-year plan also calls for acquiring 1.275 million acres within the System (id.). But the Service's performance goal to develop standardized methods to measure biological diversity and environmental health on all refuges is even more essential to the goal of healthy populations (U.S. FWS 2000a, 42–45). This will allow Congress, the public, and the agency to track progress in fulfilling the Improvement Act's mission.

Plant Conservation

The Improvement Act begins with a series of congressional findings. In them, Congress states that the System "was created to conserve fish, wildlife, and plants and their habitats" (§ 2). Although the term "conservation" appears in earlier statutes directing Refuge System management, the 1997 Act is wrong in stating that the System was created in part to conserve plants. Floral conservation, at least as separate from habitat conservation, had never been part of the System's mission. In fact, the Improvement Act is the first statute applicable systemwide to mention plant conservation, aside from references to habitat for animals. Its only antecedent is the 1996 executive order, which added plant conservation to the System's mission.

Though the 1924 Congress established the Upper Mississippi River Wild Life and Fish Refuge in part to conserve "wild flowers and aquatic plants," it was not until the 1980s that plants again received explicit mention in refuge purposes, outside of habitat for wildlife (Pub. L. No. 68-268 [1924]). Even after 1980, plant conservation establishment purposes pop up only occasionally. Plants first gain mention as a systemic concern in a 1992 bill introduced by Representative Gerry Studds that contains purpose language ultimately adopted with modifications into the 1997 Act (U.S. House 1992).

The Improvement Act echoes the congressional findings in its purpose statement by including plants among the resources to be conserved (i.e., sustained, restored, enhanced). Adding plant conservation to the Refuge System's purposes represents a significant enlargement of mission. It reflects a broader trend to expand environmental concerns beyond the animal kingdom (Campbell 1988, 20). This wider scope is consistent with the national trend toward ecosystem management, which the FWS administratively adopted for the Refuge System in 1996 (Keiter 1994; U.S. FWS *Manual*, 052 FW 1.3(B); Yaffee 1999).

The specific provisions of the Improvement Act implementing plant conservation for refuges illustrate that the embrace of the plant kingdom in the act's purpose statement is more than a mere rhetorical flourish. For instance, the Service must monitor the status and trends of plants as well as animals in each refuge (§ 5(a)(4)(N)). Also, mandated new comprehensive conservation plans for each refuge must include descriptions of the distribution and abundance of plant populations, the significant problems that may harm plant populations, and the actions necessary to mitigate those problems (§§ 7(a)(2)(B), (E)).

Nonetheless, plants do not enjoy equal treatment in all respects. The emergency power granted to the FWS to "temporarily suspend, allow, or initiate any activity" is conditioned on a finding that the activity is necessary to protect the "health and safety" of the public or any animal population (§ 8(a)(k)). A direct threat to plants alone would not satisfy the conditions for exercising emergency authority.

More troubling from the standpoint of systematic plant conservation is the Service's animal focus in implementing the Improvement Act. Despite the expansive taxonomic embrace of the statute's conservation mandate, the Service incorrectly hews to a "wildlife first" policy (65 Fed. Reg. 33,892 [2000]). The FWS states that "we will prepare refuge plans that, above all else, ensure that wildlife comes first on national wildlife refuges" and "the first and foremost goal of the Refuge Improvement Act is to ensure that wildlife conservation is the principal mission of the Refuge System" (id. at 33,893). The Service also employs a "wildlife first" policy in its compatibility regulation (65 Fed. Reg. 62,458, 62,461 [2000]). Most surprisingly, the Service's policy implementing its mandate to maintain biological integrity, diversity, and environmental health refers to "wildlife conservation" as the fundamental mission of the System (601 FW 3.7).

Although "fish and wildlife" generally means all animals, the FWS has assumed conservation responsibilities for certain plant species at least since the enactment of the ESA of 1973. The Service is now the lead agency responsible for protecting and recovering approximately 750 listed plants. It should build on this experience to implement the 1997 Improvement Act's new *phyto*-emphasis. The FWS culture and terminology continue to lag behind the ecological perspective adopted in the Improvement Act, which recognizes plants as the foundation of the ecological pyramid.

Modern Scientific Research Programs

The definition of conservation and management in the Improvement Act requires the use of "modern scientific resource programs" as a means of achieving the mission. This term receives no explanation in the legislative history. Perhaps this modifier in the definition of conservation and management does little to limit the range of tools the Service may employ: any approach that is currently associated with resource programs elsewhere might be used in refuges.

On the other hand, Congress may have intended the phrase to disapprove of certain extant approaches. For instance, one could emphasize "modern" and infer a disapproval of old-fashioned management practices. What those old practices might be, however, is unanswered in the legislative history. Classic game management, promoting favored sport hunting species, would be a prime candidate for "nonmodern" scientific management that does not meet the criteria for ecological health. The management of the National Elk Refuge to maximize the size of the elk herd would be vulnerable to charges that it violates this interpretation of the System mission. In the Elk Refuge, the maintenance of a large concentration of game has impaired the overall biological diversity. Elk over-browse woody vegetation, thereby reducing valuable habitat for trout and many bird species (Clark 2000; Matson 2000).

But most wildlife management in the United States today *is* oriented toward hunting concerns. As Jonathan Rosen observes, "'wildlife management' basically means maintaining the area to facilitate hunting" (Rosen 2001, 64). And, many problems with game management center on the narrow measures of success (e.g., single species populations) more than the actual practices employed (e.g., habitat enhancement). So even incorporating "modern" into the definition of conservation and management will not necessarily improve the refuge programs.

Alternatively, an emphasis on "scientific" might limit some experimental management practices that do not have the imprimatur of mainstream scientists. Perhaps, then, this provision would limit the FWS from experimenting with techniques, such as Alan Savory's "holistic resource management" involving "nonselective" and "short-duration" grazing prescriptions, which remain unendorsed by the majority of the range management academic community (Donahue 1999, 82–83, 141–142; Olinger 1998, 692). Yet this interpretation is also unsatisfying because experimentation is the lifeblood of the scientific method.

Another, more satisfying, way to emphasize "scientific" would be to insist that all conservation in the System employ "adaptive management." Adaptive management responds to ecological characteristics by "[r]ecognizing that every land management practice is an experiment with an uncertain outcome" (Noss 1994, 907). Adaptive management is based on feedback from continual management experimentation. So, in adaptive management, authorized activities are coordinated and monitored to determine their effects on biological integrity. The information gained then feeds back into the plan "to adjust management in a desirable direction" (Noss 1994, 907). This reading of "scientific" gains support from the substantive management criterion in the Improvement Act requiring the FWS to monitor animals and plants.

This puzzling phrase, "modern scientific research programs," may be a tribute to the influence of the 1968 Leopold report, which promoted a Refuge System that retains or expands and restores native biota wherever practicable. The House report accompanying the Improvement Act characterizes the Leopold report as recommending that the Refuge System "stand as a monument to the science and practice of wildlife management" (U.S. House 1997a, 9). Although the U.S. Forest Service receives mixed reviews for its leadership in modern forestry, it has supported the development of new tools, such as the "sloppy clearcuts" of "new forestry." Sloppy clearcuts result when even-aged logging techniques retain scattered live trees, standing dead trees, and coarse woody debris to create a more diverse structure on the logging site. In experimenting with this sort of technique, the Forest Service has been better able to incorporate some ecological protection concerns into the practice of timber management (Dower et al. 1997, 236–237; Franklin 1989; Gillis 1990; Noss and Cooperrider 1994, 210–213; Thomas 1995).

The FWS should use its new mandate to spur innovation in wildlife management and to become a premier practitioner of what one might call "new conservation." Unfortunately, this will be a difficult challenge for the FWS. Unlike the Forest Service, which contains a research division within its ranks, the FWS relies principally on scientists in the U.S. Geological Survey for its research (Wagner 1999). The lack of internal scientific expertise at the FWS will hamper its ability to be a leader in establishing modern scientific research programs and practicing adaptive management.

Habitats, Utilitarianism, and Agency Discretion

Three other terms in the mission statement are worth brief mention. First, the statement is applicable not just to animals and plants, but to their habitats as well. It is now a fundamental axiom of wildlife management and resource administration that animals and plants cannot be conserved without providing for their habitat (National Research Council 1995; Noss et al. 1997). Still, the explicit recognition of habitats in the mission statement helps promote the move toward ecosystem management.

Second, the mission statement mandates conservation "for the benefit of the present and future generations of Americans." This phrase adds a utilitarian flavor to a mission that otherwise eschews the language of costs and benefits, in contrast to the multiple use mandates of the Bureau of Land Management and Forest Service. But there is an ambiguity in the meaning of the phrase. One interpretation of the phrase is declaratory: Congress has found that conservation of life benefits present and future generations. Another interpretation is conditional: the Service should conserve only under those conditions that benefit present and future generations. Because the cost–benefit criterion is largely absent from the rest of the statute, it seems unlikely that Congress intended the phrase to be conditional. This is particularly true given the difficulties of applying the utilitarian calculus to future generations (Farber 1999, 133–162; Heinzerling 1999; Parfit 1976; Sagoff 1988, 60–65).

Third, both the mission statement itself as well as the definition of conservation and management employ the phrase "where appropriate" to limit the mandate as it applies to restoration and enhancement. This grant of discretion to the FWS is probably most significant in contrast to its absence in the part of the mission that commands sustaining populations. The tradition of public land and resource management is one of great deference and broad delegation (*Udall v. Tallman* 1965; *United States v. Grimaud* 1911). But Congress explicitly endorsed this traditional flexibility for the Service in one part of the mission (restore and enhance) but not in another (sustain). Therefore, the FWS does not enjoy its normal proprietary management discretion for that part of the mandate requiring healthy populations to be sustained. This makes the Refuge System mandate similar to the ESA, which provides wide latitude for agencies to choose and tailor actions to restore listed species, but very strictly constrains agencies to sustain populations to avoid jeopardizing the continued existence of species (16 U.S.C. § 1536). It also echoes the 1982 National Forest Management Act (NFMA) regulations binding the Forest Service to "maintain viable populations" of vertebrate species. The regulations effectively shut down the timber program in the Pacific Northwest when courts found that the Forest Service could not ensure viability of the northern spotted owl population if planned logging occurred (*Seattle Audubon Society v. Moseley* 1992). The Improvement Act's alteration of traditional, broad discretion for sustaining populations reflects the trend toward stricter backstops for biological protection.

At the very least, the mission statement is a useful tool of interpretation for resolving ambiguities and conflicts. The mission also serves as a broad-brush goal statement to act as a navigational aid for long-range planning. Congress sought to endorse ecological protection and enhancement in refuge management over the often-competing commercial or economic goals.

Coordination

In addition to the definitions in the Act, the legislative history offers some indication of how Congress meant the mission statement to guide the System. In explaining the mission, the overriding theme in the legislative history is coordination. The most obvious goal of the purpose statement is to respond to disparate administration by "managing a series of refuges in a coordinated manner to meet the life-cycle needs of migrating species, providing habitat for threatened or endangered species, or representing the various habitats that provide for the conservation of the Nation's wildlife resources" (U.S. House 1997a, 8).

The legislative history also adumbrates coordination of refuges with state programs (id.). Indeed, the act itself requires coordination with states in the administration of the System generally and in planning (§§ 5(a)(4)(E), 7(e)(3)). This partnership with states is, of course, limited by federal preemption of state law that conflicts with FWS management control on refuges. For instance, a state may not impose its own hunting/ trapping regulations or property law restrictions on the Refuge System under circumstances where they would frustrate decisions made by the Service or Congress (*National Audubon Society v. Davis* 2002; *North Dakota v. United States* 1983).

Nonetheless, the FWS has always worked closely with states, especially on hunting and fishing issues, where states have traditionally exercised comprehensive, default management. Coordination areas, where states manage federal Refuge System lands, are the most extreme example of Service deference to state wildlife programs. However, even on national wildlife refuges, the Service continually renews its commitment to respond to state interests. Service policy emphasizes state participation in most refuge decision making, especially for comprehensive conservation planning (U.S. FWS 2002c).

Coordination across jurisdictional boundaries is necessary for ecosystem management and long-term protection of biological diversity. By highlighting coordination, Congress expressed its interest in adopting the fundamental insights of conservation biology in the new charter for the System. This may help to broaden the management focus of refuges from the old "inviolate sanctuary" model of the fenced preserve to more contemporary ecological conservation strategies of establishing diverse networks of lands and waters with connecting corridors. The Service policy implementing its ecological management criteria, which I analyze in chapter 8, for instance, provides important practical guidance in addressing external threats to refuge conservation.

The mission statement in the Improvement Act succeeds in concisely and sharply focusing and shifting the overarching goals of the System. It adequately incorporates the current insights of conservation biology by updating the conservation impetus that has driven expansion and management of the System over the decades. It gives plants their ecologically warranted, equal consideration. It emphasizes the bottom-line performance measure of sustaining healthy plant and animal populations. Nonetheless, the mission of the System is weakened by its subservience to conflicting purposes in establishment documents and ill-defined, superfluous terms.

6 | *Designated Uses: The Hierarchy*

Although agreement on the conservation purpose of the Refuge System is largely unanimous, disputes continue over the kinds of uses that have a legitimate place in the System. The 1997 Refuge System Improvement Act builds on the tiered use framework developed in the 1996 executive order and the Alaska National Interest Lands Conservation Act (ANILCA) to create a hierarchy of uses. The standard, simplified description contains three basic tiers, from highest to lowest priority: 1. conservation, 2. wildlife-dependent recreation, and 3. other uses (Coggins and Glicksman 2002 § 14A:5). However, as I show in this chapter, a closer reading of the statute (reprinted in Appendix B) reveals a more nuanced hierarchy with five categories of use priorities.

Conservation, the overarching mission of the System, is the maintenance and, where appropriate, restoration and enhancement of healthy populations of animals and plants (§ 3(a)(4)). Conservation occupies the apex of the hierarchy of uses unless displaced by a purpose or mandate from a refuge unit's establishment document (§ 5(a)(4)(D)). In this respect, the top tier of the hierarchy of uses may itself be subdivided into two levels: a top subtier for establishment purposes and a bottom subtier for the System conservation mission.

President Clinton, when he signed the act, identified conservation as the "dominant" priority (Clinton 1997). Dominant use schemes of public land management have historically received less attention from commentators than multiple use approaches. However, the dominant (or primary) use model promoted in the early modern era by the Public Land Law Review Commission continues to grow as an important paradigm. Jan Laitos and Thomas Carr have recently asserted that recreation and preservation are becoming the dominant uses of all of the federal public lands, including those governed by a multiple use, sustained-yield mission (Laitos and Carr 1999). Certainly this is true of the Refuge System where preservation has always been a principal use and where certain types of recreation have been elevated under the Improvement Act to priority status.

The 1997 Improvement Act actively promotes "wildlife-dependent" recreation uses, including hunting and fishing, subject to the substantive management criterion that they comply with the compatibility standard. "Wildlife-dependent recreation" is the same category that the 1996 executive order termed "priority general public uses," and the new U.S. Fish and Wildlife Service (FWS) *Manual* policies use the two terms interchangeably (65 Fed. Reg. 62,487 [2000]). The list of activities defining this category in the hierarchy of uses differs only slightly, and insignificantly, between the executive order and the Improvement Act. Both include hunting, fishing, wildlife observation and photography, and environmental education (Executive Order No. 12,996 § 3(a); Improvement Act of 1997 § 3(a)(2)). The Improvement Act adds environmental interpretation, but environmental interpretation is generally considered part of environmental education (Knapp 1997). Trapping is not included in the priority wildlife-dependent uses category; it is not a kind of hunting.

Conservation as a Dominant Use

An important semantic issue that causes confusion in refuge management is whether to consider the individual refuge purposes and mission of the System "dominant uses." Before the 1996 executive order, hunting, fishing, and other wildlife-dependent forms of recreation were commonly described as secondary uses. This terminology links to the dominant use idea by suggesting that the individual and systemic refuge purposes, which the compatibility criterion protects, were primary uses.

However, in the enactment and implementation of the 1997 Act, the Interior Department moved away from the conception of the mission and purposes as uses. Secretary of the Interior Bruce Babbitt, commenting on an earlier version of the 1997 Act, persuaded Congress to distinguish between the conservation *purpose* of the System and wildlife-dependent recreation *uses*. Babbitt feared that the earlier bill, which categorized both as purposes, would provide a basis for legal challenges by some wildlife-dependent recreationists complaining that their uses were impaired by other wildlife-dependent recreationists. He criticized this enlarged category of purposes as "scrambl[ing] the distinction between purpose and use" (U.S. House 1997e, 10). Actually, Babbitt's real complaint was that the bill did not clearly subordinate wildlife-dependent recreation to conservation. However, his means of expressing the dominant–subordinate use distinction as one between purpose and use has taken root in the Service's policy implementing the designated uses hallmark.

Whether we call something a purpose or a use, the framework adopted in the 1997 Act clearly elevates conservation above wildlife-dependent recreation and provides no recourse to wildlife-dependent recreationists who find their activities impaired by other types of wildlife-dependent recreation. The compatibility regulation states that "in case of direct conflict between these priority public uses, the Refuge Manager should evaluate, among other things, which use most directly supports long-term attainment of refuge purposes and the System mission" (65 Fed. Reg. 62,490 [2000]). Nonetheless, I believe it is important to categorize conservation as an affirmative use to counter critics who regard nature protection as a lock-up that "embalms" public land (Rasband 2001, 619). If we relegate conservation to a nonuse status, we fail to appreciate that preserved land sustains many uses, such as ecosystem services, that provide real value to the nation (Fischman 2001, 499–500, 502). As the "dominant use" moniker suggests, conservation lands are being used—by people, in fact—even if people are not present on the lands. A person living downstream of natural areas may be using their flood control services. Undeveloped natural habitat is used by farmers who depend on its pollination and nutrient cycling services. Hunters and anglers, of course, use the animals sustained by refuge habitat.

Joseph L. Sax has observed that separating the conservation functions from use categories supports the traditional, dualistic treatment of land as a passive entity, doing nothing until transformed by development, rather than as a functioning, productive system vulnerable to damage (Sax 1993, 1442). Viewing habitat protection as nonuse has legal consequences, such as the Idaho Supreme Court's denial of water rights to wildlife refuges based on the notion that there is a dichotomy between conserving habitat for migratory birds and advancing the interests of people (*United States v. State of Idaho* 2001). The Refuge System should be at the forefront of educating the public and courts that refuge conservation is a use that works for people too.

Support for the Service's view that the System mission is not a "use" can be inferred from the 1966 Administration Act's exclusion of activities "performed by persons authorized to manage" System areas from the compatibility criterion (§ 4(c)). This provision of the 1966 Act is unchanged by the 1997 legislation. Therefore, the Service excludes from the definition of refuge use "refuge management activities," which are conducted to fulfill a refuge purpose or the System mission, if the activities do not generate commodities that can be sold or traded, such as hay or timber (50 C.F.R. § 25.12). The Service defines a refuge use as a "recreational use," "refuge management economic activity," or some "other use" (50 C.F.R. § 25.12).

Therefore, the compatibility determination, which is a public process designed to ensure that the System's mission is not impeded by refuge uses, does not apply to "refuge management activities." A federal district court upheld this FWS interpretation in finding that no compatibility determination is necessary for the National Elk Refuge elk and bison feeding program. The court endorsed the view that the statutory compatibility criterion applies only to "uses" and that all of the examples of uses provided in the legislation are "meant to be performed by third parties or the public" (*Fund for Animals v. Clark* 1998).

The FWS includes in the management activities category water level management, invasive species control, scientific monitoring, historic preservation activities, and routine maintenance (65 Fed. Reg. 62,488 [2000]). Water level management is a controversial issue in some refuges because of conflicts between habitat requirements and recreation demands. For instance, the General Accounting Office (GAO) found that maintaining water levels to facilitate boating at the Des Lacs refuge impaired wetland habitat conservation (U.S. GAO 1989, 22). The 1966 compatibility mandate did not apply to water level management because it is performed by refuge managers. However, because boating is not a purpose of the System or the Des Lacs refuge, this resource management decision in support of boating would fail to meet the Service's regulatory definition of a "refuge management activity" (50 C.F.R. § 25.12). Therefore, under the compatibility regulations, some water level management might be subject to the dominant use test of compatibility even though this result is not compelled by statute.

Without the public scrutiny afforded use approvals, including compatibility determinations, Service refuge management activities may drift away from their core function of furthering the refuge purposes and mission. But the issue of whether management activities ought to be subjected to the compatibility determination need not constrain our understanding of the term "use." Even if the Service recognized the purposes and mission as uses of refuges, it still could have exempted management activities from the ambit of the compatibility test.

Primary Uses (achieved, in part, through "refuge management activities," e.g., water level management, invasive species control, routine maintenance)	1. Individual refuge purpose 2. Conservation WHERE IT DOES NOT CONFLICT WITH INDIVIDUAL REFUGE PURPOSES
Secondary Uses	3. Wildlife-dependent recreation (Priority general public use) (hunting, fishing, wildlife observation/photography, and environmental education/interpretation) WHERE IT IS COMPATIBLE WITH PRIMARY USES • Reevaluation every 15 years • Exempt from Recreation Act funding criterion • Service mandate to promote
Tertiary Uses	4. Other recreational use (e.g., snowmobiling, boating, off-road vehicle use) WHERE IT IS COMPATIBLE WITH PRIMARY USES AND DOES NOT CONFLICT WITH SECONDARY USES • Reevaluation every 10 years
Quaternary Uses	5A. Refuge management economic activity (e.g., timber thinning, trapping, hay cropping) 5B. Economic use of natural resources ("other use") (e.g., logging, grazing, oil/gas production, electricity transmission) WHERE IT IS COMPATIBLE WITH PRIMARY USES, DOES NOT CONFLICT WITH SECONDARY USES, AND CONTRIBUTES TO ATTAINING A PRIMARY USE • Reevaluation every 10 years

Note: Non-economic management activities (e.g., water level management, invasive species control, and scientific monitoring) are not considered uses.

FIGURE 6.1. The Hierarchy of Refuge System Designated Uses

Overview of the Hierarchy of Uses

Wildlife-dependent recreation is a lower-priority use than conservation because it must be consistent with the conservation mission of the Improvement Act to be permitted. Any conflict between conservation and what the Service defines as a "refuge use" must be resolved in favor of conservation in the absence of contrary intent manifest in the establishment document. Figure 6.1 displays this subordination of wildlife-dependent recreation to what I call primary uses.

Wildlife-dependent recreation, in turn, enjoys a higher priority than nonwildlife-dependent recreation and a wide range of other nonconservation uses. These other uses include logging, grazing, oil and gas production, and electricity transmission (143 Cong. Rec. S9,093-94 [1997]). Many of these other uses are identified in the reports criticizing System management as the sources of environmental degradation. The Service compatibility policy, incorporated in the FWS *Manual*, states outright that "[w]here there are conflicts between priority [wildlife-dependent recreational] and nonpriority public uses, priority public uses take precedence" (65 Fed. Reg. 62,490 [2000]). "Priority public uses" is synonymous with "wildlife-dependent recreational uses." Because "other," nonpriority public uses include electricity transmission and oil/gas development, the Bush administration national energy policy may drive an early round of conflicts and cases on the hierarchy of uses. These other uses are often referred to as secondary uses by the Service today, but in some cases it would be more accurate to refer to them as tertiary, or even as quaternary, uses.

As figure 6.1 illustrates, I categorize conservation as a primary use and make the compatibility-conditioned wildlife-dependent recreation a secondary use. The tertiary, nonwildlife-dependent recreational uses must not only demonstrate compatibility with the primary uses of conservation and individual refuge purposes, they also must not conflict with the secondary wildlife-dependent recreational uses. The names for the categories of uses I define in the left column of figure 6.1 are my own invention to make sense of and bring order to the hierarchy of uses in refuge management; they are not terms used by the Service. However, the priority system they describe, indicated by the five-tier set of purposes and uses in the right column, is an accurate rendering of the current state of dominant use law in the System.

The Wildlife-Dependent Recreation Priority

The 1997 Improvement Act expresses the preference for wildlife-dependent recreational uses over other uses in five ways. First, the Improvement Act sets out a number of policies for the administration of the System that favor wildlife-dependent activities including:

1. "[C]ompatible wildlife-dependent recreational uses are the priority general public uses of the System and shall receive priority consideration in refuge planning and management;" and
2. compatible wildlife-dependent recreation should be "facilitated, subject to such restrictions or regulations as may be necessary, reasonable, and appropriate." (§§ 5(a)(3)(C), (D))

Though not defined by the statute, the word "facilitated" conveys strong encouragement, but not a requirement, to permit wildlife-dependent uses if they are compatible. As Secretary Babbitt stated, "[t]he law will be whispering in the manager's ear that she or he should look for ways to permit the use if the compatibility requirement can be met" (U.S. House 1997a, 9). By the same token, however, the legislative history recognizes that there will be occasions when, based on sound professional judgment, the manager will determine that such uses will be found to be incompatible and cannot be authorized (id.).

Though only policy declarations, these provisions highlight the consistent and repeated desire of Congress in the statute, legislative history, and prior bills to clarify its view that hunting and fishing are generally consistent with the System's conservation mission. For instance, Senator Kempthorne, who was one of the three cosponsors of the Senate bill that became the Refuge Improvement Act, understood the priority public use provision to, "for the first time . . . , establish hunting and fishing as priority uses on wildlife refuges" (U.S. Senate 1997, 3). This reflects, in part, the strength of hunting and fishing interests (and the state agencies they fund through license fees). They financed the acquisition of many refuges and wish to continue to use the refuges for their sports.

The Improvement Act policy statements are important because at least one wildlife-dependent recreational activity, hunting, is not always associated with dominant use conservation. The National Park Service has a statutory conservation mission very similar to the Refuge System. Even though the Park Service gives priority to public "enjoyment," it bans hunting from National Parks absent special legislation or unusual circumstances (36 C.F.R. § 2.2). The policy declarations separate refuge conservation from this aspect of national park dominant use.

Hunting and fishing are longstanding uses of refuges. Indeed, the Duck Stamp and other revenue sources derived from the hunting and fishing community helped acquire many refuge lands. Prioritizing wildlife-dependent recreation recognizes this traditional relationship between the hunting and fishing constituency and the System. It also acknowledges the on-the-ground, existing activities of many visitors to the System. The Service permits hunting to occur on a majority of refuge units and over 98 percent of the land in the System (U.S. FWS 2000a). Courts routinely uphold Service decisions to expand hunting. This is the case despite the fact that the 1989 GAO report identifies hunting as one of the uses that causes harm to refuges (U.S. GAO 1989, 20).

Second, and more importantly, the Improvement Act includes mandates that, in administering the System, the Service shall:

1. ensure that opportunities are provided within the System for compatible wildlife-dependent recreational uses;
2. ensure that priority general public uses . . . receive enhanced consideration over other . . . uses in planning and management; and
3. provide increased opportunities for families to experience compatible wildlife-dependent recreation, particularly opportunities for parents and their children to safely engage in traditional outdoor activities, such as fishing and hunting. (§ 5(a)(4)(I), (J), (K))

Again, though not absolute commands for wildlife-dependent recreation, these provisions stress their priority. In particular, the third mandate reveals the unstated impetus behind much of the tiered use framework: the desire of sport hunters and anglers to promote their activities and perpetuate their traditions. The Service has quantified this mandate by setting a 2005 performance review goal of increasing the number of compatible wildlife-dependent recreational visits to the System by 20 percent from the 1997 levels. Achieving the goal would result in an increase from 38.3 million visits to 41.4 million visits (U.S. FWS 2000–2005, 43; U.S. FWS 2000a, 11). This is a reversal of the direction urged in the 1976 comprehensive environmental impact statement (EIS), which called for a reduction in System recreation to free up resources for conservation programs. It is a confirmation that the Improvement Act increases pressure on the Service to boost recreational use of the System.

The difference in the way the Service evaluates wildlife-dependent recreational uses as compared to other uses in making compatibility determinations is another way in which these mandates for System administration express themselves in management decisions. Where there is insufficient information to document compatibility, the Service *Manual* instructs refuge managers to deny the use unless it is in a wildlife-dependent recreation category. For those priority public uses, the refuge manager "should work with the proponent of the use to acquire the necessary information before finding the use not compatible based solely on insufficient available information" (65 Fed. Reg. 62,492 [2000]).

Third, wildlife-dependent uses are favored over other uses by the schedule for review of compatibility determinations. The Improvement Act requires a reevaluation of the compatibility of all uses whenever conditions change significantly or significant new information arises regarding the effects of the use. Even if there is no significant change in conditions or new information, the act requires the Service to reevaluate most existing uses at least every ten years to determine whether they are still compatible with the mission of the System (§ 6(a)(3)(B)(vii); 50 C.F.R. § 25.21(h)). However, existing wildlife-dependent recreational uses must be reevaluated only every 15 years, allowing their perpetuation over a longer term (§ 6(a)(3)(B)(viii); 50 C.F.R. § 25.21(f)).

Fourth, bolstering the act's mandates to provide and enhance wildlife-dependent activities, the Improvement Act requires that the Service prepare comprehensive resource management plans for each refuge. Although I will discuss planning in greater detail in chapter 7, it is important to highlight here that the statute requires each plan to include, among other things, "opportunities for compatible wildlife-dependent recreational uses" (§ 7(e)(2)(F)). Plans are not specifically required to include opportunities for other kinds of uses. The act does not even require plans to include projects for the restoration of fish, wildlife, and plants, an element of the System mission. But each refuge has to come up with something to say in its plan about opportunities for wildlife-dependent recreation and to justify any lack of prospects. Projects included in comprehensive plans are more likely to receive funding and implementation priority than those excluded.

Fifth, the 1997 statute repeals the 1962 Refuge Recreation Act requirement that the Service make a finding that funds exist to develop, operate, and maintain wildlife-dependent recreation. The Improvement Act states that "no other determinations or findings [except for the compatibility considerations in the Improvement Act] are required to be made by the refuge official under this Act or the Refuge Recreation Act for wildlife-dependent recreation to occur" (§ 6(3)(A)(iii)). Because the compatibility criterion in the Improvement Act duplicates the "not interfere with" criterion of the Recreation Act, it is only the budgetary analysis that the Improvement Act waives for priority uses. Nonwildlife-dependent recreation, such as snowmobiling or boating, however, must continue to meet the Recreation Act requirements. Therefore, for nonwildlife-dependent recreation only, the Service has a statutory mandate to determine that funds are available to develop, operate, and maintain the uses. It is important to note, however, that the Service includes the consideration of whether available resources can adequately manage a proposed use, including wildlife-dependent recreation, within its compatibility policy (65 Fed. Reg. 62,468 [2000]). However, this element in administrative compatibility policy is weaker than the stark congressional command of the Recreation Act.

Another important issue the Service will have to settle is how to resolve conflicts among the wildlife-dependent uses. The new compatibility regulation sensibly commands that managers give priority to uses that "most positively contribute to the achievement of refuge purposes" and the System mission. In addition, "in case of direct conflict between these priority public uses, the Refuge Manager should evaluate, among other things, which use most directly supports long-term attainment of refuge purposes and the System mission" (65 Fed. Reg. 62,490 [2000]).

Nonwildlife-Dependent Uses

An additional category—"economic uses of the natural resources" of a refuge—occupies the lowest position in the Improvement Act's hierarchy. Even commercial operations facilitating approved programs on refuges, such as offering boats or guides for hire, constitute an economic use. These uses, which include grazing, harvesting hay and stock feed, logging, farming, and removing a variety of natural products from the ground, face an additional requirement not applicable to other uses. The Service may authorize these economic uses only where they contribute to the achievement of a refuge purpose or the System mission (50 C.F.R. § 29.1). The Service compatibility regulations distinguish "refuge management economic activity," which is conducted by the Service (or an authorized agent) to fulfill a refuge purpose or System mission and results in the generation of a commodity, from other sorts of economic uses conducted by private parties (50 C.F.R. § 25.12; 50 C.F.R. § 29.1). However, the test for both types of economic activities boils down to a showing of some affirmative contribution to a refuge purpose or the System mission. Also, the economic uses may not conflict with wildlife-dependent recreation. Because they face even greater hurdles to approval by the Service, I categorize these "economic" uses in figure 6.1 as quaternary, subordinate even to the tertiary, nonwildlife-dependent recreational uses.

The studies of incompatible uses in the 1980s found nonwildlife-dependent uses to be the cause of many of the problems preventing the System from achieving conservation goals. An alternative approach to creating a multilevel hierarchy would have banned nonwildlife-dependent uses entirely. That would have left the top priority of conservation and individual refuge purposes, followed only by wildlife-dependent recreation, where compatible. No other uses would be allowed on refuges. This was the thrust of the original 1997 House bill, ultimately amended to conform to the Senate approach, which eventually became the Improvement Act. By removing consideration of "other" uses from the Service's discretion,

Congress would have made it easier for the Service to defend locally un-popular actions (Fischman 1992, 6).

Also, a legislative nonwildlife-dependent use ban would have solved the problem of Service control over destructive uses in refuges with di-vided management. For instance, on some refuges, jurisdictional arrangements with the Army Corps of Engineers give the FWS little if any authority to control harmful uses that may be associated with navigable waters adjoining or within refuge boundaries (U.S. GAO 1989, 31). Over-all, there are 40 refuges where the majority of acreage is under the pri-mary control of the Bureau of Reclamation, the Corps of Engineers, or the Tennessee Valley Authority (U.S. House 1989, 96). The Corps need not heed the Service, but it must abide by statutory proscriptions.

The case of *McGrail and Rowley v. Babbitt* presents an interesting ap-plication of the preference rules governing economic uses, though it was not decided under the 1997 Act. In *McGrail and Rowley*, a federal district court upheld a Service denial of a permit to operate a commercial boat service to Boca Grande Key in the Key West National Wildlife Refuge. The applicant sought to bring tours of people to the island in a catamaran that would be anchored in deep water. "Passengers would wade ashore, advised to stay below the high tide mark" (*McGrail and Rowley v. Babbitt* 1997, 1390). Some would kayak around the island while others would be pro-vided kites, paddleballs, and Frisbees for play in the water. The Service distinguished this application from another for which it had granted a permit on the basis that the other tour boat operator ran a program that was, according to the refuge manager, "passive and education oriented" (id., 1393). The refuge manager found that the unit lacked the resources to monitor and control the catamaran use.

Though the new compatibility regulations exclude guiding, outfitting, or boat rental from the priority public use category, *McGrail and Rowley* illustrates how the Service can encourage prospective commercial users, like the catamaran operator in Key West, to alter their commercial pro-grams to support the wildlife-dependent recreational values. Environ-mental education, environmental interpretation, wildlife observation and photography, and fishing are all uses that fall in the wildlife-dependent recreation category. If the catamaran operator were to replace the Frisbees, kites, and paddleballs with reels, underwater cameras, and a biologist in-tern, it would have a better case under the act to compel the Service to grant a permit. In this respect, the use preferences create incentives for competition among commercial users to better advance the purposes and preferred uses of refuges.

7 | Comprehensive Planning

Few attributes of public land organic legislation better character-ize the modern era than comprehensive planning mandates. Begin-ning with the national forests in 1974 and 1976, and extending through legislation for Bureau of Land Management (BLM) lands in 1976 and national parks in 1978, Congress has required land management agencies to commit to writing long-term plans for re-source use and conservation. Comprehensive planning prompts an agency to forecast and coordinate future demands and develop-ment. Ideally, planning establishes a basis for adaptive manage-ment. Comprehensive planning also provides the public with an op-portunity to participate more effectively in the strategic decisions that drive project choices during the term of the plan. I describe the key public participation components of planning in chapter 9.

Broad-Scale Plans

Comprehensive planning for public lands generally occurs on three different scales. First, agencies may plan systemwide. Refuge Sys-tem planning has occurred sporadically under the National Environ-mental Policy Act (NEPA), which requires that federal agencies use a "systematic, interdisciplinary approach" in planning and prepare environmental impact statements for major actions significantly af-fecting the quality of the human environment (42 U.S.C. § 4332(2)(A), (C)). Although the NEPA mandate to conduct an in-terdisciplinary analysis when planning is strong, its mandate to engage in long-term planning is difficult to enforce and often ignored. NEPA remains significant, however, as a partner with authorizing statutes in requiring analysis of alternatives (42 U.S.C. § 4332(2)(C)(iii), (E)).

The Service prepared an impact statement in 1976 to plan for and evaluate the direction of the System over the next ten years. A 1994 Senate committee report described the Service's subsequent attempts to engage in systemwide planning:

> In February 1986, the USFWS [U.S. Fish and Wildlife Service] published its notice of intent to develop a System plan and EIS [environmental impact statement]. A draft EIS was released on the management of the Refuge System in December 1988. Following its release, the USFWS received many comments questioning whether the draft EIS fully complied with the provisions of NEPA. As a result, the Service withdrew the document and prepared a new Plan/EIS addressing the management needs of the System through the year 2003. . . . The USFWS released a new draft Plan/EIS in March 1993. (U.S. Senate 1994, 7–8)

The Service never issued a final EIS or plan. But it is not alone in its failure to conclude systemwide, long-term planning.

The national forests are the only public lands system with a national planning requirement in its organic legislation. The Forest and Rangeland Renewable Resources Planning Act of 1976 (commonly referred to as the Resources Planning Act, or RPA) requires, among other studies and plans, that the Forest Service prepare periodic five-year programs, based on decennial assessments, to plan for "protection, management, and development of the National Forest System" (16 U.S.C. § 1602). The Forest Service produced RPA program plans in 1979, 1989, and 2000. However, even this specific systemwide planning mandate has failed to chart a course that the agency and Congress can agree to follow. Though the Forest Service continues its assessment activities, congressional appropriation bills lately have blocked the agency from preparing the five-year plans.

The Improvement Act manifests the recent trend to downplay or ignore systemwide planning. Instead of formal plans, the Service articulates systemic or national goals in such documents as the Fish and Wildlife Service (FWS) *Manual,* the North American Waterfowl Management Plan, and several other "vision" policies (602 FW 1.7(A)). Strategic plans, required by the Government Performance and Results Act (GPRA), must contain specific benchmarks for measuring progress toward long-term, programmatic goals (5 U.S.C. § 306(a)(4); 31 U.S.C. § 1115(a)). These plans are now the most important current engines for systemwide planning. In addition, Congress recently required the Service to report on long-term plans to address priority operation, maintenance, and construction needs in the System (Fish and Wildlife Programs Improvement and National Wildlife Refuge System Centennial Act 2000, § 304(a), 16 U.S.C. § 669). This report, however, will duplicate some of the material under the goal of "stewardship of FWS facilities" contained in the GPRA strategic plans.

The second level of planning occurs on a regional level. Like systemwide plans, but to a lesser extent, regional efforts have, in the past decade, declined in importance; however, migratory flyway plans and regional fishery resource plans may sometimes offer guidance for refuge management. More importantly, the FWS divides the country into 53 ecosystems, generally defined by watersheds. Regional ecosystem teams write strategic plans that establish conservation priorities. These plans also may guide refuge management so that it contributes to regional ecosystem restoration objectives. Contributing to regional ecosystem plan goals furthers each refuge's mission to coordinate management to create a network supporting plants and wildlife.

Comprehensive Conservation Plans

The third major type of comprehensive planning occurs at the unit level. Unit-level resource management planning is common and has played an important role in public land management legislation since 1976, when the National Forest Management Act (NFMA) and Federal Land Policy and Management Act required unit-level planning for national forests and BLM districts, respectively. Congress required the National Park Service (NPS) to prepare general management plans for national park units in 1978 and even required the FWS to prepare refuge plans for the Alaska units in the 1980 Alaska National Interest Lands Conservation Act (ANILCA). Also, some pre-1977 refuge establishment documents outside of Alaska required unit plans.

Beginning in the late 1970s, the Service began to develop guidelines for refuge planning and created a section in the refuge *Manual* on master planning. However, application of and compliance with national guidelines remained decentralized (Loomis 1993, 364; U.S. House 1997a, 14). Although these administrative guidelines covered both plan procedure and content in greater detail than the Improvement Act, they lacked the binding power of a statute and did not mandate a term of years after which plans would need revision.

The 1997 Act closed an important gap in public land management by requiring unit-level comprehensive resource planning for all refuges. The Service excludes from its comprehensive planning process state-managed coordination areas, even though they are part of the Refuge System (602 FW 1.6(F)). Unit-level, "comprehensive conservation plans" (CCPs) include a description of the important resources in the unit, the uses currently occurring in the unit, management zones within the unit that will be designated for special conservation practices or human uses, development (including recreation) opportunities in the plan, environmental consequences of the plan, and (as compelled by NEPA) a range of alternative management regimes and their effects on the environment. The Improvement Act implements the mandate through a number of specific provisions that apply to all refuges not covered by ANILCA or by planning requirements in their establishment documents (§ 7(e)(1)(A)). To ensure that all refuge units in the System align site-specific goals with the conservation mission, each unit plan describes the desired future conditions on the refuge (602 FW 3.4(C)(1)(g); 603 FW 2.6(C)). This should provide a target for long-term management.

Following the model established by the NFMA, the Improvement Act requires the Service to prepare a CCP for each unit within 15 years and to update each plan every 15 years, or sooner if conditions change significantly (§ 7(e)(1)(A)(iv), (E)). In contrast, the Alaska refuges' comprehensive conservation plans, the BLM resource management plans, and the NPS general management plans have no statutory schedule for periodic revision after a certain number of years have elapsed. The Improvement Act's action-forcing deadline for revision limits agency latitude to focus resources where the planning challenges are greatest, but also makes it more difficult for the agency to skirt controversies. Also, with statutory expiration dates for plans, Congress may not withhold adequate planning monies without causing flagrant violations of statutory mandates. Administratively, the Service has strengthened the ANILCA planning requirement by putting the Alaska refuges on the same 15-year revision schedule as the rest of the System (602 FW 3.2, 3.4(C)(8)(b)).

The FWS will prepare a CCP by October 2012 for each refuge in existence on October 9, 1997, when Congress passed the Improvement Act. Until that time, the Service will continue to manage each refuge or planning unit with existing plans effective prior to October 9, 1997, to the extent these plans are consistent with the Refuge Administration Act (602 FW 3.2). For refuges established after passage of the Refuge Improvement Act, the FWS will prepare a CCP when the refuge is staffed and it acquires a land base sufficient to achieve refuge purposes, but no later than 15 years after the FWS establishes the refuge (602 FW 3.2).

Once approved, the unit plan becomes a source of management requirements that bind the agency (§ 7(e)(1)(E)). The Service would, barring emergency, have to modify a plan before it could approve an action that conflicts with the plan (§ 8(a)). The Service, therefore, is really bound by two consistency standards: (1) the statutory mandate to allow only uses compatible with the conservation mission of the System and individual refuge purposes, and (2) the requirement that management actions comply with the parameters established by the refuge plan. In this way, a plan adds site-specific substantive management mandates to the broader ones contained in the Act and discussed in chapter 8. This dual source of management standards has proved to be an important feature in the NFMA framework for citizens seeking judicial review of activities in the National Forest System and promises to be important for the Refuge System as well.

The Improvement Act lays out a typical set of procedural and content requirements for the CCPs. The content requirements for comprehensive conservation plans are generally unremarkable. With the exception of two specific mandates related to visitor use of the refuges, the statutory content requirements are all topics that NEPA requires be analyzed and discussed in the environmental impact statement (EIS) accompanying a comprehensive plan. These include the purposes of the refuge, a description of the plants and wildlife, archaeological and cultural values, significant problems adversely affecting resources, and mitigation measures (§ 7(e)(2)). The specific visitor use mandates require identification and description of

1. [areas] suitable for use as administrative sites or visitor facilities, and
2. opportunities for compatible wildlife-dependent recreational uses. (§ 7(e)(2)(D), (2)(F))

The visitor use content requirements distort the unifying effect of planning to coordinate units to achieve the larger System mission. Managers concentrating on meeting the operative mandates risk losing sight of the tasks necessary to conserve the ecological resources of the System. To best implement the mission, Congress should have balanced these specific facility and recreation location mandates with equally detailed requirements to delineate affirmative opportunities for ecological enhancement and restoration. Instead, the Improvement Act requires only that the plans describe significant adverse ecological effects and actions necessary to mitigate those effects. This merely duplicates what NEPA would require in an EIS (42 U.S.C. § 4332(2)(C); 40 C.F.R. § 1502.16). The affirmative content requirement in ANILCA, mandating specific conservation programs in plans, would have better linked the new planning provisions to the new Refuge System mission. Moreover, imperiled species reintroduction programs ought to be a specific category addressed in planning. Certainly, the Service may take (and has taken) on these tasks in the implementing policy for planning, but a mandate from Congress makes a stronger impact. The statutory content requirements reflect an overall disparity in the act between the overarching conservation mission and the focus of the detailed mandates on wildlife-dependent recreation. The Service's policy governing the content of plans counteracts somewhat the imbalance of the statute in detailing numerous categories that plans must address (602 FW Exhibits 3, 4).

Comprehensive Conservation Plan Procedures

The Improvement Act's procedural requirements for CCPs add little to the existing mandates of NEPA and the Administrative Procedure Act. They include:

1. consultation with federal, state, local, and private landowners and relevant state conservation agencies;
2. coordination with relevant state conservation plans; and
3. opportunity for the public to participate in the plan development. (§ 7(e)(3)(A), (3)(B), (4))

Like agency regulations and EISs, conservation plans are first published as drafts for public comment and then republished in final form after the agency has considered the comments. Typically, a draft EIS will accompany a draft plan, and a final EIS will accompany the final plan.

The FWS policy implementing its planning mandate fleshes out the details of the process. Compatibility determinations for all anticipated and current uses are folded into the planning efforts (602 FW 3.4(C)(5)(b)). An important tool for planning is "scoping," a term originating in the Council on Environmental Quality regulations implementing NEPA. Scoping is "an early and open process for determining the scope of issues to be addressed and for identifying the significant issues related to a proposed" plan (40 C.F.R. § 1501.7).

Though the Service employs scoping for all CCPs, it does not commit to preparing EISs for all plans (602 FW 3.4(C)(2)). Indeed, the Service has already prepared many CCPs, such as those for Wyandotte, North

Platte, and Tewaukon national wildlife refuges, with environmental assessments. Accompanying the assessments are "findings of no significant impact" that attempt to justify a decision not to prepare an EIS. This will prove to be a weakness of the comprehensive planning process. The FWS will better comply with NEPA and its organic mandate if it prepares EISs for all comprehensive conservation plans. Few decisions at the refuge level have greater significance for the environment than adoption of the place-based rules and standards in a CCP. Because the context of agency actions is a factor in determining their significance (40 C.F.R. § 1508.27), it is difficult to envision a situation where a comprehensive plan for a national wildlife refuge would not require an EIS due to the national importance of the Refuge System mission. Relatively benign decisions that might not be significant on ordinary lands rise in importance when made on the nation's preeminent network of nature protection lands. The FWS will squander scarce resources debating whether a proposed CCP crosses the NEPA threshold of significance. It would better concentrate its planning efforts by committing, from the start, to prepare an EIS, absent unusual circumstances.

The Park Service learned this the hard way when it attempted to couple some of its park-unit general management plans with environmental assessments. After a 1991 settlement of litigation challenging the North Cascades National Park general management plan, which had no EIS, the NPS agreed to prepare EISs for unit plans (Louter 1998, 205; U.S. NPS 1998, § 3.3.1.6). However, recent statements from the Forest Service and Park Service indicate a weakening of the commitment to EISs for unit plans that is consistent with the FWS position (67 Fed. Reg. 72,770 [2002]; U.S. NPS 2001, § 2.3).

Chapter 9 covers scoping and other public participation opportunities in the FWS process. For the purposes of understanding the basic parameters of comprehensive conservation planning, however, a few additional provisions administratively adopted by the FWS in its operational manual are worth discussing. The CCP policy establishes eight steps for the preparation of plans: preplan; initiate public involvement and scoping; review the vision statement and goals and determine significant issues; develop and analyze alternatives; prepare a draft plan and NEPA document; prepare and adopt a final plan; implement, monitor, and evaluate the plan; and review and revise the plan (602 FW 3.4). Here is how the eight steps work.

First, preplanning begins when the regional chief appoints a planning team leader, who then assembles the planning team. The planning team prepares a public involvement/outreach plan, which indicates how and when the FWS will invite the affected public to participate in the development of the CCP (602 FW 3.4C(1)(i)). The FWS also carries out an internal scoping process during which it identifies planning policies, the purpose and need for the plan, the planning area, data needs, and available information relevant to the CCP.

Second, initiation of public involvement and scoping begins when the FWS publishes in the *Federal Register* a Notice of Intent to prepare a CCP with appropriate NEPA compliance (602 FW 3.4C(2)(a)). The Notice of Intent will state whether the Service plans to write an EIS or whether it needs to prepare an environmental assessment (EA) to determine whether the CCP is likely to have a significant impact on the quality of the environment. Public scoping continues until the FWS prepares a draft CCP/NEPA document.

Step 3 requires the team to analyze all comments submitted during scoping (602 FW 3.4C(2)(c)). It also identifies any new information or issues, data needs, significant problems, and potential solutions. Based on this review, the FWS may modify the vision and goals for the refuge.

The next two steps comprise the work of developing the CCP and the associated NEPA and compatibility determination documents. These steps also contain the formal and direct public notice, review, and comment process for the draft CCP and the draft EIS/EA (602 FW 3.4C(5)(e)). The FWS first publishes a Notice of Availability of the draft CCP and NEPA document in the *Federal Register*, but may also notify the affected public of the availability of these documents through other means identified in the public involvement/outreach plan. The development of alternatives and their comparative analysis in the CCP are extremely important. The evaluation of alternatives is the "heart" of the EIS (40 C.F.R. § 1502.14) and should be central to CCP development. It is the principal basis on which the FWS will ultimately choose its management direction.

In step 6 the Service prepares and adopts its final CCP (602 FW 3.4C(6)). In doing this, the FWS must document, review, and analyze all public comments received in steps 4 and 5. The Service then prepares a summary of the public comments received and the agency's responses, noting where the agency has changed the documents or why it did not make changes. This summary is incorporated into the final documents, usually in the NEPA document or a CCP appendix. The Service then prepares the final CCP, EIS/EA, and compatibility determinations, as well as a decision document adopting them.

Step 7 begins the implementation of the CCP and calls for monitoring and evaluation. This reflects the CCP policy's commitment to adaptive management. A successful adaptive management program will treat implementation as an experiment in management, requiring adjustment in light of its outcomes. Refuges may develop "step-down management plans" (SDMPs), discussed in the following text, to fulfill this step.

Finally, the eighth step in the CCP policy calls for review and revision of the plan (602 FW 3.4C(8)). The FWS must review the CCP at least annually to determine whether any revisions are required. It will revise the CCP when significant new information becomes available, ecological conditions change, major refuge expansion occurs, or the Service identifies the need to do so during plan review (602 FW 3.4C(8)(b)). As already discussed, this revision must occur at least every 15 years. When the FWS decides to revise a CCP, it begins again with step 1.

In addition to CCPs, other, smaller-scale planning may occur on refuges. The Service will tier SDMPs (step-down management plans) to CCPs for more specific implementation programs, as needed. Such programs may include pest management, hunting, special area management, environmental education, and pollution control (602 FW 4). The SDMP also may be used to describe strategies and schedules for implementation of CCP objectives (602 FW 1.3, 1.6U, 1.7E). After completing a CCP, the FWS modifies existing SDMPs to reflect the new unit-level objectives (602 FW 1.7E).

Another type of planning effort is land acquisition planning, which applies to situations where the FWS establishes a new refuge or expands an existing refuge. Land acquisition planning usually results in a land protection plan (LPP) and associated NEPA document. An LPP is intended to inform landowners and the local interested public of the FWS's proposal to protect land and how the proposal may affect them (341 FW 1.6H). The FWS integrates land acquisition planning efforts into CCP preparation whenever possible. Some proposed new refuges or refuge expansions may warrant CCP development at the time of acquisition planning (602 FW 1.7C). Planning for proposed new refuges or major expansions to existing refuges not undergoing a CCP will include the development of a conceptual management plan (CMP) for the new unit. The CMP provides general, interim management direction. It should identify refuge purpose(s), interim goals, and preexisting compatible wildlife-dependent recreational uses that the FWS will allow to continue on an interim basis. The interim period is the duration of time between the establishment of a new refuge or refuge expansion and the completion of an approved CCP. The FWS may also develop an SDMP for a refuge functioning under a CMP (602 FW 1.7C).

8 | *Substantive Management Criteria*

In addition to the standards for management established in the individual comprehensive conservation plans, there are also statutory criteria that bind agency administration of refuge resources. A substantive management criterion is a mandate from Congress to fulfill a specific statutory objective. The objective marks the boundaries limiting resource management discretion.

The criteria help shape plans but apply to refuge activities irrespective of the plans. A specific management action, even if consistent with a plan, may still run afoul of the Improvement Act if it would violate a substantive management criterion (1997 Improvement Act § 5(a)(4)). Therefore, along with the planning mandate that applies them, the substantive management criteria exert the greatest influence over Refuge System management. The substantive management criteria include compatibility; maintenance of biological integrity, diversity, and environmental health; acquisition of sufficient water rights; biological monitoring; and a general conservation stewardship mandate.

The criteria are also important because they will be footholds for litigation over management of the System. At the hearing for S. 1059, the bill that became the Improvement Act, Secretary Babbitt (himself a lawyer) expressed the view that the compatibility standard would be judicially enforceable (U.S. Senate 1997, 9, 13). The House committee report is unrealistically optimistic in expecting that the Improvement Act "will diminish the likelihood of future lit-igation by providing a statutory compatibility standard" (U.S. House 1997a, 4). Given the tradition of deference to the proprietary discretion of federal land management agencies, these substantive criteria are crucial in spurring courts to review federal resource management decisions. However, sometimes the mere ability to litigate resource management issues serves as a prophylactic, discouraging an agency from disregarding the position of stakeholders or from overlooking an environmental harm to satisfy a local or powerful interest.

The importance of substantive criteria for litigation is illustrated by the relative success plaintiffs have experienced challenging national forest management under the National Forest Management Act (NFMA), compared to Bureau of Land Management (BLM) or national park management. Although courts have overturned BLM and National Park Service (NPS) management actions, it has usually been for violations of statutes, such as the Endangered Species Act (ESA) or the National Environmental Policy Act (NEPA), other than the applicable organic acts. The NFMA contains more extensive substantive criteria, such as the mandate that timber be harvested only on lands that will be restocked in five years, than the organic acts for the BLM and NPS (16 U.S.C. § 1604(g)(3)(E)). Therefore, the NFMA better serves as a foothold for effective court challenges. In contrast, the NPS Organic Act provides little more than a vague mandate "to conserve the scenery and the natural and historic objects and the wildlife therein and to provide for the enjoyment of the same in such manner . . . as will leave them unimpaired for future generations" (16 U.S.C. § 1). Similarly, the Federal Land Policy and Management Act of 1976 (FLPMA) , which provides the comprehensive management provisions for the BLM, merely offers a general criterion of avoiding "unnecessary and undue degradation" (43 U.S.C. 1732(b)). Even the NFMA standards, however, provide limited restrictions on agency discretion (Cheever 1999).

The substantive criteria in the Improvement Act are more specific than those for the National Park System or BLM lands. They are even more specific than many in the NFMA, though no single Improvement Act criterion is as specific as the NFMA strictures on timber management. The greater statutory detail and more binding management prescriptions in the 1997 Act, as compared with earlier organic legislation, reflects Congress's growing interest in controlling public land management. This strengthening of legislative mandates at the expense of agency discretion in public land administration parallels the contemporaneous trend toward greater statutory detail in pollution control law (Fischman 1997).

The Service has now begun to implement the 1997 Improvement Act's substantive criteria through revisions to the U.S. Fish and Wildlife Service (FWS) *Manual*. These *Manual* revisions are sometimes called policies and, with the exception of the compatibility guidelines, are not promulgated as regulations in the *Code of Federal Regulations*. Nonetheless, the Service puts them through the same notice and comment procedure that rules must receive under administrative law (5 U.S.C. § 553). This process involves publishing a draft policy in the *Federal Register* and opening a comment period for public input. When the Service adopts its final policy, it again publishes the policy in the *Federal Register* along with a substantive discussion addressing the comments it received.

The most innovative conservation guidelines to emerge from the Improvement Act have been the Service's policy implementing the compatibility and the biological integrity, diversity, and environmental health criteria. As with the Forest Service's 2000 planning regulations, which broke new ground in applying conservation biology to federal lands management, the FWS policy signals the next wave of ecosystem management. In particular, the policy provisions prohibiting habitat fragmentation and requiring managers to respond to external threats to refuges now stand at the forefront of protective public land administration.

This chapter analyzes the five substantive criteria that I have distilled from the Improvement Act. The act itself does not specifically highlight these five provisions, with the exception of the compatibility standard. However, I have chosen to focus on these criteria because of both their mandatory character and their substantive contribution to the overall conservation mission of the System. The Service has issued detailed interpretations for most aspects of the five substantive criteria. In some cases, the statutory criteria await further legal developments to ascertain their meaning.

The first section analyzes the components of the compatibility standard, the keystone concept of dominant use management. In large part because of the critical reports of the 1980s described in chapter 3, the Improvement Act stresses the importance of compatibility. The second section explores the most innovative and potentially far-reaching criterion, the mandate to maintain biological integrity, diversity, and environmental health. The third section explains the significance of the Service's new duty to acquire water rights for refuges. The fourth section looks at the obligation to monitor wildlife and plants, an issue that has sparked great controversy when applied through other statutes. Finally, the fifth section describes the vague affirmative stewardship requirement.

The Compatibility Standard

The compatibility standard refers to the requirement that the Service "not initiate or permit a new use of a refuge or expand, renew, or extend an existing use of a refuge, unless the Secretary has determined that the use is a compatible use" (1997 Improvement Act § 6(3)(a)(i)). The legislative origins of compatibility date to at least 1945, when Congress passed appropriations for "facilities incident to such public recreational uses of wildlife refuges as are not inconsistent with the primary purposes of such refuges" (Act of July 3, 1945, ch. 262; U.S. House 1961). Congress had earlier applied the compatibility principle to particular refuges, as opposed to applying it systemwide (Act of April 21, 1910, ch. 183). Congress has required the Service to make individual determinations of compatibility for all recreational uses since the 1962 Recreation Act. The 1966 Refuge Administration Act broadened the scope of uses subject to the compatibility standard through the authorization of general use regulations, but failed to require individual determinations. The 1997 law borrows from the strength of both prior statutes: it requires individual determinations of compatibility for all nonprimary uses of the Refuge System. In addition, it adds the conservation mission to the particular refuge establishment purposes as the touchstone for determining what uses may be allowed in refuges.

A compatible use is one that, "in the sound professional judgment of the [FWS,] will not materially interfere with or detract from the fulfillment of the mission of the System or the purposes of the refuge" (1997 Improvement Act § 5(1)). The House bill originally limited compatible uses to those that are wildlife-dependent. However, after the Senate adopted language that broadened the definition to include wildlife-dependent and other uses, the House endorsed the Senate approach. Other uses may include grazing, oil and gas production, and electricity transmission. There are three important elements of this statutory definition, taken from the administrative interpretation the Service had long been using: (1) the extent of discretion afforded the Service in applying "sound professional judgment," (2) the meaning of "not materially interfere with or detract from," and (3) the applicability of the compatibility standard to both the systemic mission and the establishment purposes of the refuge. I will explore, in detail, each of these three elements in subsections below.

The compatibility standard is important because it is the key mechanism to ensure that the new conservation mission of the System effects real change in the refuges. For instance, the Service policy finding incompatible all uses that managers "reasonably may anticipate to reduce the quality or quantity or fragment habitats" on a refuge will bolster conservation efforts by ensuring that ecosystems supporting wildlife do not degrade through permitted uses (65 Fed. Reg. 62,486 [2000]).

Courts already have called into question whether uses such as docking facilities, roads, canals, airstrips, utilities, and pipelines in the Yukon Delta National Wildlife Refuge; an oil support facility in the Alaska Maritime National Wildlife Refuge; and permissive boating and waterskiing regulations in Ruby Lake National Wildlife Refuge are compatible with individual refuge purposes (*National Audubon Society v. Hodel* 1984; *Defenders of Wildlife v. Andrus* 1978). The new compatibility standard, which now incorporates the Refuge System mission, will likely constrict further the range of compatible activities.

Congress enacted the Improvement Act largely to respond to reports that incompatible uses were a chief threat to the Refuge System. Nonetheless, uses meeting the compatibility standard are not guaranteed a place in the System. Compatibility is a necessary but not sufficient condition for allowing a use (U.S. House 1997a, 13). To determine which compatible uses should be permitted in a refuge, the Service is preparing a policy on "appropriate refuge uses" (66 Fed. Reg. 3,673 [2001]). It is likely that the "appropriate" use test will screen out some uses before they are evaluated for compatibility.

To understand the effectiveness of the compatibility standard, one must consider two issues. First, the scope of application of the standard is important. Even the most stringent management criterion will not improve management unless applied to a wide range of activities. Second, considering the means by which the standard operates, when applied, is important to determine how the criterion will shape resource management. This section will address these two issues before considering the key elements of the actual compatibility test.

Scope and Means

Though the vast majority of uses in the Refuge System are subject to the compatibility test, not all are. Like comprehensive conservation planning, compatibility determinations do not apply to management of coordination areas, even though these units are part of the System. Further, as discussed in chapter 6, "refuge management activities," such as water level maintenance, are excluded from the compatibility test. In contrast, refuge

management activities that generate commodities, such as farming, grazing, haying, timbering, and trapping, are included in the definition of
refuge uses, the domain to which compatibility determinations apply.

The compatibility criterion also does not apply to military overflights
or "activities authorized, funded, or conducted by" a federal agency other
than the FWS that has "primary jurisdiction over a refuge or portion of a
refuge, if the management of those activities is in accordance with a memorandum of understanding between" the Service and the other agency
(1997 Improvement Act § 6(3)(4)). Conflicts arising from these refuges
where other agencies have shared management authority or where the
military conducts airborne exercises continue to raise conservation concerns. In its influential 1989 report, the General Accounting Office (GAO)
listed overflights as one of the five activities most harmful to the refuges
(U.S. GAO 1989, 21–23). This exception will be a significant loophole for
uses that thwart the System mission.

Second, aside from the scope of its application, there are serious operational problems with the emphasis on compatibility as a management
mandate. Compatibility tends to divert management focus from affirmative initiatives designed to advance the System's conservation mission. Instead, refuge management attention focuses reactively on the prediction
and mitigation of impacts from allowable uses. The conservation stewardship mandate, yet to be discussed here, will shoulder the burden of affirmative improvements in a vague, weak provision that does not have the
procedural triggers or written determination requirements of the compatibility mandate.

Also, the compatibility mandate requires the Service to approve or disapprove a particular level of impact as meeting or violating the mandate.
This binary, or categorical, approach to conservation finds a use either
compatible or not. In contrast, the ecological view teaches that "different
kinds and intensities of human use will affect various aspects or components
of biodiversity to differing degrees" (Gergely et al. 2000, 115; Redford and
Richter 1999, 1247). A more forthright approach to compatibility would
ask the Service to describe and mitigate the degree to which uses impede
the conservation and establishment goals. To its credit, the Service endorses consideration of avoidance and minimization in making compatibility determinations but limits compensatory mitigation as a means to
make a proposed use compatible (50 C.F.R. § 26.41(b)). This limitation
on the use of compensatory mitigation will be especially important in end-
ing the practice of allowing roads in exchange for donations of land (Eckl
1999, 3).

The Improvement Act gives less emphasis to the scientific basis for compatibility determinations than did prior bills. For instance, a 1993 Senate attempt at organic legislation for the Refuge System would have required compatibility regulations to "describe the biological, ecological, and other criteria to be used in making the determinations" (U.S. Senate 1993, § 5(6)(B)). The use of biological criteria in making compatibility determinations will be one of the most important challenges for the Service. The 1989 GAO report recommended greater use of biological criteria to improve System conservation (U.S. GAO 1989, 5). The Service's current effort to develop "standardized protocols to monitor the biological integrity, diversity, and environmental health" of refuge habitats may address this challenge (U.S. FWS 2000a, 42). Still, a stronger statutory mandate would have made biological criteria a high priority rather than an administrative initiative.

Although the compatibility standard itself is a weak test for forcing the Service to implement its mission assertively, it nonetheless represents a significant statutory improvement over the pre-1997 law. As implemented, though, the difference between the 1986 FWS *Manual* provisions governing compatibility determinations and the 2000 regulation (and *Manual* revisions) is narrower than the legislation might suggest. The new *Manual* provision replaced the old 5-step compatibility determination with a 15-step process, but the basic procedures are fundamentally the same. This should raise some skepticism about the ability of the new *Manual* provisions to abate incompatible uses where the 1986 provisions failed.

Nonetheless, there are several important improvements in the new compatibility process. First, the requirement to provide written determinations of compatibility, the greatest difference between the old *Manual* provision and the new statutory standard, ought to spur greater agency and public investigation of the range of uses occurring on the refuges and their effects. Indeed, the 1989 GAO report linked incompatible uses with the lack of written determinations by the Service (U.S. GAO 1989, 13).

Second, the notice and comment regulations required by the 1997 Act help to facilitate public participation, which is independently required under the Act (§§ 6(3)(B), 7(3)(B)(4)(A)). The Service's *Manual* now folds compatibility determinations into the comprehensive conservation planning process, which assures heightened public participation (602 FW 3.4(C)(5)(b); 65 Fed. Reg. 62,470 [2000]). Even when managers make determinations after a plan is adopted, the compatibility process requires public review (603 FW 2.11(I), 2.12(A)(9)). Chapter 9 details the specific steps in the compatibility determination procedure where the public can most effectively participate. The FWS could promote greater public participation if it adopted a management policy like that of the NPS requiring decision makers to conduct investigations when they become aware that ongoing activities might lead to impairment of resources or values (U.S. NPS 2001, § 1.4.7).

Third, refuge management economic activities are now covered by the compatibility criterion and face a more stringent standard for approval. Fourth, the new policy clearly places the burden on a proponent of a new use to show compatibility. Finally, the substantive considerations for making compatibility determinations explicitly require a review of indirect and cumulative impacts, limit compensatory mitigation, and prohibit habitat fragmentation. These considerations will likely give the compatibility criterion new vitality in promoting Refuge System conservation.

The following subsections discuss the three key elements in the statutory definition of compatible use: sound professional judgment, the "not materially interfere with or detract from" standard, and the System mission and refuge purposes (§ 3(a)(5)(1)). The FWS regulations required by the statute and the *Manual* provisions detailing the compatibility determination process illustrate an important interpretation of the statute and are incorporated into the following discussion.

Sound Professional Judgment

To what extent does the compatibility criterion provide an objective basis for reviewing actions of the Service? The 1997 Act defines "sound professional judgment" as a "determination or decision that is consistent with [1] principles of sound fish and wildlife management and administration, [2] available science and resources, and [3] adherence to the" Improvement Act and other applicable law (§ 3(a)(5)(3)). Although this definition succeeds in establishing some independent principles against which to test management decisions, the Service retains great discretion under the compatibility standard.

The legislative history makes clear that courts should play a role in ensuring that the Service applies appropriate standards and procedures (U.S. House 1997a, 7). At the very least, the "sound professional judgment" standard endorses the approach taken by the D.C. district court in the Ruby Lake litigation. There, the judge refused to defer to Service assertions of compatibility without evidence in the record supporting the determination and responding to indications that recreational boating was harming refuge resources (*Defenders of Wildlife v. Andrus* 1978).

However, courts and the public would benefit from more specific guidelines promulgated as Service policy that go beyond ensuring that the Service followed relevant procedures.

According to the statutory definition, there are three components to "sound professional judgment." First, and most importantly, the judgment must be consistent with principles of "sound fish and wildlife management and administration" (§ 3(a)(5)(3)). This component of sound professional judgment neglects to include the applied botanical sciences, despite the inclusion of plant conservation in the System's mission. It would seem odd to make compatibility decisions with respect to plant conservation (other than for animal habitat use) based on the principles of animal management.

As with all applied fields related to the natural sciences, fish and wildlife management principles are neither codified nor uncontroversial. Therefore, in disagreements where outside experts challenge the Service's expert determinations, courts can be expected to defer to the agency. Also, because fish and wildlife management is what the Service has done for decades, continuation of poor management practices may be justified by their longstanding use as principles in refuge administration.

Courts already had been yielding to the compatibility judgments of refuge management staff before 1997 (Bean and Rowland 1997, 293–298). Applying the arbitrary and capricious standard of examining whether the Service took account of all the relevant factors in making compatibility determinations under the pre-1997 legislation, courts uniformly deferred to the Service's assertions about ecological management. In contrast, courts are less likely to defer to the Service on matters of interpreting legislation and establishment documents (*Schwenke v. Secretary of Interior* 1983). Even courts applying the NEPA hard-look doctrine accepted the Service's biological justifications of compatibility decisions (*Humane Society v. Hodel* 1988; *Friends of Animals v. Hodel* 1988). Going further still, a district court that found bias in the statements of the refuge's biologist, upon whose findings the refuge manager had based an incompatible determination for a commercial boating operation, nonetheless upheld the Service's permit denial (*McGrail and Rowley v. Babbitt* 1997).

The tendency of courts to defer to all resource management determinations as sound professional judgment is countered somewhat by the Improvement Act's overall commitment to conservation biology principles. The conservation mission and the substantive criterion to maintain biological integrity, diversity, and environmental health, read together with the compatibility standard, require application of science to achieve ecologically protective results. The implementation policies will be key sources of objective, scientific standards binding refuge managers' judgments to the methods of conservation biology. The promulgation of these policies through the notice and comment procedures of the Administrative Procedure Act makes them binding on the Service.

The Forest Service operates under organic legislation that has virtually no language harkening to conservation biology. In resolving a challenge to two national forest plans in Wisconsin, a federal court of appeals deferred to the Forest Service's rejection of the theory of island biogeography in meeting the NFMA diversity mandate. Island biogeography would have supported the establishment of large, unfragmented habitat reserves "to protect at least some old-growth forest communities" (*Sierra Club v. Marita* 1995, 620). The court explained that the Forest Service "acknowledged the developments in conservation biology but did not think that they had been shown definitively applicable to forests" like the ones in Wisconsin (id., 623). As a result, the Forest Service is able to use its own methodology, "unless it is irrational" (id., 621). In contrast to the NFMA, the Improvement Act's ecological language and the emerging Service policies, such as the linking of habitat fragmentation with mission incompatibility, provide clearer parameters for the meaning of sound management (65 Fed. Reg. 62,486 [2000]). This should lead to stricter judicial scrutiny of Service actions that clearly depart from the tenets of conservation biology than would be the case if the Improvement Act made no reference to conservation biology in other provisions.

The second component of the definition of "sound professional judgment" requires that the Service make decisions consistent with "available science and resources" (§ 3(a)(5)(3)). This component raises the troubling potential for the Service to justify uses that may harm refuge purposes. Agencies frequently lack the resources to determine the full range of consequences of permitting uses on public lands. In exercising "sound professional judgment," ignorance can become an excuse for acquiescing to consumptive refuge uses based on the lack of scientific data. The legislative history explicitly excuses the Service from developing new information on which to base compatibility determinations (U.S. House 1997a, 12). The compatibility regulations instruct refuge managers to use available information and do not require them "to independently generate data to make determinations" (65 Fed. Reg. 62,486 [2000]).

The Service suffers from low annual appropriations for refuge administration and a dearth of scientists. The refuges receive smaller appropriations per acre managed than any other federal public land system (U.S.

House 1997b, 4). One illustration of the low appropriations is the backlog of maintenance projects in the System. As of 2002, the deferred mainte-nance backlog stood at $663 million, about twice the annual appropriation for refuge operation and maintenance (Congressional Research Service 2002, 10; U.S. Department of the Interior 2002).

In 1993 the interior secretary transferred most FWS scientists to the ill-fated National Biological Survey, which Congress incorporated into the U.S. Geological Survey in 1996 (Clarke and McCool 1996, 124). So, without sufficient scientific expertise to determine the full range of consequences of a use, and without funding for new studies to better understand impacts, the Service may fail to forecast many interferences with or detractions from the purposes of the refuge. This "ignorance is optimism" scenario has historically characterized management of the System. The Ruby Lake lit-igation illustrates its deleterious effects on refuge resources (*Defenders of Wildlife v. Andrus* 1978). The "available resources" component of the definition of sound professional judgment, coupled with the elimination of the funding criterion (from the 1962 Refuge Recreation Act) for per-mitting wildlife-dependent recreational use, reduces the incentives for user interests to lobby for greater Refuge System appropriations.

However, judicial review and the new compatibility regulations have placed the legal burden on the Service to build a record that shows lack of harm from a proposed activity to the purposes of the refuge. This will serve to counteract the "available science and resources" limitation on sound professional judgment. Also, the FWS compatibility policy does forbid a refuge manager from allowing proposed uses without sufficient information to document that they are compatible (603 FW 2.12(A)(8)).

Moreover, where compatibility determinations lead to authorization of uses, NEPA will require new information to be developed for environ-mental impact statements (EISs) in some circumstances. Compatibility determinations themselves are not actions triggering NEPA. But they may lead to authorization of uses, which are NEPA actions. Also, many com-patibility determinations will occur as part of comprehensive conserva-tion planning, which will involve the NEPA process (65 Fed. Reg. 62,475, 62,494 [2000]). EISs must develop new information where it "is essen-tial to a reasoned choice among alternatives and the overall costs of ob-taining it are not exorbitant" (40 C.F.R. § 1502.22(a)). Judicial review will also require refuge managers to document how their "field experience and knowledge of the particular refuge's resources," both permissible compo-nents of sound professional judgment in the new compatibility regula-tions, support their compatibility findings (65 Fed. Reg. 62,481 [2000]).

Furthermore, the House report accompanying the bill that became the 1997 Act interprets the "available resources" component of the "sound professional judgment" test as requiring that compatibility determinations include considerations of whether funds, personnel, and infrastructure exist to manage permitted activities adequately (U.S. House 1997a, 6). The compatibility regulations echo this view of sound professional judgment in requiring the Service to "consider lack of adequate budgets for all uses, including priority public uses" in exercising sound professional judgment (65 Fed. Reg. 62,468 [2000]). The FWS incorporates this requirement in its policy defining "sound professional judgment." The Service position is that compatible use determinations must find "that adequate resources (including financial, personnel, facilities, and other infrastructure) exist or can be provided by the Service . . . to properly develop, operate, and maintain the use. . . . If adequate resources cannot be secured, the use will be found not compatible and cannot be allowed" (603 FW 2.12(A)(7)).

This interpretation is a sensible, if roundabout, restoration of the 1962 Act's funding availability criterion as applied to wildlife-dependent recreation. But, it is contradictory that Congress would explicitly exempt wildlife-dependent recreation from the funding determination requirement in the text of the statute (§ 6(3)(A)(iii)), only to incorporate it in the committee report defining the kind of judgment that the Service should exercise in making compatibility determinations. Nonetheless, the legislative history repeatedly stresses that the Service should not permit uses where the agency lacks resources to ensure compatibility.

At the same time, though, the House committee clearly expected the FWS to seek out sources of funding to sustain wildlife-dependent recreation. For instance, the committee report describes a hypothetical situation where

> a manager determines that a bird-watching program could be conducted in accordance with principles of sound fish and wildlife management and administration, but that the program is incompatible because adequate financial resources are not available to design, operate, and maintain the use so as to prevent trespassing on sensitive nesting areas and adjacent private lands. It is the Committee's expectation in this case that the manager would take reasonable steps to obtain outside assistance from States and other conservation interests before determining that the activity is incompatible. (U.S. House 1997a, 9)

The new compatibility regulations interpret the Improvement Act to require refuge managers to make "reasonable efforts to secure resources" that are needed to make a priority public use compatible (65 Fed. Reg. 62,468 [2000]). This is part of the larger policy to facilitate wildlife-dependent recreational uses discussed in chapter 6.

The third component, "adherence to the law," adds little to the definition of "sound professional judgment." The adherence component refers to compliance with both the Improvement Act itself as well as other applicable law (1997 Improvement Act § 3(a)(5)(3)). Failure to abide by any applicable law would be an independent basis for finding that the Service has acted in an arbitrary and capricious manner under the Administrative Procedure Act, so it need not be part of sound professional judgment.

The legal question of what constitutes applicable statutory or regulatory requirements ought not dilute the meaning of "sound professional judgment." After all, the phrase does not refer to the legal profession; it is aimed at the resource management or science profession. Additionally, adherence to the 1997 Act is, in part, what "sound professional judgment" helps determine. It is circular to define the standard of judgment, which determines compliance with a management mandate, in terms that refer to adhering to the mandate.

The "Not Materially Interfere With or Detract From" Standard

The standard for determining the requisite degree of consistency with purposes cuts to the core of the substantive meaning of the compatibility criterion. The requirement that a use should not materially interfere with or detract from the mission of the System or the purposes of a refuge continues the tradition of Refuge System management that tests uses against a no interference standard. One could imagine a substantive standard that requires uses to contribute affirmatively to the mission of the refuge. Indeed, that is the standard for authorizing economic uses, such as grazing, haying, timbering, or quarrying (50 C.F.R. § 29.1). Instead, in an effort to promote uses, especially wildlife-dependent recreational uses, Congress has encouraged the Service to find ways to accommodate uses as long as they do not impair other goals of the refuges.

The conservation mission of the System establishes a backstop to prevent uses that degrade the ecological integrity of an area (65 Fed. Reg. 62,489 [2000]). The Service interprets the materially interfere/detract aspect of the compatibility definition to prohibit uses that reasonably may be anticipated to fragment habitats (65 Fed. Reg. 62,486 [2000]).

Conservation biologists agree that fragmentation of wildlife habitats is a direct threat to biological integrity (National Research Council 1995; Noss et al. 1997). The prohibition on fragmentation may prove to be the most promising litigation handle for searching judicial review in the revamped policy regime for refuge management.

Also, in evaluating the effects of uses, the Service has committed itself to consider direct, indirect, and cumulative impacts irrespective of whether it prepares an EIS (65 Fed. Reg. 62,489 [2000]). The FWS *Manual* includes the diversion of "resources from an activity that would support fulfilling the System mission or refuge's purposes" in the indirect effects refuge managers must consider in making compatibility determinations (65 Fed. Reg. 62,492 [2000]). Moreover, new Service policy places the burden of proof on the proponent of a new use to show that a proposed use does not materially interfere with or detract from a purpose (65 Fed. Reg. 62,489 [2000]). The FWS *Manual*, however, makes clear that although the burden to show compatibility rests with the prospective user, even if the use is a priority, wildlife-dependent use, the refuge manager has an obligation to work with proponents of a wildlife-dependent use "to acquire the necessary information before finding the use not compatible based solely on insufficient available information" (65 Fed. Reg. 62,492 [2000]). All of these policy provisions significantly strengthen the Service's commitment to use the best science to vigorously protect the refuges.

In considering the impacts of a use on a refuge, the Improvement Act creates an initial threshold below which Service regulations should provide expedited approval. Uses that "will likely have no detrimental effect" on the purpose of the refuge or mission of the System qualify for the streamlined process (1997 Improvement Act § 6(3)(B)(v); 65 Fed. Reg. 62,493[2000]). This trigger is similar to the ESA threshold that allows expedited approval of federal actions that agencies find will likely have no adverse effect on a listed species (16 U.S.C. § 1536(a)(2); 50 C.F.R. §§ 402.12, 402.13(a)). An important difference, however, is that ESA-expedited consideration requires the action agency to solicit confirmation of its determination from another, specialized agency that has less institutional investment in going forward with the proposal (16 U.S.C. § 1536(c); 50 C.F.R. § 402.12). The Improvement Act lacks such an independent check. Though the compatibility regulations require regional chiefs to concur with determinations made by refuge managers, these chiefs will likely come from the same FWS culture as the refuge managers (65 Fed. Reg. 62,462–62,463 [2000]). It is unrealistic to expect these superior System officers to provide critical scrutiny. The absence of independent administrative oversight, the act's promotion of wildlife-dependent recreational uses, and the pressure that interest groups can bring to bear on the Service threaten to lead to superficial findings of "likely to have no detrimental effect."

System Mission and Refuge Purposes

The benchmarks against which the standard for compatibility is measured are the System mission and the refuge purposes. The Improvement Act clearly establishes the mission of the System: conservation. However, the refuge purposes against which effects of uses are measured for compatibility require some interpretation. The Improvement Act defines refuge purposes to include goals identified in instruments that establish, authorize, acquire, or expand a refuge (§ 3(10)). The purposes of the Wilderness Act apply to those parts of refuges designated by Congress as wilderness (50 C.F.R. § 25.12).

The statute and regulations list the following documents in which refuge purposes may be found: laws, proclamations, executive orders, agreements, public land orders, donation documents, and administrative memoranda. There may be a tangle of several purposes for refuges that have accreted through a combination of these instruments. I explore the sources and nature of these individual refuge purposes in chapter 10.

To clarify the compatibility determination, it is significant that Congress explicitly included acquisition and expansion documents in the sources of individual refuge purposes. In contrast, the 1966 Administration Act's compatibility test, superseded by the 1997 law, employed only purposes "for which such areas were established" (§ 4(d)). The 1962 Act lacked consistency on this issue and used the phrase "acquired or established" in one description of the sources of purposes but then used only the phrase "established" in two subsequent descriptions of the management criterion (§ 1). Throughout this book, I use the term "establishment document" or "establishment instrument" broadly to include significant sources of individual refuge purposes regardless of whether they derive from an initial designation or a subsequently authorized acquisition. After 1997, with respect to the Refuge System, there is no longer any question that purposes in acquisition documents are included in compatibility analyses.

However, the 1997 statute does not resolve the question of whether a purpose contained in an instrument authorizing acquisition of additional land for a refuge applies to the refuge as a whole, or just to the addition. The Service takes the position that the initial establishment/acquisition purposes apply to the entire refuge unit but that subsequent acquisition purposes apply only to the specific tracts acquired (U.S. FWS 2001b, § 14; U.S. FWS 2000b, 32). This creates a very complex zoning problem for refuges acquired piecemeal over time.

Although the Improvement Act amended the organic law for the System by adding a definition of compatible use that employs "the purposes of the refuge" (§ 3(a)(5)(1)), it did not repeal the provision of the 1966 Refuge Administration Act that authorizes the Service to issue regulations to open refuges to uses compatible with "the major purposes" (Administration Act of 1966, § 4(d)(1)). This creates an ambiguity in the law, which the Service has resolved in favor of the unmodified "purposes" language from the 1997 Act (65 Fed. Reg. 62,460 [2000]). This comports with the primacy placed on all individual purposes elsewhere in the 1997 Act (e.g., § 5(a)(4)(D)).

In one respect, the broader scope of the 1997 Improvement Act's compatibility definition will be easier to implement. This is because the Service will not have to determine which of the establishment purposes are major or primary. However, in another respect, it will be more difficult to implement because the Service will have to evaluate how uses might interfere with a larger number of stated goals in many refuges. Some of these goals may be relatively unimportant but would nonetheless trump the conservation mission of the System in case of conflict (U.S. FWS 2001b, § 13). It is not clear that Congress understood this change it made to compatibility. The legislative history does not mention it. To the contrary, the statute and legislative history anticipate that the Service should rely on existing compatibility determinations, made prior to 1997, until the Service develops new comprehensive plans (§ 6(3)(A)(iv)). However, these existing compatibility determinations should have applied to a narrower range of purposes than the ones required in the 1997 Act. The Service claimed that its practice prior to 1997 did not distinguish between "major" and other refuge purposes when determining compatibility (65 Fed. Reg. 62,460 [2000]). In light of the Service's lax implementation of the compatibility criterion before 1997, as documented in GAO and other critical reports discussed in chapter 3, it is not surprising that the Service failed to make the finer distinctions required in its 1962 and 1966 mandates.

Although the 1997 Act bends the conservation mission where it conflicts with establishment purposes, the compatibility standard will usually require that uses interfere with neither. This will be important. Certain recreation, even wildlife-dependent recreation, may clearly be consistent with sporting purposes mentioned in establishment documents. However, so long as those purposes can be interpreted in a way that *could* coexist with the conservation mission, then conservation remains a benchmark for determining whether a use would detract from the refuge goals. And, the conservation touchstone will likely create greater friction with sporting purposes in a compatibility determination than it will with other establishment purposes. Although Congress littered the 1997 Act and its legislative history with exhortations to promote hunting and fishing, the compatibility standard may yield surprising limits on recreation when applied to the System mission. Don Barry, the former assistant secretary of the interior responsible for the FWS, who served while the department developed and promulgated the compatibility regulations, adds "cooperative farming and timber harvest for wildlife management purposes" to this list of uses that may face new limits under the new compatibility standard (Eckl 1999, 3). However, refuge management activities are not considered uses subject to the compatibility criterion even though many game management practices, such as the creation of wildlife openings, contribute to habitat fragmentation, which the Service policy regards as incompatible with the System conservation goal.

Biological Integrity, Diversity, and Environmental Health

Building on the 1996 executive order (Executive Order No. 12,996, § 3(e)), the Improvement Act's ecological mandate to ensure the maintenance of "biological integrity, diversity, and environmental health" (§ 5(a)(4)(B)) catapults the Refuge System to the front lines of conservation biology. This is appropriate given the strong connection between the development of the System and endangered species conservation. Even before the term "endangered species" entered the resource management lexicon, many early refuges, including the first at Pelican Island, were established to prevent extinction. Congress enacted the 1966 Administration Act as part of a bill also containing an endangered species protection program.

Today, besides managing the Refuge System, the chief job of the FWS is implementing the ESA. Overall, almost a quarter of all United States species listed under the ESA occur in the System (U.S. GAO 1994, 2). Nearly 100 individual refuges derive at least some of their land from the ESA acquisition authority. More broadly, Bradley Karkkainen makes the point that the Alaska refuges, especially, are almost unparalled in their potential to provide for biological diversity over a large scale (Karkkainen 1997, 36). The 1997 Act builds on all of these attributes of the System in reaching for a new way to articulate nature protection goals. No other organic mandate employs as unconditional or specific a series of ecological criteria to constrain management and promote conservation.

Senator Bob Graham's 1992 proposed organic legislation was the earliest bill to contain a provision similar to the ultimate biological integrity, diversity, and environmental health maintenance mandate of the 1997 Act. The 1992 bill required the Service to protect the System from threats to its ecological integrity (U.S. Senate 1992b, § 4(a)(4)(B)). That language reappeared in two 1993 bills (U.S. House 1993, § 4; U.S. Senate 1993, § 5). The proposed language inched closer to the 1997 formulation in 1995 and 1997 bills calling for maintenance of biological integrity and environmental health (U.S. House 1995a, § 5(4)(A); U.S. House 1997c, §5(4)(A)).

Before 1997, the NFMA was the organic statute providing the most specific ecological management criterion. It requires regulations that guide comprehensive plans for national forests to "provide for diversity of plant and animal communities," but softens this mandate by subordinating it to "overall multiple-use objectives" (16 U.S.C. § 1604(g)(3)(B)). The NFMA further conditions the requirement of tree species diversity preservation with the "where appropriate" and "to the degree practicable" conditions that are commonplace in public land law. Indeed, the Improvement Act conditions the restoration prong of the conservation mission with a "where appropriate" condition (§ 3(a)(4)) and mandates the achievement of the mission of the System only "to the extent practicable" (§ 5(a)(4)(D)) while protecting the establishment purposes of a refuge. So the absence of these typical terms preserving proprietary discretion in the mandate to maintain biological integrity, diversity, and environmental health (as well as in the other two prongs of the System mission, conservation and management) is significant in interpreting this criterion as a stringent substantive management standard.

However, as the 1982 Forest Service regulations implementing the NFMA diversity provision illustrate, the binding agency policy applying statutory criteria will determine the effectiveness of statutory language. In the case of the NFMA, the implementing regulation required Forest Service plans to "provide for adequate fish and wildlife habitat to maintain viable populations of existing native vertebrate species" (47 Fed. Reg. 43,050 [1982]). It was the strength of this regulation, as compared to the text of the statute, that effectively halted the timber program in the Pacific Northwest during the late 1980s and early 1990s. Courts found invalid Forest Service timber plans for failure to maintain viable populations of the northern spotted owl (*Seattle Audubon Society v. Moseley* 1992).

The new Fish and Wildlife Service policy implementing the integrity, diversity, and health mandate, though not as stringent as the 1982 Forest Service regulations, significantly advances ecological protection in the Refuge System. It also corresponds closely to the 2000 Forest Service planning regulations, which gave top priority to ecological sustainability in management. Both are part of the larger effort to reinvigorate public land management with the insights of conservation biology. The Improvement Act reverses the prior position of the Service, which was that "[t]he attainment of natural diversity is not an overriding objective of refuge management," though it should be an underlying consideration (Gergely et al. 2000, 114 [quoting 1998 FWS *Manual*]).

As with the other policies revised in the wake of the Improvement Act, the Service employed the Administrative Procedure Act's notice and comment rulemaking procedures to establish the policy on maintaining biological integrity, diversity, and environmental health. The rulemaking procedure makes the final policy on maintaining the biological integrity, diversity, and environmental health of the Refuge System binding on the Service. When the George W. Bush administration took office, it delayed until April 16, 2001, this policy's effective date, originally set at Feb. 15, 2001 (66 Fed. Reg. 9,593 [2001]). The Bush administration designated no other Refuge System policy for the special review period. This reflects the relative importance of the directives for integrity, diversity, and environmental health.

The Service biological integrity, diversity, and environmental health policy, incorporated in the FWS *Manual*, fills in many details for defining planning goals and the conservation mission (601 FW 3). Therefore, the policy is important not only in implementing its own substantive management criterion, but also in providing substance to the compatibility criterion, the conservation stewardship criterion, and the comprehensive planning mandate. The Service facilitates this connection to other policies by employing interchangeable terms. For instance, the definitions of biological integrity, diversity, and environmental health in the planning policy are almost identical to the definitions in the policy on maintaining biological integrity, diversity, and environmental health (65 Fed. Reg. 33,906 [2000]; 66 Fed. Reg. 3,818 [2001]). The 2000 policy on comprehensive planning uses the shorthand "ecological integrity" for biological integrity, diversity, and environmental health (65 Fed. Reg. 33,906 [2000]). But, the Service has since abandoned the term "ecological integrity" for the awkwardly worded criterion of biological integrity, diversity, and environmental health (66 Fed. Reg. 3,810 [2001]).

Also, out of concern for biological integrity, the Service compatibility policy prohibits uses that fragment wildlife habitats (65 Fed. Reg. 62,486 [2000]). In addition to prohibiting habitat fragmentation, the mandate to maintain biological integrity, diversity, and environmental health is a basis for limiting farming, haying, logging, livestock grazing, and other extractive activities to situations where they are "prescribed in plans to meet wildlife or habitat management objectives, and only when more natural methods, such as fire or grazing by native herbivores, cannot meet" the goals and objectives (66 Fed. Reg. 3,822 [2001]). These extractive activities are considered refuge uses and must comply with the compatibility criterion.

However, unlike the 1982 Forest Service regulation mandating maintenance of viable populations or the 2000 Forest Service rule employing focal species as surrogate indicators of ecosystem integrity, there does not appear to be an easily measured bottom line for determining whether the Refuge System is meeting its ecological mandate. This is the greatest weakness of the FWS policy because measured outcomes tend to "drive out work that produces unmeasured outcomes" (Wilson 1989, 161).

Though the Service separately defines each of the three components of this substantive management criterion, they are interrelated. The Service defines "biological diversity" in terminology familiar to the federal government since the landmark 1987 Office of Technology Assessment report and 1986 National Academy of Sciences/Smithsonian Institution conference: "the variety of life and its processes, including the variety of living organisms, the genetic differences among them, and communities and ecosystems in which they occur" (66 Fed. Reg. 3,818 [2001]; Office of Technology Assessment 1987; Wilson 1988).

Under the Service policy, "environmental health" is the "composition, structure, and functioning of soil, water, air, and other abiotic features comparable with the historic conditions, including the natural abiotic processes that shape the environment" (66 Fed. Reg. 3,818 [2001]). Because more than one-third of refuge acreage is wetlands, an important aspect of environmental health, as applied in the substantive management criterion, is water quality. The "historic conditions" benchmark in the definition of environmental health refers to "the landscape in a particular area before the onset of significant, human-caused change" (66 Fed. Reg. 3,811 [2001]). The Service notes that it does not expect "to reconstruct a complete inventory of components, structures, and functions for any successional stage occurring during the frame of reference" (66 Fed. Reg. 3,821 [2001]). The draft policy had established the specific, post-

Pleistocene, pre-European time period of 800 to 1800 C.E. to serve as a "natural conditions" benchmark containing a range of historic variability. The final policy dropped the more specifically defined "natural conditions" and substituted the somewhat more open-ended "historic conditions" (66 Fed. Reg. 3,811 [2001]). However, both terms serve the same function to provide a standard against which to measure degradation from a condition of environmental health.

The Service considers "biological integrity" to be the "biotic composition, structure, and functioning at the genetic, organism, and community levels comparable with historic conditions, including the natural biological processes that shape genomes, organisms, and communities" (66 Fed. Reg. 3,818 [2001]). Of course, this definition suffers from the same difficulties surrounding the meaning of "historic conditions" as does the one for environmental health. On its face, the biological integrity definition appears to add little not already incorporated into the diversity definition.

The only other significant federal statute to use the term biological integrity is the Clean Water Act, which establishes the objective "to restore and maintain the chemical, physical, and biological integrity of the Nation's waters" (33 U.S.C. § 1251(a)). Service policy places under environmental health most of the issues addressed in the Clean Water Act (CWA). Nonetheless, the CWA integrity objective has also been used to protect biological diversity (Fischman 1992). Kevin Gergely, J. Michael Scott, and Dale Goble argue that "a principal idea behind biological integrity is that ecological systems are self-perpetuating and fully functioning" (Gergely et al. 2000, 113). This formulation bolsters the connection between health and integrity. Also, in contrast to diversity, which lends itself to quantitative counts of variety, health and integrity present greater measurement challenges because of their strong qualitative attributes.

Despite the similar definitions and closely related concepts, are there practical distinctions among the three ecological components—biological integrity, diversity, and environmental health? The Service policy answers this question, in part, by illustrating situations in which advancing one may impair another. For instance, a refuge might compromise environmental health to maintain biological diversity. To eliminate invasive fish from a pond, the Service might use a chemical poison or physically alter the aquatic system to restore the composition and functioning of the ecosystem to historic conditions (66 Fed. Reg. 3,820 [2001]). Another example, not raised in FWS policy materials, is suggested by the mandate of the Julia Butler Hansen Refuge for Columbian White-Tailed Deer. This refuge promotes recovery of a rare subspecies of deer. To provide the interspersed mixture of woodland and grassland that the deer need, the refuge must maintain and promote fragmentation of woodland habitat. This creates a conflict between the biological integrity mandate, which prohibits habitat fragmentation, and the biological diversity mandate to recover subspecies on the verge of extinction.

In another example, the Service asserts that maintaining or restoring biological integrity is not the same as maximizing biological diversity. A refuge may focus on maintaining the habitat for a critically endangered species (or migratory waterfowl through an intensively managed feeding or resting area) at the expense of local biodiversity to protect biological integrity and national species diversity (66 Fed. Reg. 3,820 [2001]). This FWS example, however, does not really show the difference between biological integrity and diversity; rather it illustrates how the scale of concern (local, watershed, national) can alter management objectives. The Service policy elsewhere recognizes that biological integrity, diversity, and environmental health cannot be considered solely on the scale of a single refuge. Instead, larger watershed objectives (such as bay restoration), national policies (such as the North American Waterfowl Management Plan or Partners in Flight), and Refuge System goals (such as those established through the Government Performance and Results Act) may influence management decisions (66 Fed. Reg. 3,814, 3,818, 3,819, 3,821 [2001]).

The core meaning of the biological integrity, diversity, and environmental health criterion is that Congress tried three ways to express its intent to ensure that conservation biology and ecological science are deployed in the Refuge System to protect nature in the long term. Rather than try to distinguish among biological integrity, diversity, and environmental health, I believe it is more constructive to understand the elements together. Circumstances where the three components align in pointing toward a particular management direction are more likely than occurrences of conflict amongst the ecological components. Many of the refuge management problems, cited repeatedly in GAO and Interior Department reports, such as maintaining high lake levels for boating at the expense of nesting habitat (U.S. GAO 1989, 22) or permitting overgrazing (Gergely et al. 2000, 108), run afoul of all three prongs of the ecological mandate.

Now that the binding policy is in place, the Service is more vulnerable to judicial intervention where it fails to remedy degrading uses of the System. This should embolden Service officials to remove, condition, and deny uses harming refuges. Though the 1997 Act did little to change the compatibility criterion that the Service had been using administratively since the 1980s, the mandate to maintain biological integrity, diversity, and environmental health requires more protective compatibility determinations. Also, refuge management activities, such as water level or forest opening maintenance, are not subject to the compatibility standard but must nonetheless meet the substantive ecological management criteria.

An important new *Manual* provision states that "refuge managers should address" threats to biological integrity, diversity, and environmental health that originate from actions that occur outside of the refuge boundary (66 Fed. Reg. 3,822 [2001]). The policy prefers voluntary or collaborative attempts to forge solutions to external sources of refuge problems. However, if those attempts fail, the *Manual* advises refuge managers to seek redress before local planning and zoning boards, and state administrative and regulatory agencies. Though tempered by cautionary language, these are nonetheless bold instructions for a traditionally timid agency. Dealing with external threats to federal resources has been a perennial problem even for the Park Service, an agency with greater political capital to expend on external affairs (Clarke and McCool 1996; Keiter 1985; Sax and Keiter 1987; Simon 1988).

The external threat to public lands is one of the most serious challenges facing conservation. Moreover, because so many refuges are at the lower reaches of watersheds, compared to national forests and national parks, the Refuge System faces particularly difficult problems that necessitate work outside of boundaries to stem degradation. For instance, chemical run off and soil erosion from upstream farm practices threaten refuge conservation in the Upper Mississippi River refuge (National Audubon Society undated a). The State of Louisiana has issued a fish consumption advisory for the Upper Ouachita National Wildlife Refuge due to mercury levels in the fish (U.S. FWS 2002d). Oil and gas development, industrial effluent, and contaminated sediment runoff are all likely external sources of the mercury (U.S. FWS 1992). Upland residential and commercial development threatens the Pelican Island and Great Dismal Swamp refuges (Criss 1999). How the Service responds to these external threats will be an early indication of the effectiveness of the strong language in the refuge policy to secure biological integrity, diversity, and environmental health.

The *Manual* provision on external threats joins with mandates for planning and other management criteria to strengthen transboundary coordination. For instance, the Improvement Act instructs the Service to "complement efforts of States and other Federal agencies to conserve" and requires the Service, in preparing unit conservation plans, to "(A) consult with adjoining Federal, State, local, and private landowners and affected State conservation agencies; and (B) coordinate the development of the conservation plan or revision with relevant State conservation plans" (§§ 5(a)(4)(C), 7(a)(3)). Though transboundary coordination is universally acclaimed as necessary to achieve ecosystem conservation, the statutory provisions for agencies to consult and cooperate seldom amount to more than exhortations. This is as true for the Improvement Act as it is for most other organic legislation. The policy provision explicitly instructing managers how to deal with external threats could help transform desirable collaboration into real management. But, when refuge managers set priorities, transboundary coordination may continue to languish. For example, the manager of the National Elk Refuge, which protects an elk herd that ranges far outside the borders of the refuge, generally does not seek to influence relevant management decisions on neighboring public and private lands. The reason, in part, is that involvement in external management decisions "would require additional funds and manpower" and it might arouse "the latent antifederal sentiment that pervades" the region (Halverson 2000, 28). Neither the 1997 Act nor the implementing policy does much to change those circumstances.

The Refuge System policy, fleshing out the substantive management criterion to maintain biological integrity, diversity, and environmental health, describes a broad conservation mission consistent with the current scientific discourse of conservation biology. For instance, Grumbine, in a follow-up study of his seminal article on ecosystem management, identifies ecological integrity as an important aspect of the cutting-edge conservation practice (Grumbine 1997). The System policy is also consistent with the overarching servicewide "ecosystem approach" to administration of its myriad responsibilities (U.S. FWS 2002e). The Service's policy can be seen as part of a larger Clinton administration effort to bring ecological and conservation sciences to bear on public land management. This effort was evident in the Clinton executive order for Refuge System management, which directed the interior secretary to "ensure that the biological integrity and environmental health of the Refuge System is maintained" (Executive Order No. 12,996, § 3(e)). Also, the Service policy categorizing fragmentation of habitat as incompatible with the Refuge System's conservation mission is based on the same principles as the controversial Forest Service roadless rule limiting the construction of new roads and logging on 58.5 million acres of inventoried roadless areas in national forests (66 Fed. Reg. 3,244 [2001]).

The Clinton reform of the national forest planning regulations, which placed priority on "the maintenance and restoration of ecological sustainability," is yet another example of this effort (65 Fed. Reg. 67,517

[2000]). Similarly, the National Park Service adopted new management policies in the last months of the Clinton administration that identified the natural integrity of parks as a key resource protected from impairment under the Park System organic legislation (65 Fed. Reg. 56,003 [2000] (§ 1.4)). The tenet that long-term economic prosperity depends on healthy ecosystems and biodiversity is part of the international movement promoting sustainable development (World Commission on Environment and Development 1987, 331).

The convergence of the national forest planning regulations and the Refuge System management criteria is significant for two reasons. First, the Forest System has had more than two decades to refine its management to the current iteration of its planning rules. The Refuge System has essentially leapfrogged over that gap in experience to the cutting edge of management prescriptions. Second, the Forest System is widely regarded as the prototypical multiple use public land system. The close match of the National Forest System's ecological management constraints with the Refuge System's dominant use ecological criteria reflects the general convergence of U.S. public lands systems toward the middle of the use continuum described in the introduction to this book. However, the current Bush administration is backpedaling on the Clinton administration's Forest Service rules. Its next logical step may be to weaken the Refuge System policy to maintain biological integrity, diversity, and environmental health.

Water Rights

Though the 1997 Improvement Act itself creates no new water rights, it does establish a clear duty for the Service to acquire water rights needed for refuge purposes (§ 5(a)(4)(G)). This will be important for the protection of all aquatic organisms. Many flagship animals of the Refuge system, such as waterfowl, are dependent on aquatic habitat for parts of their life cycles. Indigenous freshwater fish and mussels are two of the most imperiled categories of animals in the United States (Wilcove 1999, 106). Though healthy water flows are under greater threat in the arid West, many rivers and bays in the East also suffer from water deprivation. Water can be acquired by purchase or asserted as a reserved right under federal law.

Securing instream water flows for conservation purposes on public land has been a controversial topic at least since the Supreme Court found a federal reserved water right to protect the desert pupfish at the Devil's Hole National Monument in 1976 (*Cappaert v. United States*). Water rights, like property rules generally, are usually established under state law. However, federal lands may have water rights arising from federal law. A holder of a water right has a property interest in the *use* of water, rather than in the actual possession of a designated volume of water.

In the arid West, where many reserved refuges require water to conserve waterfowl, fish, and other species, most states apply the doctrine of prior appropriation to allocate scarce water. Prior appropriation requires diversion of water to a beneficial use in order to establish a water right. In times of drought, water users whose rights are older fill their allocation entirely before more junior holders of rights can get any water.

Refuges are often downstream of and junior to irrigators, the main water users in the West. In contrast to the national forests, wildlife refuges tend to be located at lower elevations, below numerous diversions that reduce stream flows. John Loomis has noted that

> water diversion and groundwater pumping for irrigated agriculture have often resulted in reducing the natural flows of water to many refuges. Irrigated agriculture often poses an additional threat from the discharge of agricultural drainage water containing toxic trace elements from pesticides and fertilizers. Such contamination made national news in 1984 with the discovery at Kesterson National Wildlife Refuge that agricultural drainage water flowing into the refuge contained many toxic trace elements, such as selenium. (Loomis 1993, 400)

Refuges, therefore, often find their water unavailable during dry seasons and years. This misfortune befell Bosque del Apache National Wildlife Refuge in 2002 and the Klamath Basin refuges in 2001. Water quality concerns are more likely to raise issues under the biological integrity, diversity, and environmental health criterion than under the duty to acquire water rights.

Refuges generally put water to nondiversionary uses, such as maintaining stream flows, wetland moisture, or lake levels. Although some states now permit acquisition of water rights for instream uses, many do not. All prior appropriation states except New Mexico have some provision for protecting instream flows in rivers (Getches 2001, 30). However, many states implement this protection through public interest limitations on private diversions or minimum stream flow regulation. Most prior appropriation states that permit acquisition of instream flow water rights limit the privilege to state agencies (Covell 1998; Tarlock 2002, § 5:28). A 1994 survey revealed that only 98 of the 226 western refuges responding to a questionnaire had adequate existing water rights to provide for refuge needs even during an average year of precipitation (Western Water Policy Review Advisory Commission 1998, 5-34).

Reserved Water Rights

The Service may assert a federal reserved water right for instream flows based on a refuge establishment document. The federal right can exist even in states that do not permit instream water rights under state law. Such a right has a priority date of the time that Congress or the president established a reservation for a particular purpose. The amount of the reserved water right is the minimum necessary to prevent the frustration of the primary purpose of the reservation (*United States v. New Mexico* 1978).

Courts have determined that these federal reserved rights may be created implicitly, even if the establishment document is silent on its intention for water rights. As long as the reservation's primary purpose requires water for fulfillment, the federal right is created for that amount at the time of establishment. Courts will assume, absent evidence to the contrary, that when Congress (or the president) reserves federal land for a particular purpose, it intends to reserve a federal water right sufficient to ensure the purpose can be achieved. For instance, the proclamation establishing the 40-acre Devil's Hole unit of the larger Death Valley National Monument declared its purpose to preserve "the unusual features of scenic, scientific, and educational interest" of a "remarkable underground pool" (Proclamation No. 2,961 [1952], *quoted in Cappaert v. United States* 1976, 132–133). The Supreme Court interpreted this purpose to include an implied reservation of water to maintain pool levels at a sufficient height to sustain the existence of a rare pupfish that lives in the pool. The Court found the fish to be one of the monument's features of scientific interest.

The rationale of the reserved water rights cases and the Department of Justice support the extension of the doctrine to acquired federal lands, in addition to reserved public domain (U.S. Department of Justice 1982). However, the courts have yet to decide a case challenging a federal claim of a reserved right for an acquired refuge holding. In general, state courts adjudicating federal reserved water rights have been reluctant to recognize instream flows (Getches 2001, 32; see, e.g., *United States v. State of Idaho* 2001).

A refuge has an implied federal reserved water right, therefore, to fulfill only the primary purposes of its establishment document, with a priority date of the act of establishment. So, even though the 1997 Act removes the need to identify major, or primary, purposes for compatibility determinations, primary purposes remain important in determining the reserved water rights. Where a refuge has grown through multiple reservations that are silent on the issue of reserved rights, different reserved water rights may be established to fulfill different primary purposes with different priority dates.

Because a federal reserved water right can trump state requirements such as diversion and continual use, and because federal courts have ruled that such a property interest may exist by implication, this issue has generated a great deal of controversy in Congress. Congress has recently begun to make explicit statements about its intent with respect to reserving water rights. For instance, in the California Desert Protection Act of 1994, Congress explicitly reserved "a quantity of water sufficient to fulfill the purposes of this Act" (16 U.S.C. § 410aaa-76). In the Improvement Act, Congress explicitly refused to create a new overlay of 1997 priority-date reserved water rights for all the refuges to fulfill the new mission of the System (§ 8(a)(n)(1)).

Nonetheless, implied reserved rights continue to exist (even if not yet adjudicated) on some refuges, based on the establishment documents. For instance, the U.S. Supreme Court found federal implied reserved water rights for the Havasu Lake National Wildlife Refuge and Imperial National Wildlife Refuge in 1963 (*Arizona v. California* 1963). However, some courts will read establishment documents narrowly to avoid disrupting the expectations of state water rights holders. For instance, the Idaho Supreme Court recently found that the establishment documents for the Deer Flat National Wildlife Refuge implied no federal reserved water rights (*United States v. State of Idaho* 2001). The Deer Flat refuge consists of approximately 94 islands over 110 miles of the Snake River and was established, like the majority of refuges, to preserve native migratory birds and their breeding grounds (id., 120–122). The Deer Flat decision followed closely on the heels of a politically charged rehearing of a wilderness reserved water rights determination by the same court. In that 2000 case, the Idaho Supreme Court reversed itself and found no implied reserved water rights for wilderness areas (*Potlatch Corp. v. United States* 2000). The 3-2 reversal occurred "after the author of the earlier decision upholding federal water rights for wilderness areas was defeated for reelection in a controversial judicial campaign in which her wilderness water rights opinion became a centerpiece of her opponent's election strategy" (Blumm 2002, 177). At best, the court's Deer Flat decision reflects a tragic misunderstanding of the absolute need for water flows to support the establishment purpose of preserving migratory birds. Unfortunately, the federal government chose not to appeal the Idaho court's decision.

The Duty to Acquire

Though it is not an independent basis for federal reserved water rights, the Improvement Act created an important new mandate for securing water rights to sustain the instream flows necessary to fulfill the conservation mission of the System. The Act requires the Service to "acquire, under State law, water rights that are needed for refuge purposes" (§ 5(a)(4)(G)). The Act also requires the Service to "assist in the maintenance of adequate water quantity and water quality to fulfill the mission of the System" (§ 5(a)(4)(F)). "Assist" is a mandate that incorporates a greater degree of agency discretion than "acquire" because it includes a wider range of consultation and informal procedures. Whether the Service fulfills a mandate to assist is likely to be a matter of degree, of determining whether the agency did enough procedurally. In comparing these two mandates, the House committee report characterized the mandate to "acquire" as imposing "a new, more specific, obligation" (U.S. House 1997a, 10). The legislative history clarifies the acquisition mandate as requiring the Service to exercise existing authority to meet new obligations. Included in the existing authority that the secretary could employ is the power to "acquire water rights with appropriated funds; improve the operations of Federal agencies with respect to the identification and protection of relevant water rights; purchase water; and participate in State water rights adjudications to perfect and defend relevant water rights" (id.).

The water acquisition mandate is important because it addresses, with respect to the Refuge System, a fiduciary issue that has been the subject of controversy in public land management for over two decades. Early suits by environmental groups unsuccessfully attempted to compel the Park Service to claim reserved water rights in the Sevier River in Zion National Park, which faced reduced stream flows due to upstream energy development (Tarlock 2002, § 9.52). Litigation over protection of Redwood National Park in the mid-1970s alleged that the Park Service failed in its statutory duty to conserve park resources (*Sierra Club v. Department of the Interior* 1974; *Sierra Club v. Department of the Interior* 1975). Although Congress ultimately resolved the particular conservation issues with respect to Redwood National Park, the court decisions raised the possibility that an affirmative public trust duty might exist on the part of the agency to protect park resources. Subsequent attempts to apply the trust responsibility to force federal land management agencies to assert water rights (or to pursue them more aggressively) have failed. But the judicial opinions never entirely dismissed the idea that there are some circumstances where a court would impose a duty on an agency to assert water rights.

The mandate in the Improvement Act to acquire water rights is more specific and stronger than mandates found in the legislation involved in the public trust litigation over federal lands. Therefore, the FWS duty will likely trigger relatively greater judicial scrutiny of agency passivity during proceedings adjudicating water rights. The Improvement Act fails to create new reserved rights, but it does mandate the Service to participate in adjudications to protect and defend water reserved rights arising from establishment documents (U.S. House 1997a, 10). Nonetheless, it will be difficult for conservation advocates to challenge mild FWS advocacy that falls short of a zealous assertion of rights.

In addition to asserting reserved rights, the Improvement Act mandates that the Service go further to purchase conventional water rights (id.). Any refuge that has establishment purposes requiring more water than would be necessary to meet just the *primary* purposes (the limit of the implied federal reserved right) will need acquired water. Acquiring water is especially necessary in two circumstances, even for nonacquired lands, because the 1997 Act does not create reserved rights to meet the needs of the conservation mission.

First, refuges that do not have some version of the System's conservation mission as their primary purpose will need to acquire water rights under state law because they do not possess sufficient federal reserved rights. A significant problem with this approach is that many states still do not permit acquisition of water rights for application to instream, conservation flows. On the other hand, an application from the FWS to a state permitting agency for "natural flow" to support wildlife may provide an opportunity for a state to expand its concept of "beneficial use" "to reflect changes in society's recognition of the value" of new instream uses (*In re: Water Right Claim No. 1927-2* 1994). This is what happened when South Dakota issued the FWS a water permit to assure the continued flow of springs providing waterfowl habitat on the LaCreek National Wildlife Refuge. In upholding the permit against a challenge by neighboring landowners, the South Dakota Supreme Court established an important precedent that may make it easier for others to acquire rights to instream conservation flows. The international interest in migratory bird protection and national interest in national wildlife refuge conservation can provide a strong set of facts for extending the traditional property doctrines of water law.

Second, because federal reserved water rights date back only to the time of establishment, there are many refuges that have relatively junior rights. For those refuges, the Service might have to purchase more senior rights to ensure seasonal instream flows for conservation. This will be the case for the Klamath Basin refuges. A recent drought has created a crisis for migratory birds using the now dry wetlands in the Klamath Basin refuges, which have junior claims to the little water going to farmers through a 1905 federal reclamation project. The Klamath refuges include the Upper Klamath, Bear Valley, Lower Klamath, and Clear Lake national wildlife refuges. The Department of the Interior currently allocates water in the Klamath basin for purposes in the following order of priority: (1) species listed under the ESA, (2) tribal trust responsibilities, (3) irrigated agriculture, and (4) national wildlife refuges (Henry 2003; U.S. House 2001).

Unfortunately, unless Congress substantially increases appropriations for purchasing water rights, the Service will have limited options to meet its duty. The lack of budget monies for water actually threaten more than just the System's purchasing power. The 1998 report of the Western Water Policy Review Advisory Commission found that the Service lacks funds even to document adequately the water uses and needs on refuges. The Advisory Commission's recommendations include development of a program to "improve data collection and analysis for use in defense of refuge water rights" and "increase the efficiency and effectiveness of existing water management" (Western Water Policy Review Advisory Commission 1998, 5–34).

Congress missed a critical opportunity in failing to establish new federal reserved water rights for the System with a 1997 priority date. There is no question that conservation of plants and animals is now the primary purpose of the Refuge System. Also, there is little doubt that lack of water would frustrate this mission in many circumstances. By establishing new rights with a 1997 priority date, Congress could have bolstered long-term environmental protection without taking water rights away from any existing users, all of whom would have priority dates earlier than 1997, and without having to rely on states to update their water law regimes to incorporate nature protection concerns. Instead, Congress mandated the FWS to accomplish the goal with a limited set of tools not up to the task at hand.

At the same time, though, Congress deserves credit for dealing directly with the issue of federal reserved water rights. The organic acts for the other federal public lands systems skirt the issue of reserved rights and leave it for the executive and judicial branches to sort out. Typical is the

Federal Land Policy and Management Act, which states that it neither expands nor diminishes federal or state rights in water resources development or control (43 U.S.C. § 1701). The Improvement Act's mandate directing the FWS to acquire water is a pathbreaking management mandate that will require vigilance on the part of the federal government to protect instream flows.

Biological Monitoring

The Improvement Act requires the Service to "monitor the status and trends of fish, wildlife, and plants in each refuge" (§ 5(a)(4)(N)). This monitoring requirement originated in the Senate bill and entered the act when the House adopted amendments to reconcile its bill with the Senate's (U.S. Senate 1997, 2; 143 Cong. Rec. S9,092 [1997]). This simple substantive criterion will prove to be important because it is a binding duty for a key, yet chronically missing, element of adaptive management. Adaptive management requires feedback about the consequences of decisions in order to adjust them continually. The FWS *Manual* defines adaptive management as "[t]he rigorous application of management, research, and monitoring to gain information and experience necessary to assess and modify management activities. It is a process that uses feedback from refuge research and monitoring and evaluation of management actions to support or modify objectives and strategies at all planning levels" (602 FW 1.6(A)). Public land management, generally, lacks a research component that adequately informs decision makers and the public about the success or failure of predictions, such as a prospective finding of compatibility (Doremus 2001; Fischman and Meretsky 2001). Therefore, implementation of biological monitoring is a necessary condition for the success of the Service's policy of employing adaptive management in planning (65 Fed. Reg. 33,907 [2000]).

One of the problems leading to incompatible uses and environmental degradation on refuges is ignorance about the distribution and needs of nongame species of animals and plants. For instance, as of 1994, for 13 percent of the threatened and endangered species that occur on refuges, the Service did not know whether populations were improving, stable, or declining (U.S. GAO 1994, 7). The 1994 GAO report describes refuges where managers lamented inadequate funds to conduct studies and surveys necessary for species recovery (id., 10). An earlier GAO study found that the FWS could not assess the effects of oil and gas operations on refuges because of lack of data (id., iii). Indeed, most of the reports documenting incompatible uses in the System in the 1980s were based on sub-jective surveys because the Service lacked monitoring of uses and impacts.

Sadly, this is typical of federal lands generally. The monitoring re-quirement directly remedies this weakness by forcing reluctant managers to invest in better information, even where it reveals disquieting conflicts. However, monitoring will be an unfulfilled mandate if it remains an un-funded mandate. Congress needs to appropriate adequate money to allow refuges to engage in adaptive management. The Senate sponsors recog-nized this need and the other important aspects of monitoring when they introduced the monitoring criterion by amendment into the version of the Improvement Act passed by the House:

> Monitoring is often one of the first casualties of budgetary constraints. In addition, given some of the past problems with secondary uses on refuges, monitoring will be very important in measuring the success of the recent administrative and legislative changes that we are now undertaking. Lastly, monitoring will ensure that our scientific knowl-edge regarding wildlife and natural resources continues to grow. (143 Cong. Rec. S9,093 [1997])

The only other public land system employing a similar monitoring re-quirement is the National Forest System. Unlike the Improvement Act, the NFMA does not explicitly mandate monitoring. But courts have nonetheless compelled the Forest Service to monitor wildlife and habitat in response to planning regulations, as well as to the resulting plans. For instance, in *Sierra Club v. Martin,* a federal appeals court suspended sev-eral national forest timber sales because the Forest Service failed to ob-tain population trend data for certain indicator species (*Sierra Club v. Martin* 1999). The then-governing Forest Service regulation stated, in a requirement similar to that in the Improvement Act, that "population trends of the management indicator species will be monitored and the re-lationships to habitat changes determined" (36 C.F.R. 219.19(a)(6) [1999]). Despite the "great deference" the Forest Service received from the court, the court rejected as inadequate the Forest Service's claim that it met the monitoring requirement by making site visits and consulting maps to evaluate habitat in the area. The court insisted on actual popu-lation surveys. The forest plan's provisions requiring monitoring bolstered the case for actual population surveys in *Sierra Club v. Martin* and the other recent case that suspended logging for the same reason (*Oregon Natural Resources Council v. U.S. Forest Service* 1999).

The refuges, with a more stringent statutory requirement than the NFMA, may well face the same judicial intervention if they fail to gather and consider biological inventory information. With clear statutory language applicable to a broader range of species than the old Forest Service regulation, the Service will likely need to conduct actual population surveys even where its conservation plans lack strong language. However, unlike the Forest Service regulation at issue in *Sierra Club v. Martin* and the other cases, the Improvement Act's mandate does not include the word "population." This may allow the refuges to monitor size of available habitat only, a practice rejected in many national forest management challenges (see, e.g., *Utah Environmental Congress v. Zieroth* 2002).

Conservation Stewardship

Despite the statutory and regulatory focus on the compatibility test, which relies on finding that uses will not interfere with or detract from the mission and purposes of a refuge, the Improvement Act also contains a broad affirmative mandate. The act requires the Service to manage the System to fulfill the mission of conservation (§ 5(a)(3)(A)). The legislative history refers to this provision as the "stewardship responsibility" (U.S. House 1997a, 10).

Though less specific than the affirmative duty to acquire water, the conservation stewardship criterion nonetheless shares that provision's fiduciary quality. It requires more active, protective management than merely ensuring compatibility. For instance, the stewardship criterion might limit boating on Deer Flat National Wildlife Refuge more stringently than the compatibility analysis would call for (Tredennick 2000, 98–99).

The conservation stewardship responsibility may be relegated to the background as mere policy because the Improvement Act contains many more specific requirements designed to advance the mission. Indeed, though in the section of the act dealing with administration of the System, the subsection containing the conservation stewardship mandate is labeled "policy." However, the recent FWS "policy" defining biological integrity, diversity, and environmental health as components of the conservation mission, adopted under the procedures of informal rulemaking and incorporated into the agency *Manual*, provides a wealth of specific standards that the Service must meet.

The conservation stewardship mandate is what William H. Rodgers Jr. calls a sleeper provision. A sleeper provision is a statutory provision that receives little attention during enactment but that has "consequences exceeding the formal legislative vision" (Rodgers 1993, 57). Sleepers frequently lie dormant during the early years of implementation of a statute and then emerge as important provisions as a program matures.

We can expect the Service's and the public's initial attention on implementation of the Improvement Act to focus on the compatibility determinations. This parallels the early focus in ESA implementation on determinations that agency actions will not jeopardize species (i.e., interfere with the goals of the ESA) (Fischman and Hall-Rivera 2002). These determinations are specific, written findings that deal with activities that often threaten acute harms. They are rallying points for controversies and litigation.

However, as the new refuge organic act matures, we may witness some growth of substantive detail on the skeleton of the broad affirmative duty. Like the affirmative duty to fulfill the Refuge System mission, the ESA's statutory requirement for affirmative species conservation (defined as species recovery) contrasted sharply with its negative partner (avoid incompatible uses for refuges in the Improvement Act and avoid jeopardy to species in the ESA) in having no procedure or written determination associated with compliance. Therefore, the affirmative recovery mandate was a lower priority for agency implementation and citizen oversight in the early years of the ESA program. Although courts consistently hold that fulfilling the duty to conserve requires some action, or some reason why the agency has not acted, they seldom set out precisely what it requires, or rely on it as the sole basis for overturning an agency's decision (Fischman and Squillace 2000, 182–183; Ruhl 1995, 1110). Therefore, the duty to conserve has not yet played a prominent role in the implementation of the ESA. Although some recent cases show signs of breathing life into the duty to conserve (*Sierra Club vs. Glickman* 1998), it currently remains overshadowed by the overlapping, but separate and more specific, duty of the Services to prepare recovery plans.

The mandate to make affirmative contributions toward the System mission provides a statutory basis for application of the public trust doctrine. This doctrine, rooted in water law, has long held attraction for advocates of federal public land conservation. It posits an enforceable duty for the government to husband natural resource use in a manner that protects the collective interests of the public. However, nonstatutory bases for its application have always proven weak (Huffman 1986, 1989; Lazarus 1986). The Improvement Act's conservation duty may, then, finally generate a body of public trust case law and practices for the federal public lands. In contrast to federal law, most western states have developed bodies of law governing their school trust lands. Those lands, originally part of a package of federal land grants at the time of statehood, are managed by trustees operating under fiduciary constraints (Fairfax 2000).

Even if it is a weak offensive weapon for conservationists to compel Service action, the stewardship responsibility serves as a basis for the Service to defend more assertive protection of the refuges, especially when dealing with external threats. In this respect, the stewardship criterion bolsters the FWS biological integrity, diversity, and environmental health policy requiring refuge managers to address external threats to refuge conservation goals. Moreover, the conservation stewardship mandate supports an "ecosystem management" approach to resource conservation, implied in the idea that System resources cannot be protected in the long term solely by controlling activities within the boundary of the refuges.

The Service can clarify and strengthen its stewardship responsibility by establishing procedures that require periodic evaluations of refuges' progress toward fulfilling the Improvement Act's conservation mandate. The *Manual* provisions governing preparation of comprehensive refuge plans would be a logical place to begin. If plans establish specific performance goals for conservation, then the stewardship duty can be measured continually as progress in meeting those goals. In this way, the comprehensive conservation plans can steer individual refuges closer to the System mission in the same way that annual Government Performance and Results Act reports spur measurable improvement for the Service as a whole.

9 | Public Participation

One of the great modern attributes of federal land management is public involvement. Although the National Environmental Policy Act (NEPA) opened management decisions to public scrutiny and involvement through environmental impact analysis, the Service remained largely free of any additional requirements until the enactment of the Improvement Act. Public participation improves management because it forces administrators to defend clearly their choices to a critical audience. It also brings more information to bear on the decisions the manager must make. This information is important to answer hybrid questions of refuge management containing both technical and social components: what quantities of goods (e.g., waterskiing areas, game, wetlands flora) to produce, which lands are suitable for which uses, and what conditions should be placed on activities. Public participation provisions recognize that land management is not simply applied natural science, it is also conflict management (Bobertz and Fischman 1993, 374).

Effective public participation is particularly important for the Refuge System because the ecological goals inevitably require partnerships across jurisdictional boundaries. However, the Improvement Act requires only passive participation, where the agency presents ideas to which the public responds. Though the Act calls for coordination, it does not contain any strong incentives for cross-boundary ecosystem management through interactive participation, where the public and the agency share in joint analysis of problems.

Interactive participation facilitates active learning through the synthesis of multiple perspectives (Clark and Brewer 2000, 14–16).

Public participation takes many forms in organic legislation. Avenues for participation open when agencies are required to set out guidance through notice and comment rulemaking, to provide a process for planning and appeals, to submit to citizen suits, or to consult advisory committees. The Improvement Act promotes public participation in System management in standard, unimaginative ways. This is particularly striking when compared with the Act's strong, detailed, and creative provisions in the other hallmarks of modern organic legislation. The Improvement Act does little to advance the cause of public participation beyond what existing law requires and encourages. However, the U.S. Fish and Wildlife Service (FWS) has, on its own initiative, employed some of these methods.

The public is not a monolithic bloc. The FWS *Manual* defines the "public" to include private individuals, organizations, and groups; governmental officials; Indian tribes; and foreign nations. Some members of the public have special expertise in an area of study that has a bearing on important refuge management decisions. Others might have a particularly deep knowledge of the resources located on a particular refuge. These members of the public have better opportunities to affect refuge management decisions. However, even the ordinary concerned citizen with a special interest in a refuge issue can participate in some agency decisions.

Most means of public participation are direct in the sense that the interested person communicates concerns, opinions, or information directly to the responsible Service official. However, indirect participation can also be an important tool for the public to shape Service policy. The FWS examines a variety of outside information and data in the course of evaluating its management options. The public can participate indirectly by influencing or contributing to these outside sources. For example, the FWS must consider endangered species recovery plans and tribal and state wildlife management plans when engaging in comprehensive conservation planning for a refuge (602 FW 1.7). Influencing these relevant plans or the studies on which they are based is a form of indirect participation in the comprehensive conservation plan.

This chapter discusses opportunities for public participation in several key Service procedures. The chapter begins with an evaluation of the way in which the Service solicits public comment in making rules and policies. The chapter next describes the public participation provisions in the Service's comprehensive conservation planning activities. Chapter 7 covers the basic criteria, goals, and procedures for comprehensive refuge planning.

This chapter homes in on the key steps in planning where public participation is most effective. In addition to refugewide comprehensive conservation planning, this chapter also covers the key steps in making compatibility determinations that offer the public opportunities to influence the Service. Finally, this chapter concludes with a discussion of advisory committees and avenues for challenging FWS decisions.

Rules and Policies

Under the Administrative Procedure Act (APA), most federal agency regulations binding the public must go through notice and comment rulemaking (5 U.S.C. § 553). Though public land management rules are generally exempt from this broad APA requirement, organic legislation sometimes mandates that the APA procedure be followed. The National Forest Management Act (NFMA) requires the Forest Service to employ notice and comment rulemaking for forest planning standards and procedures, and the Improvement Act requires the FWS to employ it only for compatibility standards and procedures (16 U.S.C. § 1604(g); 16 U.S.C. § 668dd(d)(3)(B)). But even when not required, land management agencies, including the FWS, often turn to the notice and comment procedure to facilitate public participation in creating binding national policies to implement statutory criteria and other land management programs.

Before the 1997 Improvement Act, the Service seldom employed notice and comment rulemaking in issuing policies or *Manual* provisions. For instance, when the FWS first published guidance in its refuge *Manual* for compatibility determinations in 1986, it did not use notice and comment rulemaking. With the exception of the compatibility criterion, the Improvement Act is silent as to procedures the Service should follow for fleshing out important topics, including comprehensive planning. Though the Service has decided not to write its newly revised *Manual* provisions as regulations, it has decided to employ the notice and comment rulemaking *procedures* of publishing draft policy, inviting comment, and then responding to comments in promulgating final guidance (65 Fed. Reg. 62,475 [2000]). So, although they are not rules compiled in the Code of Federal Regulations, the new agency practices with respect to, for instance, planning, wilderness stewardship, and maintenance of biological integrity, diversity, and environmental health are based on the extensive discussions of public input resulting from notice and comment promulgation.

The Improvement Act requires the compatibility regulations to provide an opportunity for public review and comment on each individual determination (§ 6(3)(B)(ix)). This review and comment may be met through the comprehensive planning process. It is incongruous for Congress to require regulations for compatibility determinations but not for comprehensive planning. It is not sufficient for the plans themselves to be subject to public notice and comment, as the act requires (§ 7(e)(4)). The Improvement Act should have required planning regulations for the FWS, as the NFMA does for the Forest Service. Without such a statutory mandate, a future administration might change the current policy of employing notice and comment rulemaking procedures for *Manual* provisions related to comprehensive planning.

The U.S. experience with national forest planning indicates that management improves when the agency is subject to the discipline of an open notice and comment rulemaking to lay out planning measures. This kind of rulemaking is beneficial because it (1) allows interest groups to leverage their resources to shape the framework for planning generally, even where such groups lack the resources to participate in many individual comprehensive plans; (2) provides enforceable benchmarks to ensure the Service does what it promises to do in comprehensive planning; and (3) ensures greater systemic unity through well-vetted standards.

The Service "policies" go through the same notice and public participation as regulations under APA section 553. But, instead of appearing in the Code of Federal Regulations, the policies become chapters in the FWS *Manual*. Even the compatibility rule has a counterpart policy written to conform to the *Manual* style (65 Fed. Reg. 62,484 [2000]). Like its more celebrated cousin for the U.S. Forest Service, the FWS *Manual* provides mandatory operational instructions for land managers. Typically, manuals contain policies that do not directly regulate the public, but instead set out the duties of public officials. Still, these policies, such as the definition of the principles for maintaining biological integrity, diversity, and environmental health, frequently determine what resources the public may enjoy in a refuge.

The judiciary generally holds that *Manual* provisions scrutinized through the notice and comment process bind agencies. Therefore, public participation is also important in forcing the agency to follow its own policies. Where *Manual* provisions are not promulgated under APA section 533, they receive less public scrutiny and therefore are accorded less weight by courts. This issue arose in a pre–Improvement Act management dispute at the Key West National Wildlife Refuge. In *McGrail and Rowley v. Babbitt*, a federal district court rejected the plaintiff's contention that the Service should be bound by provisions in the refuge *Manual* dealing with public access to coastal island refuges. The court cited the following factors as important in concluding that the provisions were non-binding: (1) neither the 1966 Act nor the Service regulations referred to the refuge *Manual;* (2) the language of the *Manual* was advisory in tone; and (3) the Service did not employ APA informal rulemaking procedures in producing the *Manual* (*McGrail and Rowley v. Babbitt* 1997, 1394).

The FWS declares that it is bound by the promulgated provisions in the *Manual* and will need to employ the same notice and comment procedure to amend a policy that it used in original adoption (65 Fed. Reg. 33,902 [2000]). An incentive for the FWS to promulgate its manual through notice and comment rulemaking is that courts will then accord the substantive interpretations greater deference than *Manual* provisions adopted without the formality and public participation of notice and comment rulemaking (*Southern Utah Wilderness Alliance v. Dabney* 2000; *United States v. Mead Corp.* 2001). However, if future administrations abandon or abbreviate the APA section 553 notice and comment procedure used to promulgate policy, then the *Manual* will revert to a far inferior tool for ensuring good management.

In addition to the rise of notice and comment rulemaking procedures for *Manual* revisions, the other important administrative trend spurred by the Improvement Act is the increase in policy detail. The post-1997 *Manual* provisions reflect the new organic legislation in laying out detailed guidelines to follow and factors to consider in refuge management. A member of the public reading *Manual* sections promulgated since 1997 has a much better idea about how the Service conducts management and how to influence Service decisions. This, of course, raises the stakes for public participation in the formulation of *Manual* provisions.

As the FWS posts more chapters of its *Manual* on the Internet so that they are as easily accessible as the Code of Federal Regulations, the practical distinctions between implementing through policy rather than through regulation dissolve. For several months in 2002, though, the *Manual* was not readily available to the public because a federal court order suspended the operation of most Department of the Interior Web sites. This interruption of access to the *Manual* underscores the enduring advantage of the Code of Federal Regulations as a widely disseminated, print reference source.

Comprehensive Conservation Plans

Chapter 7 describes the eight steps that the Service employs in developing comprehensive conservation plans (CCPs). Though all the planning steps contain opportunities for public involvement, steps 2, 4, 5, and 8 require refuge managers to make special efforts to reach out for public comment. This section surveys the opportunities for direct and indirect public involvement in planning.

Personal relationships enhance influence throughout the planning process. The public should get to know the refuge manager, planning team leader, and planning team members who will be responsible for developing a CCP. Cultivating a relationship with these individuals, through phone calls, letters, or face-to-face meetings, may provide the earliest opportunity to shape the plan. One common tactic for influencing the long-term direction of a refuge is the establishment of a "friends of the refuge" group that can lobby the FWS for needed changes on the refuge, provide volunteers to implement parts of the refuge CCP and step-down management plans (SDMPs), assist with monitoring the effects of plans and activities, and develop educational programs for the refuge.

During preplanning, the FWS may seek information directly from private landowners concerning land management issues that impact or relate to the refuge. Planners may identify and consult with resource experts familiar with the key species and habitats on the refuge (602 FW 3.4C(1)(e), (f)). The Service may begin at this stage to decide what issues will be addressed in the NEPA document that will accompany the CCP and whether an environmental assessment (EA) or environmental impact statement (EIS) is more likely. Moreover, individuals or organizations can send to the planning team relevant scientific data and information. The FWS compiles and consults a large array of information and data sources such as state heritage databases and conservation plans, species lists compiled by various agencies and organizations, scientific literature, relevant EAs and EISs, and information from ongoing research projects (602 FW 3.4C(1)(e)). Any opportunity to contribute to these information sources provides an indirect mechanism to shape the CCP at its inception.

Step 2's scoping begins with a notice of intent to prepare a CCP in the *Federal Register*. The FWS also issues news releases to the local media about the opportunity to participate in the preparation of the CCP and to take part in the scoping process (602 FW 3.4C(2)(b)). The scoping process is an early and essential opportunity for the public to influence the CCP. The best time to influence the CCP is before the FWS starts writing it. The CCP is easier to shape at this early stage of development, as opposed to attempting to modify it at later stages through criticism of the draft document. At this step the public can critique or comment on the refuge's vision statement and goals as articulated by the FWS, as well as any actual or potential issues, management needs, impacts, or problems.

Issues that are likely to be relevant to a number of refuges include potential conflicts between species, especially species that compete for resources on the refuge or that are in a predator–prey relationship; conflicts between human users of the refuge; management and control of unwanted species; the quantity and quality of water on the refuge; off-refuge land uses that can impact water quantity and quality, air quality, or aesthetics on the refuge; and roads, parking, and visitor access to different areas of the refuge.

Steps 4 and 5 require the Service to develop an analysis of alternatives for a draft plan and then to publish it so that the public can comment. The Service then provides a minimum of 30 days for public review of a draft CCP with an EA and 45 days for a draft CCP with an EIS. The FWS will also make copies of the draft documents available to tribal governments, organizations, libraries, resource experts, adjacent landowners, and individuals requesting them. Drafts are now widely disseminated through the Internet as well (http://library.fws.gov/ccps.htm). The FWS will also conduct other public involvement activities as called for in the public involvement/outreach plan.

The formal invitation for direct participation through comments on draft documents presents a challenge. It is extraordinarily difficult to digest and analyze a complex document in 30 or 45 days (Mullin 2000). Nonetheless, individuals can enlist the support of other experts and agencies to cover many aspects of the draft. Of particular importance is the Environmental Protection Agency's (EPA's) special role in reviewing EISs under federal law (42 U.S.C. § 7609(a)). The EPA grades every draft EIS on two scales reflecting the adequacy of the EIS analysis and the potential adverse environmental impacts (Fischman 2001). Because EPA comments reflect officially sanctioned environmental expertise, courts and agencies pay special heed to serious EPA criticisms.

Once the formal comment period closes, the FWS need not consider any further direct public participation. In step 6, the Service works internally to respond to comments and produce final versions of the CCP, the EIS/EA, and compatibility determinations. The FWS publishes a notice of availability in the *Federal Register* and contacts the affected public when the final documents are available.

Step 7 begins the implementation of the management strategies identified in the CCP. The Service generally initiates a monitoring and evaluation program to determine whether the management strategies are having the desired effect. Though the FWS does not formally provide for any public participation at this step, the public may be able to participate in implementation and monitoring of the CCP strategies. First, the Service designs many monitoring and evaluation programs with an SDMP that has its own procedures for public participation. Second, some refuges may establish a refuge volunteer program that allows citizens to help with implementation and monitoring activities. Refuge managers typically are receptive to volunteers helping to implement educational and interpretive programs. This fits within the partnerships that are central to the FWS's overall strategic plan (U.S. FWS 2000–2005). Also, the public can independently monitor environmental parameters such as water quality, patterns of habitat use by wildlife, predator activity, bird nesting success, use of educational exhibits and trails, and unwanted human disturbance. These forms of collaboration contribute to the coordination theme of the Improvement Act's mission, discussed in chapter 5.

Finally, step 8 brings the public back into the process to help review and revise the CCP. Direct participation at this step is possible, but it may require some level of scientific expertise. Although the *Manual* does not state a direct mechanism by which the public can initiate the review of a CCP, the public can influence the decision to review by submitting to the refuge manager evidence that conditions on or bordering the refuge have changed. The Service reviews plans annually, so submissions are almost always timely. This direct participation will be most effective if derived from participation in step 7's monitoring and evaluation. Examples of the kind of information justifying revision might include the appearance or disappearance of a species, significant change in the species population size, significant change in the uses of lands bordering the refuge, or changes in refuge habitats due to succession, fire, or natural disaster. When the Service initiates a CCP revision as a result of plan review, it begins again with step 1, resetting the process for public participation.

Compatibility Determinations

Compatibility determinations for all anticipated and current uses are folded into the planning efforts (602 FW 3.4(C)(5)(b)). Many controversial refuge disputes will boil down to compatibility determinations. The refuge managers must make determinations for expansion, renewal or extension of uses, and proposed new uses. Compatibility determinations may be made as part of the development of a plan (generally, a CCP or an SDMP), as part of a land acquisition plan, or as part of the initial application or permit renewal for long-term uses.

The FWS periodically reevaluates compatibility determinations, even if they are not subject to permit renewals (603 FW 2.11H). The time frame and scope of reevaluations depend on the type of use. The FWS reevaluates compatibility determinations when (1) conditions under which the use is permitted change significantly; (2) there is significant new information regarding the effects of the use; (3) it prepares or revises a CCP; or (4) 15 years have elapsed for wildlife-dependent recreational uses, or 10 years have elapsed for other uses, since the last compatibility determination (603 FW 2.11H). A refuge manager always has the discretion to reevaluate the compatibility of a use at any time (603 FW 2.11H(1), (2)). When the FWS reevaluates a use for compatibility, it takes a "fresh look" and prepares a new compatibility determination following the standard procedures (603 FW 2.10H(5)).

The FWS may periodically reevaluate long-term uses for compliance with permit terms and conditions (603 FW 2.11H(3)). For long-term uses in existence on November 17, 2000, the compatibility reevaluation will examine compliance with the terms and conditions of the authorization, but not the authorization itself. After November 17, 2000, no uses will be permitted or reauthorized for a period longer than ten years unless the permit specifically allows for modifications to its terms and conditions. The FWS will make a new compatibility determination prior to extending or renewing a long-term use when the authorization expires.

The FWS must provide a direct opportunity for public review and comment prior to issuing final compatibility determinations (603 FW 2.11I). The refuge manager will attempt to identify individuals and organizations that reasonably might be affected by, or be interested in, a refuge use. The Service employs public review and comment to solicit relevant information and views on whether or not a use is compatible (603 FW 2.12A(9)(a)).

For compatibility determinations prepared concurrently with CCPs or SDMPs, the public review and comment requirements for the determination may be subsumed into the review and comment process of the draft plan and associated NEPA document. For compatibility determinations prepared separately from a plan, the refuge manager chooses the appropriate level of public review and comment based on the degree of complexity, controversy, and impact to the refuge (603 FW 2.11I, 2.12A(9)(a)). These factors are consistent with the ones that determine whether a proposed action "significantly" affects the quality of the human environment for the purposes of triggering NEPA's EIS requirement (40 C.F.R. § 1508.27).

For minor, incidental, or one-time uses that typically result in no significant or cumulative impact to the refuge and would likely generate minimal public interest, the refuge manager may limit public review and comment to posting a notice of the proposed determination at the refuge headquarters. Also, in these cases the refuge manager may reduce the time period for review and comment to the time available (603 FW 2.12A(9)(a)).

For all other uses, at a minimum, the refuge manager solicits public comment by placing a public notice in a newspaper with wide local distribution. The notice must contain a brief description of the compatibility determination process, a description of the use that is being evaluated, the types of information that may be used in completing the evaluation, how to provide comments, when comments are due, and how people will be informed of the decision the refuge manager will make regarding the use. The public then has at least 14 calendar days to provide comments following the day the notice is published (603 FW 2.12A(9)(a)).

For evaluations of controversial or complex uses, the FWS expects the refuge manager to expand the public review and comment process to allow for additional opportunities for comment. This may include newspaper or radio announcements, notices or postings in public places, notices in the *Federal Register,* letters to potentially interested people such as adjacent landowners, public meetings, or extended comment periods (603 FW 2.12A(9)(a)).

The refuge manager must document written public comments and this information will go into the administrative record along with the compatibility determination (603 FW 2.12A(9)(b)). The documentation includes a description of the process used, a summary of comments received, and a description of any actions taken or not taken because of the comments received.

Any person at any time may provide information to the refuge manager about changes in conditions, which may then prompt the manager to reevaluate a compatibility determination for a use. However, the refuge manager maintains full authority to determine if this information is or is not sufficient to trigger a reevaluation (603 FW 2.11H(4)). In contrast, the National Park Service requires its decision makers to conduct investigations when they become aware that ongoing activities might lead to impairment of resources or values (U.S. NPS 2001, § 1.4.7). The FWS would invite greater public participation if resource managers were bound to conduct investigations through a compatibility reevaluation when the public presented evidence that an ongoing activity might lead to impairment of conservation or establishment purposes.

Advisory Committees

The Federal Advisory Committee Act (FACA) sets out procedures that govern how agencies may constitute, convene, and use committees of people who are not agency employees (5 U.S.C. App. I). It is designed to ensure that agency reliance on private advisory groups does not result in the application of private solutions to public matters (Aman and Mayton 2001, 736–739). The FACA may play a role in refuge management because (1) private uses of refuges in ways that thwart conservation objectives have been a problem for the System; (2) a few establishment documents, such as for the Silvio O. Conte National Fish and Wildlife Refuge, call for advisory committees; and (3) advisory committees can be an effective way for the Service to generate and channel public participation.

The Improvement Act exempts from FACA any FWS coordination with state agency personnel (§ 8(o)). Otherwise, the 1997 Act does not alter the law with respect to advisory committees. Any group not composed wholly of full-time federal or state employees convened to give advice or make recommendations must comply with the FACA requirements (5 U.S.C. App. I § 3).

The FACA procedures focus on opening the selection of and deliberative process of the advisory group to public scrutiny. So, for instance, a refuge manager who consults a committee of experts and stakeholders for advice on operating water retention facilities on a refuge must make certain that the committee has a charge specifying, among other things, the group's scope, objectives, and duties (5 U.S.C. App. I § 9). All committee meetings must be announced in advance in the *Federal Register* and be open to the public (5 U.S.C. App. I § 10). All committee minutes, reports, and working papers must be available to the public (id.).

The FWS *Manual* calls for discretionary establishment of FACA committees if their functions cannot be performed by existing organizations or individuals within the federal government, or by an existing advisory committee (107 FW 1.3A). The membership of a committee depends upon its functions and may include scientists and representatives of the public interest (107 FW 3.3). Public members of advisory committees are selected on the basis of their experience or capability in the subjects on which the committee is expected to provide advice and recommendations. Public members may also be selected because they represent a part of the public that might be affected by the advice or recommendations of the committee (107 FW 3.3B).

Besides serving on an advisory committee, the public may directly participate by attending meetings, which must be held at a reasonable time and in a place reasonably accessible to the public (107 FW 4.4). Any member of the public may speak at the meeting, and any member of the public is permitted to file a written statement with the committee (107 FW 4.4). Opportunities for indirect participation in the work of advisory committees are likely to be plentiful because of the wide range of information and data sources that the committees are likely to use.

As the Service moves toward more collaborative, multistakeholder procedures in forging management, FACA will rise in importance. The Service will need to adapt FACA procedures to take part in the new adaptive management experiments in public resource management. This will require some revision of the Service *Manual* to fold the FACA requirements into the existing steps that lead to plan and project development.

Challenges to FWS Decisions

The public participates in resource management not only before an agency makes its decision but afterwards as well. Sometimes postdecisional participation, such as citizen monitoring, supports the agency course of action. Other times it takes the form of a challenge to the agency decision. The Service has the ability to resolve challenges through administrative appeals before courts will hear them. Ultimately, though, the judiciary may step in to resolve a dispute over the legality of the Service's action. The availability of administrative and judicial review of challenges to agency decisions tends to improve the quality of those decisions for two reasons. First, the availability of postdecisional review gives the public greater incentive to participate in the development of decisions. Second, the specter of review gives agency officials a greater incentive to grapple fairly and openly with public opinions and information.

Administrative Review

Administrative review allows agencies to correct errors in planning before controversies erupt in political and judicial forums over which agencies have less control. It promotes more efficient third-party examination than litigation and also resolves peripheral or minor issues to sharpen important disputes destined for judicial resolution. More specifically, in the Improvement Act context, administrative review would encourage better central oversight of unit planning to ensure uniformity in compliance with System goals. An internal Service appeals process would allow the agency to minimize adverse spillover effects from refuges and coordinate activities across refuges. In this way, administrative appeals advance the systemic purpose of organic legislation.

For these reasons, a system of administrative appeals should be viewed as part of good planning and management rather than as a separate process that occurs afterward. Currently, an administrative appeal process is available only to applicants seeking review of a permit denial (65 Fed. Reg. 62,493 [2000]). For instance, in *McGrail and Rowley v. Babbitt*, after the Key West National Wildlife Refuge manager denied a company a permit to operate a commercial tour boat with landings on Boca Grande Key, the company was able to appeal the decision to the assistant regional director for refuges and wildlife (*McGrail and Rowley v. Babbitt* 1997, 1390). A neighboring landowner or an environmental interest group, however, would not be able to make this kind of administrative appeal. Administrative appeals should be more broadly available for citizens challenging the crucial Service decisions of compatibility determinations in permitting and comprehensive conservation plan adoptions.

Unfortunately, without a statutory mandate for appeals, the Service has rejected proposals for a system of independent administrative review. Responding to comments requesting that the draft compatibility regulation be modified to provide the public with an opportunity to make administrative appeals of determinations, the Service relied on two aspects of its compatibility determination process. First, the Service argued that the new predecisional opportunities for public review and comment would obviate the need for appeals (65 Fed. Reg. 62,462–63 [2000]). Actually, administrative appeals would improve the predecisional public participation process. The seriousness with which decision makers view public comments increases with the availability of an administrative appeals process. A refuge manager who knows that the public has little recourse short of expensive and likely fruitless litigation need not worry very much about dismissing concerns raised in the comment (predecisional) phase of decision making. Likewise, the availability of postdecisional administrative review would attract more participation from a public assured that its views will receive thorough consideration.

Second, the Service argued that a new requirement for compatibility determinations, concurrence from regional chiefs, would accommodate the concerns that motivated the requests for an administrative review system (65 Fed. Reg. 62,462–63 [2000]). Though the concurrence requirement will help promote more uniform application of the compatibility standard, it is unlikely to provide the kind of critical evaluation of difficult issues facilitated by impartial adjudicators of administrative appeals. Of course, not all administrative appeal adjudicators are impartial outsiders. The Forest Service, for instance, employs superior officers to decide appeals from lower-level officers. The Forest Service appeals regime, like the Refuge System process, uses regional chiefs to decide appeals of unit managers (36 C.F.R. § 219.36). The use of adjudicators removed from day-to-day agency administration and decision making, such as those in the Department of the Interior's Interior Board of Land Appeals and the EPA's Environmental Appeals Board, is necessary to realize the potential benefits of administrative review.

Judicial Review

The Improvement Act, like most public land legislation and unlike most pollution control legislation, contains no provision specifically authorizing citizen suits. Final agency actions, such as compatibility determinations and comprehensive unit plans, are subject to judicial review through the APA. The APA opens the courts to citizens "adversely affected or aggrieved" by agency action or failure to act (5 U.S.C. § 702). If the Service ever institutes a system of administrative appeals, then actions would not be final until the administrative process runs its course. Under the APA, courts must "compel agency action unlawfully withheld or unreasonably delayed" and must overturn agency actions that are "arbitrary, capricious, an abuse of discretion, or otherwise not in accordance with law" (5 U.S.C. § 706).

Members of the public seeking judicial review of refuge management, however, face several familiar hurdles. First, federal litigation is expensive. Second, standing and ripeness doctrines prevent courts from reviewing actions until the Service authorizes a specific activity that causes particular injury to an identified party that can be redressed by a court (*Friends of the Earth v. Laidlaw* 2000; *Ohio Forestry Association v. Sierra Club* 1998). Third, the scope of judicial review is limited to determining whether the agency acted in an arbitrary and capricious manner or specifically violated a rule or statute. Courts will not remand merely poor management decisions (*Citizens to Preserve Overton Park v. Volpe* 1971).

Though Congress has lost its enthusiasm for citizen suits in recent years, they remain an important incentive for public land management agencies to be responsive to claims of the public. Compared to the multiple use regimes, Refuge System management has seldom been subject to citizen suits. With the exception of the 1992 litigation over the widespread incompatible uses, few lawsuits have affected Refuge System management. Of course, the potential for, or threat of, litigation likely has an effect on management, albeit one that is difficult to measure. The Improvement Act's substantive management criteria, along with detailed standards in the new *Manual*, will provide more footholds for citizens seeking judicial review of refuge management. To ensure the availability of judicial review, a better organic act would have a citizen suit provision that makes clear Congress's intent to allow direct judicial review of comprehensive conservation plans, even if the Service has not yet authorized individual projects. It would also "define injuries and articulate chains of causation that give rise" to citizen standing (*Lujan v. Defenders of Wildlife* 1992, 580 [Kennedy, J., concurring in part]).

PART THREE

Applying Resource Management to Individual Refuges and Resources

10 | *Individual Refuge Purposes*

In administering the 1997 Improvement Act, the U.S. Fish and Wildlife Service (FWS) encounters a fundamental challenge: reconciling the national purposes of systemic management with the individual purposes set out for each refuge. The units of the Refuge System were created and acquired under a diverse array of instruments (including statutes, executive orders, and public land orders) and authorities (including Article II of the Constitution and federal statutes) for a range of purposes.

This section surveys the hodgepodge of instruments, authorities, and purposes to illustrate the centrifugal forces that resist cohesive, systemic management. Because the Improvement Act defers to establishment documents where they conflict with a provision in the organic legislation, some refuges hew primarily to particular mandates with site-specific application. The act states that "if a conflict exists between the purposes of a refuge and the mission of the System, the conflict shall be resolved in a manner that first protects the purposes of the refuge, and, to the extent practicable, that also achieves the mission" (§ 5(a)(4)(D)).

Direct conflict between specific refuge purposes and organic legislation is rare, but it does occur. For instance, a handful of game ranges call for the improvement of public grazing lands and dedicate a certain portion of the forage to domestic livestock. The Fort Peck Game Range sets numerical quotas for the allocation of forage to support "a maximum of four hundred thousand (400,000) sharp-tail grouse, and one thousand five hundred (1,500) antelope" (Exec. Order No. 7,509 [1936]). Another group of refuges, such as Calhoun and Spring Lake, originate with establishment documents that seek to improve navigation and control flooding as their primary purpose (11 Fed. Reg. 13,397 [1946]). Then, there is the odd individual refuge purpose tailored to the special circumstances of establishment. For instance, the Kuchel Act, establishing and expanding the Tule Lake, Lower Klamath, Upper Klamath, and Clear Lake national wildlife refuges (NWRs), designates as "the major purpose" of the refuges "waterfowl management, but with full consideration to optimum agricultural use that is consistent therewith" (Pub. L. No. 88-567 [1964]).

Usually, the Service can find ways to reconcile the specific refuge purposes and organic legislation through interpretation. Specific refuge purposes often promote and limit activities over which the Service has management discretion under the Improvement Act. However, because austere funding is such an important limiting factor in management of the Refuge System, there remains the problem of setting priorities for refuges when the principal goals of an establishment instrument vie with the System mission for resources. In this respect, individual establishment objectives more often compete with rather than conflict with organic purposes.

Many refuges have purposes that derive from more than one type of instrument. Some refuges, such as those created by executive orders relying (in part) on statutory provisions, are born under multiple sources of authority with varying statements of purposes. For instance, the National Elk Refuge owes its establishment to congressional measures as well as to executive orders. Other refuges grow through accretion of additional parcels, which may be added under instruments different from the original establishment type. For instance, the Malheur NWR derives its current boundaries and purposes from no fewer than a dozen congressional, presidential, and administrative instruments. This common situation presents puzzles for managers seeking to determine which purposes should receive priority in refuge management. Therefore, in addition to the tension between organic and establishment/acquisition mandates, there is also a tension in sorting out priorities among establishment and acquisition mandates. Rather than resolve the difficulties of reconciling multiple purposes, this chapter aims to highlight these sources of tension that contribute to the management conflicts in the System.

The Improvement Act's deference to establishment purposes respects the political compromises that allow refuge creation and expansion. Retrospectively, notions of contractual fairness among the stakeholders who negotiated the terms of legislation (or, less commonly, executive and administrative orders) militate in favor of retaining the establishment instrument as the primary guidance document for a refuge unit. Prospectively, statutory interpretation that respects old deals promotes future participation by stakeholders who are able to horse-trade with some confidence that subsequent application of organic legislation will not overturn a carefully wrought compromise. Some statutory detail in establishment legislation likely results from necessary political compromises to gain support of the users of some of the resources included within a new refuge. For instance, the Bayou Cocodrie NWR establishment statute requires the Service to permit access to surface mines subject to certain specific conditions (Pub. L. No. 101-593, § 108(e)(4) [1990]). Similarly, Congress has required the Service to issue access permits across Back Bay NWR and to give special consideration to commercial timber production and allow flood control activity in Tensas River NWR (Pub. L. No. 96-315, § 3(a) [1980]; Pub. L. No. 96-285, § 4 [1980]).

Greater population, economic activity, and development make refuge establishment today a more difficult task than in the past. For each acre of new refuge land, there are likely to be more existing economic uses than occurred on an acre of refuge land established 50 or 75 years ago. Therefore, explicit compromises and trade-offs will continue to condition establishment documents in order to reach an acceptable deal. The concomitant level of detail in refuge establishment documents will rise as it has in establishment statutes for "second generation" national parks (Fischman 1997, 797–804).

The Service distinguishes between establishment purposes, which are included in the source initially creating a refuge, and acquisition purposes, which are included in the sources authorizing additions to existing refuges (603 FW 2.12A(3), (4)). The Service limits to just the new portion of the refuge the applicability of acquisition purposes (U.S. FWS 2001b). However, I use the term "establishment" broadly to include both the creation of a refuge and the addition of land to an existing refuge. An establishment document is an instrument creating, amending, or enlarging a refuge. Though establishment authorities may be called enabling authorities, I believe the latter term is best reserved for laws that provide sovereign or legislative authority to political jurisdictions.

Both the Improvement Act and the compatibility regulations list seven instruments in which individual refuge purposes may be found: law, proclamation, executive order, agreement, public land order, donation document, and administrative memorandum (§ 5(10)). I divide these sources of refuge purposes into three categories explored in the following sections: presidential (proclamations and executive orders), congressional (statutes, or law), and administrative (which includes all other instruments). The purposes in a document expanding or amending an initial establishment instrument can be important even though they may have a limited geographic scope. The FWS files many of these expansions and amendments in its purposes database, which is available to the public through the Internet (http://refugedata.fws.gov/databases/). Though purposes and priorities for refuges appear in all types of instruments, few specific management mandates occur in sources other than statutes. As the "second generation" problems of modern refuge establishment have intensified, site-specific statutory instruments have become far more common than they were before 1970.

The level of specificity with which the Service defines individual refuge purposes determines how important the centrifugal influences will be in implementing the Improvement Act. The Service has three basic choices for defining individual refuge purposes. It can employ, from most general to most specific, the broad statutory (or, less frequently, presidential) terms, the intent of the basic authorities as revealed through legislative history, or the particular circumstances that led to the approval for each refuge. The Service's current practice, though not yet endorsed by the judiciary, is to define establishment purposes in the most general way, through broad statutory terms (U.S. FWS 2001b).

For instance, the Service lists in its database the purpose of "conservation, maintenance, and management of wildlife, resources thereof, and its habitat thereon" for each refuge established under the authority of the Fish and Wildlife Coordination Act (FWCA) (16 U.S.C. § 664). The Service lists the FWCA as an establishment document for 47 refuges. For some of the units, such as D'Arbonne NWR, the FWCA is the sole source of the individual refuge purpose. For other units, such as the Charles M. Russell NWR, the FWCA is one of many establishment sources. It is difficult to imagine a situation where the general purpose, taken from the text of the FWCA, would conflict with the organic mission of the System.

However, a different and somewhat more specific approach would designate as a purpose for each FWCA-established refuge the particular goals discussed in the legislative history: public recreation, wildlife preservation, migratory bird protection, habitat conservation, disease control, provision of hunting and shooting areas, and rearing and stocking of wildlife (U.S. Senate 1958). Yet another, and even more specific, approach would abandon the practice of attaching the same establishment goals to all refuges created under the same statutory authority and instead would explore the administrative record (decision memoranda, meeting minutes, reports, etc.) to determine the particular rationale for exercising the FWCA authority in each case. More specific rationales would present a greater potential for conflict with the overall mission of the System.

The Service may have adopted the most general approach for the practical reason that it is easier than interpreting and reviewing legislative history, or researching and sifting through administrative records creating each refuge. But the general approach is the best approach under the Improvement Act for another reason. It most effectively implements the organic principle of unifying the refuges into a dominant-mission system. However, the inclusion of "administrative memorandum" in the Improvement Act as a source of individual refuge purposes suggests that the organic law may compel a more detailed accounting of establishment mandates.

The three sections that follow describe the three different sources of individual refuge purposes: presidential, congressional, and administrative. The sections provide examples illustrating the interpretive challenges presented by the historical accretion of individual purposes through successive establishment and acquisition documents. The sections also demonstrate the variety of ways in which individual refuge purposes may sway System management. Appendix C lists each named national wildlife refuge, its realty establishment date, and size.

The realty establishment date is the time when the federal government first reserved or acquired land for conservation purposes in the area that is now a refuge. A few refuges, such as the Alaska Maritime NWR and the Kodiak NWR, have realty dates that precede the official establishment of the refuge unit. This is because the federal government reserved land for some form of conservation in the Pribilof and Afognak islands before they were subsumed into the Alaska Maritime and Kodiak refuges. Other refuges have realty establishment dates later than the date of the actual document authorizing the refuge and setting out establishment purposes. This is because refuges do not receive a realty date until the federal government acquires the first property interest in the authorized area; there may be a lag between authorization and actual purchase or transfer of land.

Presidential Sources

From the time of the very first reservations of land for wildlife protection, the president has been a leader in establishing refuges. Presidential proclamations and executive orders, which differ in name only, are two equivalent instruments that the chief executive can use to establish refuges. Proclamations generally concern matters of broad interest "that directly affect private individuals," and executive orders typically concern matters directly related to "the conduct of the Federal Government" (Ashmore 1981, 2). The president has employed only proclamations to establish refuges since 1958. In recent decades the pace of presidential refuge establishment has waned substantially.

The early executive orders and presidential proclamations shaped the enduring features of the Refuge System. They established the precedent for limiting hunting, focusing on wildlife protection, and closing units to uses unless explicitly opened by agency action. The early presidential establishment orders, such as for Pelican Island, Stump Lake, Three Arch Rocks, and Mille Lacs, used the term "reservation" rather than "refuge" to categorize the units. This is consistent with the parlance of public land law, which uses the term "reservation" to refer to public land designated for a particular purpose and withdrawn from the domain of one or more resource disposal programs, such as the homesteading or mining laws.

However, beginning with a congressional appropriation in 1913 and then an executive order in 1914 for the National Elk Refuge, the term "refuge" arose for most units of the System (Federal Revenue Sharing Act, ch. 145 [1913]; Exec. Orders Nos. 1814 [1913], 2,047 [1914], 2,417 [1916]). In a sweeping order, President Franklin Roosevelt renamed as "national wildlife refuges" almost 200 units, previously known as reservations, bird refuges, migratory waterfowl refuges, migratory bird refuges, and wildlife refuges (Presidential Proclamation No. 2,416 [1940]). The term "refuge" captures the dominant purpose of most of the establishment documents: protection of life from some danger. As figure 2.1 from chapter 2 illustrates, however, there remains today a diverse array of names for System units.

The early presidential establishment documents for refuges cite no legislative basis for the reservation of the lands. Charles Wilkinson has highlighted the lack of congressional authorization for the early refuges as precedent for presidential boldness in protecting federal lands (Wilkinson 1996). As early as 1890, the Justice Department had advised the secretary of the interior, who adopted as his opinion to the president, that the president needed no statutory authority to reserve federal land for public interest (*Decisions Relating to the Public Lands* 1890). The constitutionality of presidential establishments remained uncertain until 1915, when the Supreme Court upheld the longstanding practice of the president to withdraw a tract of federal land from the application of disposal laws and designate a special purpose for the reserve, especially where Congress acquiesced to the designation (*United States v. Midwest Oil* 1915).

Beginning with Wilson's 1913 proclamation designating lands for the National Elk Refuge, presidential instruments increasingly relied on statutes, at least in part, as a basis for establishing refuges. Like the statutes cited in Wilson's Elk Refuge order, the legislation cited in presidential instruments falls into two categories. One type of legislation is a general grant of authority to the president for withdrawal of lands, such as the now-repealed Pickett Act of 1910 (Ch. 421, § 1 [1910]). The other type of legislation provides authority more specifically for the reservation of a particular area or the expenditure of funds for the purchase of refuge land. After Congress enacted the Migratory Bird Hunting Stamp Act of 1934, making funds available for refuge land purchase, the proportion of presidential instruments citing some legislation to support establishment rose dramatically.

Today, there are two factors that cause presidential instruments establishing refuges to rely on legislation as a basis for their authority. First, the 1976 Federal Land Policy and Management Act (FLPMA) purported to revoke Congress's acquiescence to the president's longstanding practice of relying on inherent executive power to make public land reservations. Second, there are now so many statutory authorities on which to base an order establishing a new refuge, or expanding an existing one, that there is little need for a claim of inherent executive power. In addition to the broad acquisition authorities, such as the Endangered Species Act and the Migratory Bird Hunting Stamp Act, FLPMA retained the withdrawal authority of the Fish and Game Sanctuaries Act and created a new basis for the president, through the Interior Department, to make withdrawals and reservations (Getches 1982). However, FLPMA did repeal many withdrawal statutes, such as the Pickett Act, which had been widely used by presidents to establish refuges.

Where an executive order provides specific, individual refuge purposes, it may dictate management priorities at variance with systemic legislation. The *Schwenke* litigation over the relative priority of livestock grazing and wildlife protection on the Charles M. Russell NWR illustrates this problem. President Franklin Roosevelt created the Fort Peck Game Range, now the Charles M. Russell NWR, in a 1936 executive order. The order established a limited priority for sustaining populations of game (with a ceiling of 400,000 grouse and 1,500 antelope), beyond which access to forage should be equally shared between livestock and wildlife. In

1976, Congress transferred game ranges and other conservation lands from shared jurisdiction with the Bureau of Land Management (BLM) to the FWS alone to secure better wildlife conservation. The *Schwenke* court rejected the Service's position that the 1976 legislation heightened wildlife priority, pursuant to refuge organic legislation (at the time, principally the 1966 Act) (*Schwenke v. Secretary of the Interior* 1983, 576–577). The court found that the 1976 statute, considered alone, did heighten the priority of wildlife over livestock in access to forage on the refuges subject to the transfer (id., 576). However, because the 1976 law failed to revoke expressly the 1936 executive order creating the refuge, the individual purposes set out in the presidential document continued to control management of the refuge. The court held that the limited priority scheme established by the 1936 executive order still bound the Service despite "congressional intent to dictate a different priority" (id., 577).

George Coggins and Robert Glicksman question this holding on the grounds that Congress, not the president, has superior constitutional power to set priorities for public lands (Coggins and Glicksman 2002, § 10D:6). Although the Property Clause (U.S. Const. art. IV, § 3) might provide a constitutional basis for an alternative rule of interpretation that would favor congressional instruments over presidential ones, there is a better reason to criticize the *Schwenke* decision. Courts should employ rules of construction that favor more systemic rather than individualistic goals. A proper understanding of organic legislation would support a canon of interpretation that required less than express revocation of old establishment documents to consolidate refuge management under systemic goals. The strengthening of organic legislation in the 1997 Act should now tip the scales toward this mode of centripetal interpretation. Such an interpretation of refuge management mandates would respond not only to the accumulation of individual refuge purposes in executive instruments, but also to the more widespread phenomenon of statutory detail in establishment laws.

Congressional Sources

Refuges with purposes derived from "law" have statutory establishment authorities. The Refuge System database includes 15 different general statutory provisions authorizing refuge establishment, including the Migratory Bird Conservation Act, the Fish and Wildlife Act of 1956, the 1966 Refuge Administration Act, and the Endangered Species Act. So, for example, if the Service establishes a refuge under the land acquisition provision of the Endangered Species Act, then the Refuge System database will list recovery of threatened and endangered species as a purpose of the refuge. This is the case for nearly 100 refuges, such as Kakahaia NWR and Attwater Prairie Chicken NWR.

The establishment purposes derived from general authorizing statutes employ broad terms to promote conservation. For instance, refuges established under the authority of the Migratory Bird Conservation Act are "for use as an inviolate sanctuary, or for any other management purpose, for migratory birds" (16 U.S.C. § 715d). Similarly broad language is part of establishment purposes authorized by the Fish and Wildlife Act of 1956 ("for the benefit of the United States Fish and Wildlife Service, in performing its activities and services") (16 U.S.C. § 742f(b)(1)) and the Emergency Wetlands Resources Act of 1986 ("the conservation of the wetlands of the Nation in order to maintain the public benefits they provide and to help fulfill international obligations contained in various migratory bird treaties and conventions") (16 U.S.C. § 3901(b)). They will not conflict with the 1997 Improvement Act's mission and mandates except in the most extraordinary circumstance.

In addition to general statutes that authorize multiple refuge acquisitions for a particular purpose or set of purposes, Congress also enacts site-specific statutes creating individual refuges or authorizing the secretary to establish particular refuges. These special statutes are much more likely to have specific purposes and mandates that dominate management of the unit at the expense of the overall System mission. Since 1970, the site-specific statutes have proliferated in number and detail.

The first part of this section will describe the rise in statutory detail for refuge establishment law and the broadening of the range of establishment purposes. This section then discusses how multiple purposes and mandates in specific legislation demand difficult choices in refuge management. In many cases, the Improvement Act can be used to interpret establishment law ambiguities in order to conform to systemic goals. In a few cases, establishment statutes will exert a centrifugal pull on the coherence of the Refuge System.

Toward Broader Purposes and Greater Detail

The early site-specific establishment statutes follow the path blazed by the early executive proclamations in designating refuge units for breeding and protection of animals. The terms "breeding place" and "refuge" or "reserve" were frequently paired in early establishment statutes and presidential instruments. Examples include the Upper Mississippi River Wild Life and Fish Refuge (ch. 346 [1924] ["refuge and breeding place for migratory birds"]) and the Bear River Migratory-Bird Refuge (ch. 413 [1928] ["refuge and feeding and breeding grounds for migratory wild fowl"]). Indeed, the very first specific statute establishing a refuge outside of the Pribilof Islands, which were long a subject of conservation law-making to maintain the fur seal skin industry, designated the Wichita Forest Reserve (now the Wichita Mountains Wildlife Refuge) for "the protection of game animals and birds and be recognized as a breeding place therefor" (Pub. L. No. 23, ch. 137 [1905]). The Wichita statute also prohibited direct takes of game animals and birds in the new reserve except where expressly permitted under the land manager's (then the Department of Agriculture's) regulations.

Over time, the establishment purposes display a trend of broadened concern to protect a wider variety of biological resources. Early purposes focused on particular animals, such as elk or bison, or relatively narrow categories of animals, such as game and native birds. Though more recent refuges display a more expansive, ecological concern than early units, single-species conservation continues to be an important purpose for refuges.

Plant protection lagged behind animal protection in establishment in-struments. The Upper Mississippi River Wild Life and Fish Refuge es-tablishment statute is the first, and one of the only, to explicitly include plants ("wild flowers and aquatic plants") as resources to be protected in and of themselves, rather than merely as habitat for animals (Pub. L. No. 268, ch. 346 [1924]). Though floral resources were a factor in the estab-lishment of some other refuges at the time, they were not significant factors. For instance, the minutes of the Migratory Bird Conservation Commission's 1936 meeting provisionally approving acquisition of the Okefenokee NWR make reference to protecting the last big stand of cy-press. However, unlike the statutory provision in the Upper Mississippi River refuge, the Service does not consider Commission minutes a source of refuge purposes. Instead, all refuges approved by the Commission have the same general purposes, provided by the Migratory Bird Conservation Act, "for use as an inviolate sanctuary, or for any other management pur-pose, for migratory birds" (16 U.S.C. § 715d).

More recently, such as for Cat Island NWR, Congress has incorporated the Improvement Act's plant conservation purpose into establishment legislation (Pub. L. No. 106-369 [2000]). The recent inclusion of plant conservation illustrates the way in which organic legislation can influence subsequent establishment statutes by highlighting new concerns. One ef-fect of the inclusion of plant protection in the organic mission of the Sys-

tem will be a greater likelihood that areas containing significant floral resources will enter the Refuge System. Though plants are certainly included
within broader purposes to protect ecological resources or biological diversity, their explicit inclusion in an establishment statute is an important
spur for the Service, which, after all, has a "wildlife first" policy.

The inclusion of plant protection in the 1924 Upper Mississippi River
Wild Life and Fish Refuge is an anomaly. It did not create a precedent for
subsequent establishment purposes. Plant protection was absent in establishment purposes outside of the Upper Mississippi Refuge until the
early 1970s, when ecological concerns haltingly emerged. The 1972 establishment statute for the Tinicum National Environmental Center, administered as a unit of the System, marked the first time Congress included
protection of "ecological features," which include plant communities, as a
purpose (Pub. L. No. 92-326 [1972]). This new purpose may have been
inspired by the Leopold report's 1968 recommendation to add a "natural
ecosystem" conservation element to refuge management. Subsequently,
the 1973 Sevilleta NWR and the 1980 Tensas River NWR establishment
instruments employed ecological terminology.

The rise in the ecological, or biological diversity, conservation purposes
in the 1980s establishment instruments did not substantially change the
wildlife focus of the refuges. However, some of the 1980s and 1990s
establishment statutes did explicitly include plants within diversity purposes, presaging the systemic missions in the executive order and the
Improvement Act. These include the Wallkill River NWR (Pub. L. No.
101-593 [1989]) (conservation of "the natural diversity of fish, wildlife,
plants, and their habitats"); the Great Bay NWR (Pub. L. No. 102-154, §
319(d) [1992]) ("to encourage the natural diversity of plant, fish, and
wildlife species"); the Rocky Mountain Arsenal NWR (Pub. L. No. 102-
402 [1992]) ("to conserve and enhance the land and water of the refuge
in a manner that will conserve and enhance the natural diversity of fish,
wildlife, plants, and their habitats"); and the Silvio O. Conte National Fish
and Wildlife Refuge (Pub. L. No. 102-212, § 104 [1991]) ("to conserve,
protect, and enhance the natural diversity and abundance of plant, fish,
and wildlife species").

Most of the 1980s establishment statutes employing a diversity purpose follow the formula for the Alaska National Interest Lands Conservation Act (ANILCA) refuge establishments, which limited their scope to
animal species. These include the Bon Secour NWR (Pub. L. No. 96-267
[1980]) ("to conserve an undisturbed beach–dune ecosystem which includes a diversity of fish and wildlife"); the Falls of the Ohio National

Wildlife Conservation Area (Pub. L. No. 97-137 [1981]) (including purpose "to protect wildlife populations and habitats in their natural diversity"); the Protection Island NWR (Pub. L. No. 97-333 [1982]) (including purpose "to provide habitat for a broad diversity of bird species"); the Connecticut Coastal (now, Stewart B. McKinney) NWR (Pub. L. No. 98-548 [1984]) (including purpose "to encourage natural diversity of fish and wildlife species"); and the Bayou Sauvage Urban NWR (Pub. L. No. 99-645 [1986]) (including purpose "to encourage natural diversity of fish and wildlife species").

Beginning in the 1970s, another, stronger trend in establishment statutes emerged that helped lay the foundation for the Improvement Act. This was the inclusion of wildlife-oriented recreation and environmental education as purposes. Examples include the San Francisco Bay NWR (Pub. L. No. 92-330 [1972]) (purposes include "wildlife-oriented recreation and nature study"); the Protection Island NWR (Pub. L. No. 97-333 [1982]) (purposes include providing "wildlife-oriented public education and interpretation"); the Bayou Sauvage Urban NWR (Pub. L. No. 99-645, § 502 [1986]) (purposes include providing environmental education and "opportunities for fish and wildlife oriented" recreation); the Pettaquamscutt Cove NWR (Pub. L. No. 100-610, § 202 [1988]) (purposes include providing opportunities for "environmental education, and fish and wildlife-oriented recreation"); and the Bayou Cocodrie NWR (Pub. L. No. 101-593, § 108(d) [1990]) (purposes include "fish and wildlife-oriented recreational activities"). Wildlife-oriented recreation and environmental education are also commonly included in establishment statutes as uses that the Service may develop, rather than as purposes. Examples include establishment legislation for Tensas River NWR, Bogue Chitto NWR, and Bandon Marsh NWR (Pub. L. No. 96-285 [1980]; Pub. L. No. 96-288 [1980]; Pub. L. No. 97-137 [1981]). However, where it is designated as a purpose, wildlife-oriented recreation raises difficulties in reconciling the primacy of the systemic conservation mission with the deference to establishment documents. Recreational purposes also defeat the compatibility criterion's ability to limit recreational activities that might impair ecological health.

With the 1976 establishment of the Minnesota Valley NWR, Congress stepped up its control over management through statutory detail. The Minnesota Valley Act is indicative of a style of establishment best exemplified (though more dramatically) by the detail pervading recent legislation creating units of the National Park System (Fischman 1997). First, the Minnesota Valley establishment act includes a section containing definitions, which is indicative of modern, complex legislation (Pub. L. No. 94-466, § 3 [1976]). Second, the act requires the Service to develop a "comprehensive plan for the conservation, protection, preservation, and interpretation" of the refuge within three years (§ 6(a)). Though the Improvement Act now requires all refuges to develop such plans, the Minnesota Valley Act is significant in setting the precedent for requiring individual refuge plans. Subsequent establishment statutes, such as for the Alaska refuges (ANILCA, § 304(g) [1980]) and Grays Harbor NWR (Pub. L. No. 100-406, § 5(c) [1988]), mandate specific procedures and content for the unit plan. Third, the Minnesota Valley Act requires the Service to construct an interpretation/education center in the refuge (§ 4(c)). Subsequently, Congress often promoted development within refuges of such capital projects as visitors' centers, boardwalks, and parking facilities through content requirements in planning mandates. Examples include establishment legislation for the Bayou Sauvage Urban NWR (Pub. L. No. 99-645, § 502(c) [1986]) (requiring the Service to prepare a master plan for development of the refuge) and the Grays Harbor NWR (Pub. L. No. 100-406, § 5(c) [1988]) (requiring the Service to prepare a plan for development that must include the construction of a year-round visitor center, boardwalks, and parking facilities).

Another, more recent, statute typifying the trend toward detailed establishment mandates is the establishment act for the Silvio O. Conte National Fish and Wildlife Refuge (Pub. L. No. 102-212 [1991]). It contains not only definitions and specific purposes but also a mandate to create an advisory committee to assist "on community outreach and education programs that further" the refuge purposes (§ 108). This detailed mandate for a committee, in which Congress specified membership terms, types of members, and how the committee should act, remains rare in the Refuge System but is now common in National Park System unit establishment statutes.

The trend toward more detailed legislation on refuge management is part of the overall movement toward greater congressional involvement in public lands. Indeed, the more detailed, modern establishment legislation makes early refuge establishment instruments appear "enigmatic" and "vague" (Gergely, Scott, and Goble 2000, 107, 108). Whether manifest in similar growth in statutory detail in national park establishment legislation, or in more specific systemic guidance in organic legislation, one of the most notable developments in modern environmental law is the increased interest of Congress in closely controlling agencies. The trend is also apparent in pollution control law (Fischman 1997).

Nonetheless, the level of substantive management requirements, the numbers of required studies, and the numbers of mandated advisory committees are much lower for refuge establishment statutes than for national park establishment statutes. Congress remains capable of establishing refuges with no special conditions that deviate from the systemic legislation. Examples include Egmont Key NWR (Pub. L. 93-341 [1974]), Bandon Marsh NWR (Pub. L. 97-137 [1981]), and Ten Thousand Islands NWR (102 Stat. 4,579 [1988]).

Balancing Multiple Purposes

Multiple establishment purposes compete for priority with the System mission. Questions about priorities will set the terms of the debate over how dominant the Improvement Act's mission and purpose will be in shaping the System. In this respect, the clear ecological conservation mission of the Improvement Act can be helpful and should be used as an interpretive tool to reduce seeming conflicts. After 1997, any ambiguities should be resolved in favor of systemic purposes and mandates. Whether designated specifically for bison, elk, or hunted animals generally, game protection will sometimes conflict with the broader ecological mission of the System. For instance, maintaining high densities of elk at the National Elk Refuge reduces woody vegetation that is valuable habitat for other species of native wildlife, including trout and many bird species (Matson 2000, 101, 107–109, 115; Clark 2000, 171–173). Maximizing deer habitat in the Julia Butler Hansen Refuge for Columbian White-Tailed Deer requires maintenance of interspersed grassland and woodland, which fragments habitat in derogation of the Service's compatibility policy under the Improvement Act (65 Fed. Reg. 62,486 [2000]). Managing refuges to maintain high populations of waterfowl is associated in some areas with farming activities and impoundment management to the detriment of native ecosystems (66 Fed. Reg. 3,812 [2001]). An FWS directive appropriately instructs refuge managers to place priority on conservation purposes over other purposes in establishment documents (U.S. FWS 2001b). Where an establishment document has multiple conservation purposes, a more specific purpose takes precedence over a more general purpose (id.).

Another issue that arises in establishment legislation is whether purpose and management language in appropriations law should receive lower priority than language in authorizing statutes. Appropriations riders usually receive less scrutiny from the congressional committee system of hearings and reports, and are generally written to be transient authorities, expiring in relevance after a short period of time. On the other hand, appropriations measures often have contained important delegations of authority, such as the 1897 "organic act" for national forests, and are constitutionally binding through the same bicameral and presentment processes that create other statutes. Refuges with legislative authorities (either original or amending some earlier instrument) contained in appropriations measures include the National Elk Refuge (ch. 284 [1912], ch. 145 [1913]) and the Great Bay NWR (Pub. L. 102-154, § 319(d) [1992]).

A similar problem of interpreting individual purposes arises from piecemeal additions to refuges. Should an initial statute establishing a refuge receive higher priority for its purposes than subsequent legislation amending or expanding the refuge? The Improvement Act's legislative history makes clear that refuge purposes can be derived from documents expanding a refuge (U.S. House 1997a, 7). However, the committee report does not speak to the relative importance or scope of purposes in expansions as compared to initial purposes. Service policy endorses the sensible view that refuge additions adopt the purpose of the original unit, but the original unit does not take on the purpose of an addition outside of the addition itself (U.S. FWS 2001b). But that policy decision does not speak to priorities in the additions between the new and original purposes.

Beyond sorting out priorities between different pieces of legislation, the Service also must evaluate the relative importance of multiple purposes listed within single establishment statutes. For instance, the Upper Mississippi River Wild Life and Fish Refuge legislation states that the refuge

> shall be established and maintained (a) as a refuge and breeding place for migratory birds included in the terms of the convention between the United States and Great Britain for the protection of migratory birds, concluded August 16, 1916, and (b) to such extent as the Secretary of Agriculture may by regulations prescribe, as a refuge and breeding place for other wild birds, game animals, fur-bearing animals, and for the conservation of wild flowers and aquatic plants, and (c) to such extent as the Secretary of Commerce may by regulations prescribe as a refuge and breeding place for fish and other aquatic animal life. (Pub. L. No. 268, ch. 346 [1924])

This statute raises the issue of whether the purposes in part (a), for the protection of birds specifically named in a cited treaty, are of greater importance than those in parts (b) or (c), which broaden the purpose of the refuge for conservation of most animals and plants in the aquatic area. Congress created two categories, in (b) and (c), because in 1924 the Agriculture

Department's Bureau of Biological Survey had yet to merge with the Commerce Department's Bureau of Sport Fisheries to create the FWS.

On its face, the establishment statute does not prefer one purpose over any other; it lists three purposes joined by the conjunction "and." But the first purpose uses the then standard terminology for refuge designation, "a refuge and breeding place," and creates a binding requirement that cannot be altered by administrative action. In contrast, purposes (b) and (c) depend on administrative action. They are purposes that can ebb and flow depending on regulatory decisions made in the management agency. Again, application of the Improvement Act's mission to resolve this kind of ambiguity is an appropriate function of organic legislation. We should expect the Improvement Act to influence the Service to exercise its discretion under the second and third purposes in such a way as to promote the conservation mission.

Other establishment statutes explicitly set out a "major purpose" followed by subsidiary uses. For instance, the Kuchel Act established for the Tule Lake, Lower Klamath, Upper Klamath, and Clear Lake refuges the "major purpose of waterfowl management, but with full consideration to optimum agricultural use that is consistent therewith" (Pub. L. No. 88-567, § 2 [1964]). Another version of ranking purposes is found in the establishment statute for Grays Harbor NWR, which lists four purposes. However, the statute conditions the fourth purpose, "to provide an opportunity . . . for wildlife-oriented recreation, education, and research," on its consistency with the prior three (conservation-oriented) purposes (Pub. L. No. 100-406, § 2 [1988]). And ANILCA provides more examples. For the Tetlin NWR, it conditions the purpose of providing opportunities for environmental interpretation and subsistence uses on consistency with conservation purposes (Pub. L. No. 96-487, § 302(8) [1980]). Similarly, ANILCA conditions the purpose of providing opportunities for scientific research, interpretation, and environmental education uses on consistency with conservation purposes for such units as the Kenai NWR (Pub. L. No. 96-487, § 303(4) [1980]).

Recall that the 1997 Improvement Act departs from prior legislation in measuring a proposed activity's compatibility with the establishment purposes of the refuge without qualifying which purposes count (§ 3(a)(1)). So, unlike the compatibility determinations conducted under the 1962 Recreation Act, which measure a proposed activity against only "primary" purposes, or the 1966 Administration Act, which measure a proposed activity against only "major" purposes, the 1997 law introduces a wider scope of analysis to the compatibility determination.

Even though compatibility determinations now need not distinguish among purposes, the Service must distinguish between true purposes and subsidiary, conditional, or discretionary goals of the instrument. Because the Improvement Act yields only to "purposes" in establishment documents, defining subsidiary goals of a refuge as something other than "purposes" would allow the Service to tip the balance toward more consistent System management. It would also require a searching analysis of the legislative intent of an establishment act, as interpreted through the lens of the organic mission.

Administrative Sources

The Improvement Act lists agreements, public land orders, donation documents, and administrative memoranda as additional sources from which individual refuge purposes may be derived (§ 3(a)(10)). These administrative sources present some difficult interpretive questions for determining priority purposes and uses. However, in practice, the Service correctly downplays the influence that these derivative sources exert on refuge management.

The administrative sources are derivative in the sense that they are exercises of specific delegated authority under some executive or congressional establishment instrument. The secretary of the interior has general statutory authority to withdraw public land for refuge establishment but may not modify or revoke most existing withdrawals that added land to the System (43 U.S.C. § 1714(j)). Public land orders, secretarial orders, and wildlife orders are all forms of administrative action authorized by statute that have been used to establish refuges. The secretarial order has only been used once for establishing refuges since 1974. Administrative establishment documents have not been important sources of particularized management mandates for refuge units. They generally contain little detail on refuge purposes or management mandates.

As the number of executive orders and presidential proclamations establishing refuges diminished after World War II, the number of administrative establishment orders increased. These orders make the *Federal Register* an important collection of establishment information. However, many informal administrative orders establishing refuges are not published in the *Federal Register*. Such refuge acquisition authority as the 1956 Fish and Wildlife Act is written so broadly as to permit the secretary of the interior to purchase whatever land he or she deems appropriate for the System (16 U.S.C. §§ 742f(a)(4), (b)(1)). Congressional approval, however, is generally required in the form of appropriation.

The Improvement Act lists "administrative memorandum" and "agreement" as sources of individual refuge purposes but does not define the terms. The legislative history and the Service regulations fail to clarify what the terms refer to. The terms likely describe types of documents not published in the *Federal Register* and not readily accessible to the public. If administrative memoranda were predecisional documents not authoritatively incorporated by reference in some kind of record of decision, then they would be weak sources for individual refuge purposes because they would not otherwise be binding in administrative law.

Most agreements relevant to refuge management are cooperative agreements with other federal or state agencies, as authorized by a section of the Fish and Wildlife Coordination Act (16 U.S.C. § 664). Like donations, cooperative agreements are authorized by many parts of the U.S. Code. They are the charters for the coordination areas of the System. These 50 units, though, are not subject to many of the key systemic mandates of the Improvement Act, such as planning or compatibility.

In practical effect, administrative memoranda and agreements contribute little to refuge purposes for compatibility analysis. The Service does not include administrative memoranda in its database of refuge purposes, an omission that reflects the practical difficulty of complying with this aspect of the Improvement Act. The Service seldom recognizes an individual agreement as the source of a refuge purpose. A rare example of a refuge purpose derived directly from an agreement was found at the entry for the Stillwater NWR in the 1999 Refuge System Database. A 1948 agreement established the "purposes of conservation, rehabilitation and management of wildlife, its resources and habitat, and for the purpose of operating and maintaining a public shooting ground and a wildlife refuge." The FWS has since removed this agreement from the list of purposes in its database.

One could interpret administrative memoranda to include the records of meetings of the Migratory Bird Conservation Commission during which refuge acquisitions are approved. Under the 1929 Migratory Bird Conservation Act, the Commission must approve all proposals for refuges established under this authority (16 U.S.C. § 715). However, the FWS refuge purposes database assigns Commission-approved refuges only the general purposes set out in the Migratory Bird Conservation Act, which created the acquisition mechanism for the Commission. The Service database does not look into the specific goals of the Commission in approving a particular acquisition. This is a wise policy that resists the aggregation of informally discussed rationales for individual acquisitions appearing in the record of Commission meetings that, if elevated to purpose status, would confound systemic management. The Commission may approve individual tract acquisitions for reasons having little to do with the purpose of the refuge, or even the Migratory Bird Conservation Act. For instance, the Commission has approved acquisitions for protection of fish and big game. An illustration of this occurs in the minutes of a meeting on January 14, 1936, when the Commission discussed acquisition of the Okefenokee swamp for such purposes as providing big game habitat, cypress stand conservation, and primitive area maintenance, in addition to waterfowl production goals.

Though the System's statutes and regulations make reference to donation documents, these grants of land, specifying particular intents of the donor to the System, are not easily accessible. The donated lands also comprise less than one percent of the System and are not recorded in the Service database. Donation of lands for refuges, however, dates back at least to 1912 (Reed and Drabelle 1984, 21). It continues to occur. For instance, in 2002, the Richard King Mellon Foundation announced a 33,805 acre donation to the Alaska Peninsula NWR (Berman 2002).

The extent to which the Service can accept purposes in a donation document that are not authorized by a statute or executive order is not clear (U.S. GAO 2000, 4). However, the Fish and Wildlife Act of 1956 authorizes the secretary to accept gifts of real property for the general benefit of the Service "in performing its activities and services" (6 U.S.C. § 742f(b)(1)). The 1956 law authorizes the Service to accept gifts "subject to the terms of any restrictive or affirmative covenant, or condition of servitude, if such terms are . . . compatible with the purpose for which acceptance is sought" (id.). It is conceivable, then, that some acquired areas of refuges could be conditioned on certain management purposes, such as maintaining a particular population of animals.

Conclusion

Presidential sources of individual refuge purposes are important for creating the key terminology and management strictures later adopted more widely in legislation. Though seldom exercised today, the presidential authority to establish refuges remains broad and can be revived to exert leadership in conservation. The litigation over the Charles M. Russell NWR illustrates the continuing vitality of old executive orders that can drive management on individual refuges decades after presidential proclamation, despite subsequent legislation.

Administrative sources of refuge purposes are important for their sheer numbers. Particularly through acquisition, but also through the secretary of the interior's delegated authority to withdraw public lands, administrative additions to the Refuge System continue to accumulate at a substantial pace. Without the existing, narrow interpretation of what constitutes an individual refuge purpose, administrative considerations could undermine the systemic operation of the Improvement Act. Nonetheless, the Improvement Act's reference to "administrative memorandum" casts doubt on the legality of the Service's existing, sensible practice.

Congressional sources of individual refuge purposes create the most difficult conflicts and competing priorities for systemic management. This is due in part to the power of statutes and their authoritativeness in delegating tasks to the Service. But statutory establishment documents are also distinguished by their specific detail in defining refuge purposes and management obligations. Establishment legislation has experienced an increase in statutory detail similar to organic legislation. Indeed, many systemic purposes first gained recognition in the System through establishment statutes.

Ultimately, a better theory of organic legislation would help resolve the interpretive challenges created by individual refuge purposes. Recognition of the special status of organic legislation would support relatively less deference to anything but explicit commands in establishment statutes. It would also guide the drafting of new establishment statutes that better conform to the framework of the Improvement Act.

11 | *The Special Case of the Alaska Refuges*

The Alaska national wildlife refuges are distinguished more by their extraordinary physical characteristics than by special resource management rules. As chapter 3 describes, the Alaska refuges are notable for their immense size and wild ecosystems. Historically, they played a precedent-setting role in advancing organic law for the System. For the most part, though, all of the law discussed in this book, including the 1997 Improvement Act, applies to the Alaska refuges in the same way it applies to the rest of the System. However, there are a few significant topics for which peculiar rules apply in the Alaskan portion of the System.

In addition to pathbreaking establishment mandates for most of the Alaskan refuges, discussed in chapters 3 and 10, the Alaska National Interest Lands Conservation Act of 1980 (ANILCA) also allows subsistence hunting and fishing for rural Alaskan residents (16 U.S.C. § 3101(c)). Subsistence uses are permitted nowhere else in the System. Moreover, ANILCA accords subsistence activities a high priority, allowing them to displace other uses and creating conflicts unique to Alaska (16 U.S.C. §§ 3112(2), 3114). The U.S. Fish and Wildlife Service (FWS) has promulgated special regulations governing subsistence and other uses in the Alaska refuges (50 C.F.R. part 36).

Nine years before Congress enacted ANILCA, it passed the Alaska Native Claims Settlement Act (ANCSA) to resolve aboriginal land claims. The claim settlement system authorized native corporations to select federal lands. The selected lands were turned over to the corporations for use as company assets to benefit the aboriginal shareholders. Though most of the selected lands transferred to native corporations were removed from federal control, section 22(g) of ANCSA limited the property rights obtained by the corporations for lands within the Refuge System (43 U.S.C. § 1621(g)). As a result, these so-called 22(g) lands are subject to partial FWS regulation and a modified compatibility standard.

Finally, no discussion of the special case of Alaska refuges would be complete without treating the dispute over oil and gas development in the Arctic National Wildlife Refuge (NWR). The political fight over drilling in the Arctic NWR, the largest refuge in the System, has dragged on for decades but intensified in recent years. Just as the development of a reservoir in Yosemite National Park's Hetch Hetchy Valley became emblematic of the conservation divide of the early twentieth century, the dispute over the Arctic NWR is symbolic as well as practical. The coastal plain of the refuge may be a "complete, pristine," undisturbed ecosystem hosting a "rich pageant of wildlife" to the FWS (U.S. FWS 2002f), but to George W. Bush's Interior Secretary Gail Norton, it is a "flat, white nothingness" (Firestone 2003). The Arctic NWR dispute reflects the larger tension between commodity development, on the one hand, and wilderness and wildlife values on the other. It is resolved under special provisions, discussed at the end of this chapter, outside of the System's organic legislation.

Subsistence Uses

As chapter 2 describes, the FWS commonly opens refuges to hunting and fishing. Indeed, the 1997 Improvement Act encourages hunting, fishing, and other wildlife-dependent recreation. When a portion of a refuge is open to hunting or fishing, state law governing those activities generally applies unless it conflicts with some federal law or a specific refuge regulation. Commercial hunting and fishing in refuges is rare and certainly does not qualify for the priority status of wildlife-dependent recreation.

However, in Alaska, some hunting and fishing is neither recreational nor fully commercial. Instead, it is part of the "customary and traditional uses by rural Alaska residents of wild, renewable resources for direct personal or family consumption as food, shelter, fuel, clothing, tools, or transportation; for the making and selling of handicraft articles out of nonedible byproducts of fish and wildlife resources taken for personal or family consumption; for barter, or sharing for personal or family consumption; and for customary trade" (16 U.S.C. § 3113; 50 C.F.R. § 36.2).

These are the subsistence uses that ANILCA provided for on refuges in Alaska.

In Alaska, ANILCA modifies the hierarchy of use preferences in the Refuge System. "Nonwasteful subsistence uses" receive priority over wildlife-dependent recreational uses (16 U.S.C. § 3114). Subsistence uses displace the usual, secondary, "priority general public uses" and are subject only to public safety, administrative, and conservation limitations (16 U.S.C. §§ 668dd(a)(3)(C), 3126(b)). As the Service acknowledged in its rulemaking implementing the subsistence provisions, the administrative limitation is potentially broad. Certainly, it is steeped in discretion. The administrative limitation may be used to protect the refuge purposes and values in the refuge area and "to otherwise manage the refuge prudently" (46 Fed. Reg. 31,825 [1981]).

ANILCA characterizes the conservation limitations on subsistence uses in two ways. First, the section establishing the priority for subsistence uses conditions them on restrictions "in order to protect the continued viability" of populations of fish and wildlife (16 U.S.C. § 3114). Second, the section limiting the applicability of the subsistence subchapter of ANILCA states that the law does not permit subsistence uses where they are "inconsistent with the conservation of healthy populations" (16 U.S.C. § 3125(1)). The FWS, relying on the ANILCA legislative history, interprets the two descriptions of the subsistence limitation as a single standard that maintains "fish and wildlife resources and their habitats in a condition which assures stable and continuing natural populations and species mix of plants and animals in relation to their ecosystems, including recognition that local rural residents engaged in subsistence uses may be a natural part of that ecosystem; minimizes the likelihood of irreversible or long-term adverse effects upon such populations and species; and ensures maximum practicable diversity of options for the future" (46 Fed. Reg. 31,823 [1981] [quoting S. Rep. No. 96-413, 233] [1979]).

The Service must provide adequate notice and employ hearings before permanently closing areas to subsistence use (16 U.S.C. § 3126; 50 C.F.R. § 36.16). Shortly after the Alaska Supreme Court overturned the state's subsistence preference program in December 1989, the federal government assumed management of all subsistence uses on federal lands, under a framework provided by ANILCA (*McDowell v. Alaska* 1989; 16 U.S.C. § 3115). The federal government divides Alaska into ten subsistence regions, each with its own regional council whose local members are appointed by the secretaries of interior and agriculture. These councils may propose modifications to subsistence regulations. The Federal Subsistence Board, composed of the Alaska directors of the four major federal land management agencies, including the FWS, exercises oversight for the federal subsistence management program.

Native Claims

Unlike the Indian tribes in the lower 48 states, Alaskan aboriginal peoples were never organized on reservations. Nonetheless, the Alaskan natives did have similar claims to natural resources based on aboriginal use and occupancy. Congress enacted ANCSA in 1971 to resolve those claims. Two overriding considerations prompted Congress to act in 1971. First, Congress needed to clear title to the public domain to allow the state to complete its selection of state lands as part of the 1959 Alaska statehood deal. Second, Congress wanted to promote development of the newly discovered, colossal oil field at Prudhoe Bay on the north coast.

To compensate the native peoples of Alaska for extinguishing their aboriginal claims, ANCSA authorized the creation of native corporations, organized under Alaska law, at two geographic levels: regional and village. ANCSA divided Alaska into 13 regions for 13 native regional corporations. It also created over 200 native village corporations. The corporations received nearly $1 billion and 40 million acres of land (Haycox 2002, 90–99). The native people received shares of stock in both the regional and village corporations covering the area in which they lived (Walsh 1985, 227–230).

The special rules governing land selection by and enterprise governance of the native corporations are tortuous and beyond the scope of this book. However, one aspect of the land selection continues to vex refuge management in Alaska: the "22(g)" land selections within national wildlife refuges. These land selections are known by the section number of the original provision of ANCSA that encumbered them with FWS regulation (43 U.S.C. § 1621(g)). Currently, 945,000 acres in seven Alaska refuges are covered by section 22(g).

Under ANCSA, village corporations were entitled to select lands in and adjoining the village townships (43 U.S.C. §§ 1610, 1613(a)). The village corporation received title to the surface estate for all selected land, and the regional corporation generally received the subsurface estate, including mineral rights. Each regional corporation could also make its own selections, for which it received both the surface and the subsurface rights (43 U.S.C. §§ 1611(a)(1), 1613(h)(9)).

ANCSA capped the number of acres village corporations could select in refuges (43 U.S.C. § 1611(a)(1)). Also, with one exception in the Kenai

NWR (discussion following here), ANCSA withheld from regional corporations the subsurface estate for selected lands in the Refuge System. These subsurface rights, which are below village corporation surface estates in refuges, remain in federal ownership. Regional corporations could select subsurface rights elsewhere, outside the System, to compensate for this loss of potentially valuable mineral deposits (43 U.S.C. § 1611(a)(1)). ANCSA also authorized an increase in the size of the Refuge System in Alaska by the same amount as the selected native corporate lands in refuges diminished its size (43 U.S.C. § 1621(e)).

The most significant impact on current resource management in refuges, however, is a consequence of ANILCA section 22(g), which limited in two ways the surface rights native corporations selected in the Refuge System. First, it gave the United States the right of first refusal if the land is ever sold by the native corporation. Second, and more importantly, it required all patents deeding refuge lands to native corporations to "contain a provision that such lands remain subject to the laws and regulations governing use and development" of the refuge (43 U.S.C. § 1621(g)). This restraint on the title of native corporation land within refuges creates a strange category of lands that are not owned outright by the federal government, but over which the Service has regulatory control.

The Service exercises its control over native corporate surface activities in the Alaska refuges principally through the compatibility criterion. By regulation, there are four major deviations from the general compatibility standards and procedures for the System, when applied to 22(g) lands (50 C.F.R. § 25.21(b)). The Service justifies the deviations on the basis that the 22(g) patent limitation is not intended to give FWS its usual proprietary power to manage the 22(g) selections (65 Fed. Reg. 62,464–62,465 [2000]). Instead, the patent merely allows the Service to function as a kind of local land use control authority, regulating the uses that the native corporation managers propose. This is an unusual role for the Service.

The first exception to the general compatibility rule for 22(g) lands is that determinations measure a proposed activity against only the individual refuge purposes; the FWS will not consider the System mission in the compatibility analysis (50 C.F.R. § 25.21(b)(1)(iii)). Though this pushes aside a key function of the 1997 Improvement Act, the ANILCA individual refuge purposes, discussed in chapters 3 and 10, have conservation mandates very similar to the System mission. Also, 15 of the 16 Alaska refuges include a purpose of subsistence use (65 Fed. Reg. 62,465 [2000]), so this deviation does not have great practical effect.

Second, compatibility determinations for 22(g) lands evaluate the effects of the proposed use only on the adjacent refuge lands, not on the 22(g) lands themselves (50 C.F.R. § 25.21(b)(1)(v)). This exception reflects the Service position that the patent condition is designed to prevent adverse spillover effects of 22(g) land uses on the federally owned portion of the refuges. Third, these compatibility determinations are not subject to the periodic reevaluation every ten years that applies outside of 22(g) lands (50 C.F.R. §§ 25.21(b)(1)(vi), (b)(1)(vii), (g)). The FWS rule does, however, call for reevaluation when significant new information affecting the determination emerges or the use changes significantly (50 C.F.R. § 25.21(b)(1)(vi)). Fourth, use proponents of 22(g) lands enjoy somewhat more favorable procedures for compatibility determinations and appeals than do other use proponents (50 C.F.R. §§ 25.21(b)(1)(i), (iv)).

The Service also treats 22(g) lands differently in other respects. First, refuge-unit comprehensive conservation plans (CCPs) do not include 22(g) lands (50 C.F.R. § 25.21(b)(1)(vii)). Because the CCP is such an important blueprint for forecasting and shaping future refuge conditions, this opens holes in the ability of Alaskan refuges to engage in ecosystem management. Second, the Service will allow any uses on 22(g) lands that are compatible (50 C.F.R. § 25.21(b)(1)(ii)). This is a departure from the general rule for the System that not all compatible uses are appropriate, or allowed, on refuges. Because the determination of appropriateness should normally depend on how well an activity conforms with the CCP (U.S. House 1997a, 13; 65 Fed. Reg. 62,468 [2000]), this exception to the general System management policy makes sense, given the limitation on the scope of CCPs. Third, the Service does not require special use permits for 22(g) land activities that pass the compatibility test (50 C.F.R. § 25.21(b)(1)(viii)).

The Kenai NWR is the only refuge in which a regional corporation, the Cook Inlet Region, Inc. (CIRI), acquired subsurface property rights (Pub. L. No. 94-204 §§ 12(b)(1-7), (c)). This occurred after 1971, as a result of federal settlements to a series of land claims by CIRI. As a result, the Kenai NWR is the only refuge in Alaska with current oil and gas production. Chapter 12 discusses how private subsurface property holders can gain access to a refuge to develop their mineral rights.

The Arctic National Wildlife Refuge

The 19.3 million acre Arctic NWR is the largest and most controversial unit in the System. The national debate over whether to drill for oil on the Arctic NWR's coastal plain or whether to preserve its wilderness character and wildlife habitat has prompted continual congressional activity in the past 15 years. Nonetheless, Congress has been unable to enact a law changing the status quo prohibition on oil development. Proposals to expand the Arctic NWR wilderness area to include the coastal plain, which would preclude drilling, also regularly fail. The unique qualities of the Arctic NWR set the tone of the dispute, which seldom focuses on the systemic issues or tools of organic legislation.

The Arctic NWR is unique, in part because it is the only protected area in the United States that contains the "complete spectrum" of arctic ecosystems, from the tallest peaks of the Brooks Range to the marine environment of the Arctic shore (U.S. Department of the Interior 1987, 46). But the coastal plain is the focus of land use conflicts because it is both the location of potentially vast hydrocarbon deposits as well as the most productive habitat for an impressive assemblage of large mammals and waterfowl.

In the 1960s, oil companies discovered and leased the Prudhoe Bay field under Alaska-owned lands just to the west of the Arctic NWR. This 11 to 13 billion barrel oil field, the largest in North America, became an important oil-producing area with the construction of the Trans-Alaska Pipeline in the 1970s (Corn, Gelb and Baldwin 2002, 1). Alaska derives most of its state revenue, close to 80 percent for the 2002–2003 fiscal year, from oil royalties (Corbisier 2002, 304–404). In addition to direct royalties from state-leased mineral resources, such as Prudhoe Bay oil, the state also receives 90 percent of the royalties collected from federally leased resources.

The extent of the oil field underlying the refuge is unknown, but the most recent federal estimate indicates it is likely as large as Prudhoe Bay (Corn, Gelb, and Baldwin 2002, 4). However, the actual volume of oil produced depends not only on the size of the field but also on the price of oil. At $24 a barrel, the U.S. Geological Survey estimates that there is a 95 percent chance that two billion barrels or more of oil could be economically produced (id., 4).

Almost everyone agrees that the ecological richness of the coastal plain of the refuge is of global importance. The debate instead focuses on the effects that oil development would likely have on the biological resources, including the migration of thousands of caribou, the nesting of hundreds of thousands of diverse migratory waterfowl and shorebirds, and habitat for imperiled species. Of particular concern is the health of the Porcupine Caribou Herd, which calves in or near the coastal plain during the summer, and the polar bears, which den in the coastal plain during the winter (id., 6). Development would also threaten the health of the wetland complex of the coastal plain (Adams 2002). Of course, oil and gas development would degrade the wilderness character of the coastal plain.

A secretarial public land order established the nine million acre Arctic National Wildlife Range in 1960, which served as the predecessor to the Arctic NWR and included the valuable coastal plain (Pub. Land Order 2,214, 25 Fed. Reg. 12,598 [1960]). Though Alaska had entered the union a year before, the area covered by the 1960 order had been segregated from the unreserved public domain since 1957. This segregation placed the area off limits for selection of state lands under Alaska's statehood statute and blocked the transfer of the beds underlying navigable and tidal waters to the state (*United States v. Alaska* 1997). Therefore, the federal government has been able to control any potential oil development in the Arctic NWR coastal plain for some time. The 1960 establishment document allowed for oil and gas leasing, though it did not occur.

In 1971, ANCSA authorized the Kaktovik Inupiat Corporation (KIC) to select lands within the Arctic range, but the federal government retained the subsurface mineral rights. These 22(g) lands total over 92,000 acres on the coastal plain. In 1983, the federal government granted the Arctic Slope Regional Corporation the subsurface estate under the KIC's 22(g) lands in exchange for the corporation's in-holdings at Gates of the Arctic National Park (Ross 2000, 272; U.S. Department of the Interior 1987, 43). However, the agreement prohibits oil/gas development unless Congress specifically authorizes it in the refuge or on the KIC 22(g) lands (Baldwin 2002, 3).

In 1980, ANILCA renamed the range as the Arctic NWR and added 9.2 million acres, mostly to the south and west (ANILCA § 303(2)). ANILCA designated as wilderness most of the original national wildlife range area of the new refuge, but excluded the 1.5 million acre coastal plain (ANILCA § 702(3)). ANILCA did not appreciably change the area of coastal plain contained in the refuge. However, Congress did designate most of the coastal plain as a special zone, known as the "1002 area," for special study to help it decide on future leasing of oil/gas (ANILCA § 1002, 16 U.S.C. § 3142). In the meantime, ANILCA prohibited oil and gas leasing, production, and development unless authorized by a subsequent act of Congress (ANILCA § 1003, 16 U.S.C. § 3143).

In 1987, the Reagan Interior Department completed the study required by ANILCA § 1002 for the coastal plain. In its report to Congress, which included an environmental impact statement, the Interior Department recommended full leasing and development of the entire coastal plain

(U.S. Department of the Interior 1987). Environmentalists bitterly disputed Interior's recommendation and sanguine assessment of oil production's impact on the coastal ecosystem (Ross 2000, 275–283). This triggered a round of law drafting that continues today. Congress frequently hosts duels, fatal to bills on both sides, between proposed legislation authorizing drilling and provisions designating wilderness on the coastal plain.

Though the 1987 report heightened congressional interest in Arctic NWR oil development, the 1989 wreck of the *Exxon Valdez* tanker, resulting in the disastrous Prince William Sound oil spill, dampened much of the enthusiasm for two years. In 1991, the Persian Gulf War renewed pressure to open the Arctic NWR to drilling. As a result, the Senate Energy Committee reported a National Energy Policy Act with a provision for leasing, but a roll call vote on the Senate floor failed to kill a filibuster on the provision. Congress ultimately enacted the law in 1992 without a provision for drilling in the Arctic NWR (Pub. L. No. 102-486).

The closest that Congress ever came to authorizing oil development occurred in 1995, when it enacted an enormous budget reconciliation bill that included a provision for drilling (U.S. House 1995b). However, President Clinton vetoed the bill, in part because he objected to the drilling measure. Congress did not override his action (Corn, Gelb, and Baldwin 2002, 3).

Though serious legislative skirmishes over oil development popped up several more times in 1995 and 2000, the next major battle over the future of the coastal plain began with President George W. Bush's energy policy recommendation to drill in the Arctic NWR. Though the House of Representatives passed a bill in 2001 supporting the Bush policy, the Senate in 2002 rejected development of the refuge in its version of the energy bill. The energy bill died in conference committee at the end of the 107th Congress.

The 108th Congress, with a Republican Senate more friendly to President Bush's agenda than the 107th, offers the best prospect for approving oil development in the Arctic NWR since the release of the 1987 report. As this book went to press in 2003, the 108th Congress was still considering new energy bills. However, although the House passed a bill approving drilling in the refuge, the Senate defeated (52–48) a similar provision. Just two weeks before the March 19 Senate vote, the nonpartisan National Research Council (2003) issued a report analyzing the cumulative effects of existing oil and gas development on Alaska's North Slope. The report highlighted the long-term damage to the tundra habitat, to bird and mammal populations, and to the people living in the region. It also forecasted continued accumulation of environmental and social harms.

Statutory approval of oil development in the Arctic NWR would require Congress and the FWS to address a number of legal and resource management issues. These include environmental standards for energy development, such as the extent to which the FWS may impose conditions based on compatibility concerns; the appropriate level of review for development of the KIC 22(g) lands; the extent to which NEPA might apply to energy-related uses; and the allocation of royalties between the federal government and the state of Alaska (Corn, Gelb, and Baldwin 2002; Baldwin 2002).

12 | *Oil and Gas Development in the Refuges*

As an economic use of natural resources, mining activity, including oil and gas development, occupies the lowest rung in the hierarchy of Refuge System designated uses, illustrated in figure 6.1. This quaternary use may occur only where it is compatible with primary uses, does not conflict with secondary uses, and contributes to attaining a primary use. Primary uses of refuges include both individual refuge purposes and the System's mission, which calls for "conservation, management, and where appropriate, restoration of the fish, wildlife, and plant resources and their habitats" (16 U.S.C. § 668dd(a)(2)). Though there may be circumstances where petroleum-related development does not frustrate plant and wildlife protection, it is difficult to imagine a circumstance where it would affirmatively contribute to attaining conservation goals. So, even putting aside the possible conflicts between oil/gas development and secondary, wildlife-dependent recreational activities, it is unlikely that the U.S. Fish and Wildlife Service (FWS) could approve new proposals for oil and gas development under the 1997 Improvement Act, absent special circumstances.

However, some type of oil or gas exploration or development activity occurs on 77 refuges in 22 different states (U.S. GAO 2001, 1). In 27 of these refuges, the oil- or gas-related activity is a pipeline running through the refuge. Some 45 refuges in 15 states actually produce oil or gas. The number of producing wells in these refuges range from 1, in the Canaan Valley National Wildlife Refuge in West

Virginia, to over 300 in the Upper Ouachita National Wildlife Refuge in Louisiana (id., 3).

Given the strategic importance of fossil fuels and the high priority of developing federal oil and gas resources, the Refuge System faces increased pressure to coexist with energy production. Nonetheless, outside of the Arctic National Wildlife Refuge, or other places where Congress might intervene with special legislation to authorize drilling, oil/gas development (and mining generally) on refuges will remain rare because of the Improvement Act's compatibility standard and hierarchy of dominant uses. This chapter focuses on the special circumstances that permit oil and gas development to go forward.

Refuge System mineral development occurs in two situations, examined in the two sections that follow. The first is where the federal government leases its own subsurface oil and gas to avoid drainage by neighboring drillers or to fulfill the terms of older leases. Since the promulgation of a 1947 rule, the Interior Department has refused to approve new leases on existing refuges except for the purpose of avoiding drainage of federal oil/gas. But some federal leases exist on refuges because they predate either the establishment or the expansion of the refuge or because they predate the 1947 rule. Federal mineral lessees must abide by lease stipulations and regulation of surface activities to ensure fulfillment of the System conservation mission. Eight units of the System currently produce federally leased oil or gas (U.S. GAO 2001).

The second, more common, situation arises where the subsurface petroleum or other mineral resources under a refuge are not owned by the federal government. These private, subsurface resource owners generally may mine their property, subject to some regulation of their surface disturbance. However, this surface regulation gives rise to greater conflicts than the regulation of federally leased minerals. This is because private oil/gas development is more widespread and because the extent of permissible regulation is less clearly defined by law. Forty-one units currently have oil or gas activity deriving from privately held subsurface mineral rights.

Federal Subsurface Ownership

Where the federal government owns subsurface resources, it may open valuable deposits to private extraction. Before 1920, oil and gas were subject to the same mineral disposal law as "hardrock" commodities, such as silver and gold. This disposal law, known as the General Mining Law, or the 1872 Mining Law, allows people to prospect federal lands designated as open to "entry." Upon discovery of valuable mineral deposits subject to the law, the mineral rights pass from federal to private ownership. However, the interior secretary and the president have broad statutory authority to close parcels of public lands to "entry" under the General Mining Law through an act called a "withdrawal." After the date of the withdrawal, no new mineral rights may be acquired under the 1872 Mining Law. Valid existing rights at the time of withdrawal are, however, retained by the private owners.

Because no organic legislation removes the Refuge System from the operation of the 1872 Law, refuges are generally open to prospecting and mineral discovery under the General Mining Law unless mining is excluded from an area for some reason (16 U.S.C. § 668dd(c)). Nonetheless, little mining under the General Mining Law occurs on refuge lands (Leshy 1987, 447). Some refuge lands are withdrawn from the operation of the General Mining Law through explicit provisions in their establishment documents (see, e.g., UL Bend National Wildlife Refuge, 34 Fed. Reg. 5,851 [Mar. 28, 1969]; Simeonof National Wildlife Refuge, 23 Fed. Reg. 8,623 [Nov. 5, 1958]; Michigan Islands National Wildlife Refuge, 12 Fed. Reg. 2,529 [Apr. 18, 1947]; Tewaukon National Wildlife Refuge, 10 Fed. Reg. 8,559 [July 10, 1945]; Columbia National Wildlife Refuge, 9 Fed. Reg. 11,400 [Sept. 15, 1944]; and Alaska refuges in the Alaska National Interest Lands Conservation Act [ANILCA] § 304(c) [2000]). Other establishment documents may close a refuge from mineral entry by inference where express purposes are incompatible with mining activity (*Pathfinder Mines v. Hodel* 1987, 1291). In upholding an administrative invalidation of a mining claim, a 1987 federal appeals court approved Interior Department precedent withdrawing from entry lands where "full exercise of rights under mining laws would jeopardize or impair or destroy the usefulness of the reserve as a wildlife refuge" (id. 1292 [internal quotations omitted]).

In addition, the secretary of the interior may withdraw refuge lands from the operation of the General Mining Law at any time (43 U.S.C. § 1714(c), (d), (e)). This authority is not reversible: the secretary may not modify or revoke existing withdrawals in the System (43 U.S.C. § 1714(j)). The ratchet effect of this authority has led to the closing of most refuge lands to mineral entry (Maley 1996, 150). Acquired refuges, like most acquired federal land, are closed to the 1872 law's disposal scheme (16 U.S.C. § 668dd(a)(5)). The Supreme Court announced this principle that acquired federal lands are closed to entry unless opened expressly by the acquiring document in *Oklahoma v. Texas* (1922).

In the Mineral Leasing Act of 1920, Congress removed oil and gas, as well as other valuable fuel minerals, from the disposal scheme of the 1872 Mining Law (41 Stat. 437). Instead of employing miner-initiated prospecting and discovery to dispose of the fuel minerals, Congress created a leasing regime that allows the secretary of the interior to control the location, timing, and terms of federal oil and gas disposal. The 1947 Mineral Leasing Act for Acquired Lands extends the Mineral Leasing Act of 1920 to acquired lands, including acquired refuges (61 Stat. 913; 43 C.F.R. § 3100.0-3(b)). By regulation, the Department of the Interior excludes refuge lands from the leasing system for geothermal resources established by Congress in 1970 (43 C.F.R. § 3201.11(e)).

All lessees of federal oil and gas are required to pay royalties of at least 12.5 percent to the federal government, as well as annual rentals of $1.50 or $2.00 per acre. Furthermore, a minimum bid of $2.00 per acre is required to secure the lease (30 U.S.C. § 226(b)). The primary period of an oil and gas lease is usually ten years. However, leases that are producing oil or gas in paying quantities beyond the primary term are extended so long as paying quantities are produced (30 U.S.C. § 226(e)). A federal oil and gas lease does not guarantee the lessee a right to drill for the hydrocarbon. Sometimes, all a leaseholder can do is exclude others from drilling for the fuel minerals. Some leases contain "no surface occupancy" (NSO) stipulations. These stipulations protect the surface directly over the leased oil and gas. The NSO lessees often can employ directional drilling techniques to extract the oil and gas from somewhere adjacent to protected land.

Although National Wildlife Refuges have generally been off limits for new leasing since at least 1947 (U.S. GAO 2001, 4; 43 C.F.R. § 3101.5-1), there are two situations in which leasing has been allowed to occur on Refuge System land where the federal government owns the oil and gas rights. First, leases can be issued when there is "drainage" of federally owned oil or gas under refuges (43 C.F.R. § 3100.2-1). Drainage occurs when an adjacent landowner's oil and gas drilling activities draw down an oil/gas field owned or leased by the federal government (30 U.S.C. § 226(f)). The drainage policy originates in a 1941 attorney general opinion stating that the executive branch has "implied authority" to "take protective measures in cases where lands acquired by the United States for a specific public purpose are found to contain oil which is being drained by adjoining owners" (U.S. Attorney General 1941).

When drainage of federally owned oil or gas is found to be occurring, the federal government can either enter into royalty agreements with the neighboring owners causing the drainage or it can issue its own leases (43 C.F.R. § 3100.2-1). When drainage agreements are made, the ten-year pri-

mary term of the lease is extended for "the period during which such compensatory royalty is paid and for a period of one year from discontinuance
of such payment and so long thereafter as oil or gas is produced in paying quantities" (30 U.S.C. § 226(j)). Service policy, however, states that
drainage leases should contain NSO stipulations "where possible" (612 FW
2.8(C)). Though the "where possible" language of FWS policy allows for
some discretion in imposing the stipulation, pertinent regulations dictate
a strong presumption against surface disturbance (43 C.F.R. § 3101.5-1).

The second situation in which federal oil and gas leasing may occur on
refuges is where a lease predates the establishment of the refuge. Currently, this situation occurs on two refuges, Bitter Lake National Wildlife
Refuge in New Mexico and Bowdoin Wetland Management District in
Montana (U.S. GAO 2001). In both instances the federal government issued the leases prior to the expansion of the refuge boundary to encompass all or some of the producing wells. Because the Mineral Leasing Act
requires extension of the lease period so long as oil or gas "is being produced in paying quantities," the wells continued to operate even after the
land became a refuge (30 U.S.C. § 226-1(d); 43 C.F.R. § 3107.2-1).

Prior to 1947, no federal policy prohibited mineral leasing on refuges.
Only one refuge, Hewitt Lake National Wildlife Refuge in Montana, produces gas from leases issued before 1947. The executive order establishing Hewitt Lake National Wildlife Refuge expressly permits oil and gas
leasing (Exec. Order No. 7,833 [Mar. 7, 1938]). The 1947 regulation prohibiting leasing of federal oil and gas on refuges contained an exception
(since abolished), that allowed leasing on refuges if the lessees, as a group,
developed a unit agreement plan that stipulated how the extraction of an
oil or gas field would occur on a refuge. Under this exception, lessees in the
Delta National Wildlife Refuge in Louisiana continue to produce oil and
gas. As with many other aspects of resource management, special rules
modify the leasing regime somewhat for Alaska (16 U.S.C. § 3149).

Where leasing is allowed to occur, the Fish and Wildlife Service, as the
agency with "sole and complete jurisdiction over such lands for wildlife
conservation purposes" (43 C.F.R. § 3101.5-1(a)), has broad authority to
manage the surface development operations associated with production.
The Bureau of Land Management (BLM), through its onshore federal
leasing program, manages the issuance and extension of the leases, so the
Service does not have the authority to terminate or extend leases. But the
Service can impose limitations on the activities of lessees for the benefit
of wildlife, even when the land comes under Service jurisdiction via an expansion of refuge borders. The Service stipulates conditions on the lease

"as to the time, place, nature and condition of such operations in order to minimize impacts to fish and wildlife populations and habitat and other refuge resources on the areas leased" (43 C.F.R. § 3101.5-4). Since 1993, the FWS has required NSO stipulations for drainage leases (612 FW 2.8(C)).

Private Subsurface Ownership

Oil and gas activities where private parties own subsurface rights occur on 41 refuges (U.S. GAO 2001, 2). This generates conflict between the Service, seeking to minimize the environmental impacts of oil and gas development, and private subsurface owners, seeking to maximize the profit from their property. The Service regulates privately owned oil and gas resources under a rule first issued in 1966 (31 Fed. Reg. 16,027). But, to avoid a Fifth Amendment taking of the private mineral rights, the regulation states that "[n]othing in this section shall be applied so as to contravene or nullify rights vested in holders of mineral interests on refuge lands" (50 C.F.R. § 29.32).

Therefore, though the regulation calls on private mineral right-holders to "prevent damage, erosion, pollution or contamination" and to avoid interference with the operation of the refuge, these requirements are conditioned on the extent to which they are "practicable" (50 C.F.R. § 29.32). Generally, practicable conditions allow restrictions only to the extent that they are affordable. The regulation of private oil or gas activity may not go so far as to make production unprofitable. This can make regulation of marginally profitable wells problematic. Similarly, the regulation restricts storage and removal of waste to the extent practicable. Physical occupation of the refuge while engaging in oil- and gas-related activities "must be kept to the minimum space compatible with the conduct of efficient mineral operations" (id.).

In addition to the regulation, there are other tools for protecting refuge resources from the adverse impacts of oil and gas development. First, oil and gas activities are subject to the same environmental laws that apply to regulate pollution on private lands. Second, there may be relevant stipulations or conditions in the deeds for acquired refuges. Sometimes the Service acquires a surface estate from a property owner who possesses both the surface and the mineral estate. Under those circumstances, the Service may expressly require the holder of the remaining mineral estate to apply for a special use permit from the Service before engaging in exploration or production. The FWS *Manual* facilitates this kind of negotiation by providing sample language to use in negotiating the deed transfer (342 FW 3, exhibit 3). The special use permit could then contain specific restoration requirements or stipulations limiting activities to certain times of year when wildlife is less likely to be disturbed.

If the FWS obtained a surface estate from a seller who did not own the mineral rights, or if the FWS did not explicitly reserve the right to condition mining on a special use permit, a refuge manager may have to ask for voluntary compliance (612 FW 2.9(B)(2)–(4)). *Caire v. Fulton* illustrates the Service's relative weakness where the refuge acquisition deed contains no express permitting authority (1986). The court held that FWS does not have the authority to apply 50 C.F.R. § 29.32, its oil/gas rule preventing refuge damage, to regulate privately owned subsurface mineral interests in D'Arbonne National Wildlife Refuge. In negotiating a settlement to a condemnation proceeding concerning the land in question, the federal government dropped language that appeared in a draft that would have explicitly adopted 50 C.F.R. § 29.32 to govern approval for the erection of structures connected to oil and gas exploration and development. The court, therefore, interpreted the final settlement language conveying property rights to the United States for the refuge and a flood control project, which was silent as to the application of the regulation, as a surrender of the authority to require Service permits or impose the regulatory conditions on the subsurface mineral owner. More typically, refuges retain their regulatory authority to condition special use permits. They also often possess bargaining leverage through their control of access to the surface site.

13 | CONCLUSION
Resource Management
through Organic Legislation

Managing the national wildlife refuges as a coordinated conservation system is an important challenge. It tests both the theory of sustainable development as well as the practice of dominant use resource management through organic legislation. The National Wildlife Refuge System Improvement Act of 1997 is significant both for its reforms of U.S. Fish and Wildlife Service (FWS) administration of the Refuge System as well as for its updated framework of nature protection.

Though one may argue whether the 1966 Administration Act provided organic legislation for the Refuge System, there is no question that the 1997 Improvement Act is an organic act in the modern sense of the term. The act sets forth a clear, affirmative conservation purpose statement; details a hierarchy of use preferences for the System; requires periodic, comprehensive resource planning for each unit; and establishes several binding, substantive management criteria. In all of these respects, the Improvement Act is an exemplar of the modern public land law meaning of the term "organic act."

The Improvement Act is the only organic statute for a system of public lands enacted since the reform spurt of the 1970s. As such, it is a rare expression of the current congressional attitudes toward public land law and perhaps a forecast for future reforms. It is the most revealing expression of the hallmarks of organic legislation. The Improvement Act is also a manifestation of the unusual circumstances and compromises that can result in passage of a sweeping new public land law in a period of divided government.

This chapter begins with a discussion of how effectively the Improvement Act may banish incompatible uses from the Refuge System. In doing so, I consider proposals to improve refuge management through institutional reform. Then I discuss the key aspects of refuge management law that may serve as models for reform of other conservation regimes.

The Persistence of Incompatible Uses

The impetus for the 1997 Act was not to provide the Refuge System with a modern organic act merely because the other major federal land systems had them. The drive to revise the Refuge System law responded both to the continuing interests of hunters and to the real ecological protection problems raised in the U.S. General Accounting Office (GAO) reports of the 1970s and 1980s. These problems centered on the persistence of uses incompatible with a variety of conservation goals. Therefore, in evaluating the act's effectiveness, we must ask: how well do the act and the Service's early stages of implementation address these concerns?

The greatest hope for reducing harmful refuge uses is the written compatibility determination, along with its periodic reevaluation folded into comprehensive planning. The Improvement Act's concrete mandate to protect wildlife, plants, and the environment will strengthen the Service's justification for and resolve to "just say no" to incompatible, nonpriority uses such as grazing, off-road vehicles, airboats, and waterskiing. Moreover, we can expect better conservation management through the monitoring requirement, the duty to acquire water rights, and the policy to maintain biological integrity, diversity, and environmental health. These substantive management criteria do not depend on use approvals, and they limit the discretion of the Service to base compatibility determinations on wishful thinking or political expedience.

As with almost all modern public land law, considerable discretion remains with the managing agency. Therefore, the executive branch will continue to set the pace of progress in achieving conservation goals. The first batch of final policies designed to implement the Improvement Act continues that tradition of leadership. For example, the new Refuge System policy prohibiting uses that fragment habitat binds the Service to strict application of the compatibility criterion and the biological integrity mandate. The new implementing policies also call for less Service passivity in the face of external encroachments.

There are limitations, however, to the Improvement Act's response to incompatible uses. In 1989, for instance, refuge managers considered waterfowl hunting to be harmful in a quarter of the refuges in which it occurred (U.S. GAO 1989, 20; Meier 1991). Yet, the 1997 Act grants hunting a priority status in the hierarchy of uses and facilitates its expansion. The immunity of hunting from restrictions applicable to many other uses is unsurprising given the history of hunting and refuges. There has been a steady increase in the influence of hunters over the Refuge System, traceable at least as far back as the Duck Stamp Act. Hunters shape refuge policy directly through their interest groups and indirectly through state game or natural resource agencies that derive much of their revenue from the sale of hunting (and fishing) licenses. The historic role that hunters have played in promoting conservation initiatives and the funds they have provided for property acquisition do justify some special treatment. However, the Service should strive to resist pressures for continual expansion of hunting and for game production where they overwhelm the System mission. The FWS will best control wildlife-dependent recreation by remaining faithful to the higher statutory priority of conservation. The new substantive management criterion for the maintenance of biological integrity, diversity, and environmental health should strengthen the Service's notoriously weak resolve in this area. Also, the decline in hunting as a recreational activity in the United States may portend a weakening of hunting interests.

The National Park Service's famous dual mandate for (1) conservation and (2) other uses that leave resources unimpaired creates a tiered system for management similar to the Refuge System (16 U.S.C. § 1). With the missions of the National Park System and the National Wildlife Refuge System now so closely aligned, the FWS could succumb to a merger with the more widely respected and better-funded National Park Service. The recreational uses allowed in national parks generally are the same as those allowed in refuges with the exception of hunting. By regulation, the National Park Service prohibits hunting in most national parks. However, national preserves (part of the Park System), which typically adjoin flagship national parks, generally are open to hunting. Although proposals to consolidate public land systems have a history of failure, the low profile of the Refuge System, coupled with the administrative proximity of the National Park System in the same cabinet department, makes a merger of the two agencies more likely to succeed.

The National Audubon Society recently reprised a proposal from the 1970s to create a new refuge management agency that, unlike the FWS, would not have any responsibilities other than land management (National Audubon Society undated b; U.S. House 1975; U.S. Senate 1975). Not surprisingly, the Service and the Interior Department responded negatively (Clarren 2001; Public Land News 2000). This type of institutional reform is a distraction. First, it is not at all clear that separating Refuge System management from the other FWS responsibilities would bring greater funds or prestige. Second, in this era of government downsizing, if the Refuge System is removed from the FWS, it is more likely to be placed in the National Park Service than it is to be reborn as an independent agency.

The failure of the effort to create an independent biological services bureau within the Interior Department offers a cautionary tale to proponents of Refuge System secession. Secretary Bruce Babbitt created the National Biological Survey (NBS) by secretarial order on October 1, 1993, reassigning hundreds of scientists from seven Interior Department agencies. The FWS lost more scientists than any other agency. In the wake of the Republican congressional election victory of 1994, debate over dissolving the NBS began in the House Committee on Resources and ultimately led to a 1996 compromise with those supporting a return of NBS scientists and employees to their original agencies. This compromise reduced the NBS budget by 15 percent and transferred the scientists into the Interior Department's U.S. Geological Survey, creating a Biological Resources Division (BRD) (Wagner 1999). The upshot of well-intentioned institutional reform creating a new agency was a reduced budget and a lower profile inside of a more powerful existing agency.

Consolidation of the public lands into fewer management systems would reduce opportunities for experimentation and innovation. What we most desperately need in the field of conservation is a wider range of case examples of sustainability. Diversity in management regimes, not consolidation, best serves that end.

Elevating wildlife-dependent recreation to a priority category for uses makes sense because it builds on the attributes of the Refuge System that distinguish it from other public lands. The provisions of the Improvement Act that give preeminence to wildlife-dependent recreation uses over other forms of recreation are sound, dominant use, tiered management mandates. However, the strong statutory counterweights, such as the inviolate sanctuary provision of the Migratory Bird Conservation Act and the adequate funding determination required by the Recreation Act, that have historically limited use preferences need to be revived and strengthened.

The exemption of wildlife-dependent recreation from the Recreation

Act's funding determination requirement is a serious flaw in the Improvement Act, and Congress should correct it. Rather than convey the message that Congress prefers some uses over others, this provision goes further to undermine the compatibility principle. The legislative history of the Improvement Act and the Service compatibility policy include "availability of resources" as only one element in the compatibility determination (U.S. House 1997a, 12; 65 Fed. Reg. 62,468 [2000]). This is a weak offset to the numerous statutory provisions and the strong interest-group pressure encouraging greater wildlife-dependent recreation. Separating the budgetary concern out of the larger conservation consistency analysis and retaining it as a separate test for recreational uses would highlight its importance.

The refuges are notoriously understaffed and underfunded. A 1999 survey of refuge managers found a vast majority believing that their refuges were not adequately staffed to meet the core conservation mission (Public Employees for Environmental Responsibility 1999). Although abstract analysis will often show consistency between wildlife-dependent recreation and conservation, actual implementation may fall short for lack of personnel to ensure compliance with limits, to reevaluate limits adaptively, and to minimize incidental damage from the recreation. Rather than reducing the uses subject to the funding determination, Congress should have broadened the applicability of the test to all permitted uses, not just recreation. This would have been more responsive to the real problems in refuge management revealed by the 1989 GAO report, which found political and local economic pressures to be a driving force behind harmful uses of refuges (U.S. GAO 1989, 24–32). The same political pressures that prompted Congress to splash approval of hunting and fishing over almost every section of the Improvement Act will make it difficult for refuge managers to resist or restrict those activities without strict statutory shields, such as the funding criterion. On the other hand, the 1962 Recreation Act's requirement had been on the books for 35 years without strict compliance, so mere retention of the funding criterion may not have prompted any shift in management practices. An effective funding criterion, therefore, would require written determinations subject to citizen challenge. Until Congress better addresses funding and staffing for refuge conservation programs and not merely facilitates maintenance, organic act reform will have little impact on the ground.

In addition, the Improvement Act should have followed the Alaska National Interest Lands Conservation Act's (ANILCA's) lead and required all unit comprehensive plans to design conservation programs. This would better translate the broad mission into site-specific programs with higher priorities for implementation. More specifically, a revised Improvement Act should require a schedule of tasks for ecological recovery in each refuge's comprehensive conservation plan (CCP). Like the Endangered Species Act's requirement for species recovery plans (16 U.S.C. § 1533(f)(1)(B)), CCPs should incorporate

1. descriptions of site-specific actions for ecological recovery and enhancement,
2. objective measurable criteria for success, and
3. estimates of the time and costs required to carry out the necessary measures.

To this list I would add a provision incorporating the biological monitoring substantive management criterion.

The 1997 Improvement Act failed to alleviate the problems in refuges created by divided jurisdiction. As highlighted by many of the commentators and government reports in the 1980s, the Service's lack of control over subsurface mineral rights (mining and oil/gas development), navigable waters (dam and river management), and easements (roads/power lines) will continue to threaten the mission of the System. Military overflights remain a problem in several refuges, and the Service has inadequate political clout to respond (Improvement Act, § 6(4)). An outright statutory prohibition on public uses other than wildlife-dependent recreation would resolve some of these issues with the political will and legal authority that the Service lacks. Other problems with divided jurisdiction will require revision of establishment instruments and real property acquisitions.

The boilerplate language in the Improvement Act exhorting the Service to coordinate with other property owners and agencies, and to encourage public participation, hardly promotes innovative collaboration. With the exception of the biological integrity, diversity, and environmental health policy provision on responding to external threats, the Service's implementation of the Act's tired language in this area has been unimaginative. Here is an opportunity where vigorous leadership within the Service can make a big difference for landscape-level conservation. Still, funding remains a tight constraint on creative collaboration.

Finally, the Improvement Act's priority for establishment purposes limits the legislation's ability to exert a strong centripetal force to unify the Refuge System. Though the act displays all of the hallmarks of modern organic legislation, it neglects to harmonize the underlying discord among the various units of the System. The fallacy of the "systemic" mandates is that they apply only where they do not conflict with establishment mandates. Congress should not allow widely variable establishment terms, some almost a century old, automatically to trump the unifying organic purpose of the Improvement Act. Some bargains struck to enact refuge establishment laws must be respected out of fairness and to provide ongoing incentives for new unit additions to the System. But Congress needs to commission a thorough study of the establishment instruments to determine which particular purposes and mandates continue to serve those aims and which merely reflect outdated views of the ecological value of refuges. Also, courts need to adopt rules of interpretation, like the one rejected in *Schwenke*, favoring systemic goals over individual refuge purposes in otherwise close cases (*Schwenke v. Secretary of the Interior* 1983).

The Refuge System as the Future of Public Land Conservation

Just as developments in the late 1960s and early 1970s heightened the standards for what qualified as an organic act, our experience with the 1997 Improvement Act should raise the bar even higher for a new round of revisions to legislation governing other public land systems. In particular, the 1997 Improvement Act substantially advances three of the five hallmarks of modern organic legislation: purpose statements, designated uses, and, most significantly, substantive management criteria.

The history of attempts to define the purpose of the Refuge System is a lesson in the evolution of how we as a society value nature. When President Franklin Roosevelt described the System in a 1940 proclamation standardizing the names of refuge units, he characterized the purpose in strict utilitarian terms: "conservation and development of the natural wildlife resources [so they] may contribute to the economic welfare of the Nation and provide opportunities for wholesome recreation" (Proclamation No. 2,416, 54 Stat. 2,717 [1940]). The 1966 Act explicitly added restoration to the mission of the consolidated system and dropped "development" (Pub. L. No. 89-669, § 1(a)). Though "development" was an important aspect of New Deal (and Progressive) era conservation, the term fell out of favor with the rise of the wilderness ethic in the mid-1960s. The 1968 Leopold committee report built on the 1966 mission in seeking to add "natural ecosystem" concerns to bolster the scientific basis of the systemic mission (Leopold et al. 1968, W-4). The 1996 executive order used the term "network of lands and waters" (Executive Order No. 12,996

§ 1) to highlight the interconnected ecological concerns of island bio-geography.

The 1997 statute retains a utilitarian tone (but phrased in more modern jargon), justifying conservation "for the benefit of present and future generations" (Improvement Act, § 4). But its definition of the mission connects strongly to conservation biology by explicitly incorporating "methods and procedures associated with modern scientific resource programs" (§ 5(4)). Broadening the purpose of the Refuge System to include plants transforms the mission from wildlife protection to true ecological conservation as we understand it today. It brings the Refuge System to the forefront of current ideas about how public lands best contribute to our welfare. The recent insights of ecological economics have clarified the great value to our economy of nature's services, such as pollination and nutrient cycling (Daily 1997; Fischman 2001).

The most important aspect of the "designated uses" hallmark manifested in the 1997 Improvement Act is the complex hierarchy of priorities. No other U.S. organic act establishes such an elaborate system of preferences. As implemented by the Service, a refuge manager cannot evaluate a use until first categorizing it to determine where it falls within the hierarchy. Under the System's use hierarchy, as illustrated in figure 6.1, the evaluation will vary depending on whether the use is an individual refuge purpose, conservation, wildlife-dependent recreation, a refuge management activity, an economic use, or some other use. In making management decisions on public lands, it is appropriate to discriminate among types of uses based on historical and cultural judgments. Also, categorical choices frequently enable managers to make progress toward goals without demanding an effects analysis that may be beyond the reasonable predictive powers of current science. This justification for categorical approaches over performance measures is particularly well developed in the pollution control area (Houck 1994).

However, the framework under the Improvement Act relies too much on categorical determinations and not enough on uniform performance standards. As a harbinger of revisions to other organic acts, the Improvement Act's hierarchy of uses is a troubling sign. The issue of properly categorizing uses is likely to generate many disputes and litigation that will divert attention from core conservation needs. An analogous pattern emerged in the implementation of the Resource Conservation and Recovery Act (RCRA) in pollution control law (42 U.S.C. §§ 6901–6992k). In RCRA, the categorization of a substance as both a solid and hazardous waste carries with it such important regulatory consequences that the EPA expends a great deal of implementation and enforcement effort merely on justifying categorical distinctions (Williams and Cannon 1991). The hierarchy of uses is simply too complex and the sorting task too unwieldly to serve as a promising model for other land management systems.

The single most important aspect of the 1997 Improvement Act is the level of statutory detail for substantive management criteria. This hallmark of modern organic legislation shows considerable movement toward increased congressional involvement in public land management. Though the 1976 National Forest Management Act (NFMA) still stands out as having the most detailed substantive management requirements for a single category of concern (timber management), the 1997 Improvement Act has a more broadly applicable array of detailed substantive congressional mandates.

The mandate to maintain biological integrity, diversity, and environmental health establishes a pathbreaking precedent for public land management. Congress now conditions even priority uses on the performance requirement that they not impair ecological elements and processes. This is an overdue statutory recognition that public lands play central roles in providing the ecosystem services, such as pollination, on which humans are utterly dependent. In this respect, the 1997 Act merely updates the long-standing public welfare rationale for conservation.

This bold mandate is also a recognition of the value of natural diversity and ecological health as ends in themselves, even if we cannot trace their direct benefit to our welfare. As a substantive management criterion supporting the Refuge System mission, this mandate reflects a change in the relative importance that the functioning of nature plays in our public land use decisions. The 2000 Forest Service attempt to effect this change through revisions to planning regulations is another indicator of this shift in thinking. The subsequent reversal of the regulatory reforms by the Bush administration illustrates the importance of establishing substantive criteria in statutes, which better resist backsliding.

The duty to acquire water rights for refuge purposes is also a significant precedent for making explicit the federal government's trust responsibility for public land resources. Rather than simply maintain current conditions or prevent harm, the Service now has an affirmative responsibility to seek water rights necessary to fulfill refuge purposes. This specific fiduciary obligation is important for two reasons. First, the issue of providing instream flows of water to maintain healthy ecosystems is particularly urgent given the junior and downstream circumstances of many refuges. Second, the duty to assert water rights has been the subject of heated debates over the public trust to protect federal lands. Therefore, Congress's decision to establish this explicit duty reflects a new assertiveness in organic legislation. It commands federal agencies to play a more active role in securing protection.

The more general conservation stewardship mandate is another (broader but weaker) provision reflecting the increased role of statutory trust language. The conservation stewardship mandate eliminates any question about the executive branch's prerogative to innovate for conservation on refuge lands. These fiduciary duties now align the refuges with other trust management systems, such as state school lands, private land trusts, and American Indian reservations.

The Refuge System's history tracks the development of conservation concerns in the United States. Early focus on hunting stock and migratory birds gradually shifted to broader endangered species protection. The Improvement Act continues the tradition of leadership of the Refuge System in biological conservation. Protections for animals have now expanded to include habitat and, ultimately, plants themselves. A park preserve attitude toward achieving conservation is giving way to the recognition that land reserves alone cannot maintain biological integrity, diversity, and environmental health; instead, the System must work outside as well as within its boundaries to create a network of lands and waters to achieve its conservation mission. Moreover, the Service interprets the Improvement Act to prohibit habitat fragmentation, a problem uncovered by conservation biologists to be a significant threat to ecological diversity.

Ultimately, the task of ecological conservation will require a change in the way we view private property. The compatibility principle, which favors some uses but allows a wide variety of activities so long as they do not materially interfere with or detract from conservation goals, can serve as a standard for public control of private land use in protective zones. Compatibility, along with the policy principles prohibiting habitat fragmentation and requiring coordination to respond to external threats, is a conservation tool that the federal government can demonstrate for the benefit of other jurisdictions struggling to achieve sustainable development.

In this respect, the Improvement Act establishes a management framework that will be helpful abroad. With the 1997 legislation, the Refuge System has become the premier public land conservation network applicable to other countries experimenting with ecological protection strategies. Although we in the United States tend to regard the National Park and National Wilderness Preservation Systems as the pinnacles of federal conservation, both these systems grew out of peculiarly American visions of monumental, pristine, uninhabited nature that are not widely shared by the rest of the world. In contrast, the Refuge System's mandate is founded on more globally accepted principles of ecology (biological integrity, diversity, and environmental health criteria) and sustainable development (permit uses compatible with the conservation mission). Therefore, the Refuge System deserves special attention and support as a model for international conservation. Existing international programs already recognize this aspect of refuge management through designations of parts of the System as biosphere reserves and wetlands of international importance.

The 2002 Johannesburg World Summit on Sustainable Development marked the tenth anniversary of an international commitment to promote economic prosperity in a manner that safeguards our natural heritage. Yet the United States has no national program for attaining sustainable development and no official criteria with which to measure progress. The National Wildlife Refuge System's operating principles, though not explicitly designed to fulfill our obligation to sustainable development, nonetheless offer a powerful case study in coordinated conservation management. Refuge management has the potential to serve as the United States' chief nonmonetary contribution to the advancement of sustainable development. The coming years will test whether organic legislation can orchestrate a national network of healthy ecosystems that coexist with a wide range of compatible uses.

APPENDIX A

A Chronology of Refuge System Development[1]

1869

Congress creates a national reservation (now part of the Alaska Maritime National Wildlife Refuge) in the Pribilof Islands, Alaska, to protect fur seals "more efficiently." The statute gives the secretary of the treasury authority to regulate use of the islands.

1885

A forerunner of the Fish and Wildlife Service, the Division of Economic Ornithology and Mammalogy, is established in the Department of Agriculture, with C. Hart Merriam as its first chief. Dr. Merriam leads the Division through its expansion and renaming as the Bureau of Biological Survey.

1892

President Benjamin Harrison designates Alaska's Afognak Island (now part of Kodiak National Wildlife Refuge) as a "fish cultural and forest reserve" under the 1891 General Revision Act. The reservation's purposes include protecting sea lions and sea otters.

1900

The Lacey Act marks the new era of federal regulation of wildlife trade. It prohibits the interstate transportation of animals killed in violation of state law.

1901

President William McKinley adds the Wichita Forest Reserve (now the Wichita Mountains National Wildlife Refuge) to the growing number of forest reserves created under the authority of the 1891 General Revision Act. But McKinley's designation makes no reference to wildlife conservation.

1903

President Theodore Roosevelt, with a presidential order citing no statutory authority, reserves Florida's Pelican Island as a "preserve and breeding ground for native birds." The proclamation gives the Department of Agriculture's Division of Biological Survey management authority. Pelican Island's first game warden, Paul Kroegel, is paid a salary of $1/month by the American Ornithologist's Union bird protection fund. Before leaving office in 1909, President Roosevelt sets aside another 51 Biological Survey reservations to protect wildlife. Roosevelt's Pelican Island reservation is generally recognized as the first unit of the National Wildlife Refuge System.

---

1. Sources include Fischman 2002; U.S. FWS 2001a; Gergeley et al. 2000.

1904

In his Annual Message to Congress, President Roosevelt urges legislators to authorize the reservation of public lands as game refuges for the preservation of the "bison, wapiti, and other large beasts once so abundant in our woods and mountains and on our great plains, and now tending toward extinction."

1905

Congress begins reserving lands that would become wildlife refuges, starting with the Wichita Mountain Forest in 1905 and followed by the National Bison Range in 1908 and the National Elk Refuge in 1912.

1906

Congress enacts the Game and Bird Preserves Protection Act (Refuge Trespass Act) to provide regulatory authority for managing uses on reservations administered by the Bureau of Biological Survey. The act makes it a misdemeanor to disturb birds or their eggs on federal wildlife reservations.

1907

As a result of intensive lobbying from noted wildlife photographer William L. Finley, President Theodore Roosevelt establishes Three Arch Rocks, Oregon, as the first federal bird reservation on the West Coast.

1908

Congressional establishment of the National Bison Range authorizes the first acquisition for a wildlife refuge.

1913

Congress enacts the first Migratory Bird Act, authorizing the federal government to regulate hunting of migratory birds. The law is later repealed as a result of the passage of the Migratory Bird Treaty Act of 1918.

1916

The United States signs the Convention between the United States and Great Britain (for Canada) for the Protection of Migratory Birds.

1918

Congress enacts the Migratory Bird Treaty Act, implementing new treaty obligations to sustain populations of certain birds. Fulfilling these obligations has been an important impetus for the creation of refuges ever since. The Act reauthorizes federal regulation of migratory bird hunting.

1924

Congress authorizes and funds the first migratory bird refuge, the Upper Mississippi River Wild Life and Fish Refuge. The refuge is also the first explicitly to include plants ("wild flowers and aquatic plants") as resources to be protected in and of themselves, rather than merely as habitat for animals. Plant protection would remain absent from other establishment documents until the 1970s.

1929

Congress enacts the Migratory Bird Conservation Act, authorizing the ongoing purchase of lands to serve as "inviolate sanctuaries" for waterfowl. This is the single most commonly used authority for creating new refuges.

1934

President Franklin Roosevelt appoints the Committee on Wild-Life Restoration. Its members, Thomas H. Beck (chairman), Jay Norwood "Ding" Darling, and Aldo Leopold, prepare a report for the secretary of agriculture recommending an aggressive program to acquire lands for waterfowl; upland game; mammals; and song, insectivorous, and ornamental birds. The report further recommends that $50 million be earmarked for acquisition and habitat restoration projects.

1934

Congress enacts the Migratory Bird Hunting Stamp Act, creating a dedicated fund for acquiring waterfowl refuges under the Migratory Bird Conservation Act from the sales of federal stamps that all waterfowl hunters must affix to their state hunting licenses. The law, therefore, is commonly called the Duck Stamp Act. Ninety percent of the duck stamp fund revenues were earmarked for acquisition of habitat and the remainder for refuge management. Since 1934, the federal government has collected more than $500 million from duck stamp sales.

1939

President Franklin Roosevelt reorganizes federal agencies, transferring the Bureaus of Biological Survey and Fisheries from the Departments of Agriculture and Commerce, respectively, to the Department of the Interior.

1940

President Franklin Roosevelt creates the Fish and Wildlife Service by combining the Bureaus of Biological Survey and Fisheries. Roosevelt appoints Ira N. Gabrielson as its first director.

1940

President Franklin Roosevelt consolidates many units of the System by changing the name of 193 reservations to "refuges," where it is "unlawful to hunt, trap, capture, willfully disturb, or kill any bird or wild animal . . . or to enter thereon for any purpose, except as permitted by law or by rules and regulations of the Secretary of the Interior."

1942

The Fish and Wildlife Service publishes the first edition of its refuge *Manual,* providing national policies and guidelines for managing national wildlife refuges.

1949

Congress increases the price of duck stamps and allows up to 25 percent of "inviolate sanctuary" refuges to be designated as "wildlife management areas" upon which public waterfowl hunting may occur.

1956

Congress enacts the Fish and Wildlife Act, which purports to "establish" the Fish and Wildlife Service, even though the Service had been in existence for 16 years. The act does give the Service a much broader scope of authority to acquire refuges than it had before.

1958

Congress authorizes another increase in the price of duck stamps and allows up to 40 percent of "inviolate sanctuaries" to be opened to hunting. The legislation also permits the secretary of the interior to use duck stamp proceeds to purchase not only "inviolate sanctuary" refuges, but also "waterfowl production area" refuges, which are not subject to any limit on the areas open to hunting.

1962

Congress enacts the Refuge Recreation Act, limiting all approved refuge recreation activities to those that are compatible with refuge purposes and those for which adequate funding exists for proper management.

1964

Congress enacts the Wilderness Act, creating an overlay National Wilderness Preservation System. The Refuge System now contains over 20 million acres of wilderness areas.

1966

Congress enacts the National Wildlife Refuge System Administration Act, consolidating all of the Fish and Wildlife Service conservation lands into a "National Wildlife Refuge System." The act also provided the first comprehensive management mandate for the Refuge System, borrowing the compatibility principle from the 1962 Refuge Recreation Act.

1968

Congress enacts the Wild and Scenic Rivers Act, creating an overlay National Wild and Scenic Rivers System. The Refuge System now contains over 1,400 miles of wild and scenic rivers.

1968

The Interior Department's advisory committee for the Refuge System, chaired by A. Starker Leopold, proposes adding a "natural ecosystem" component to refuge management.

1971

Congress enacts the Alaska Native Claims Settlement Act authorizing Alaska Natives to select and receive 44 million acres of public land in the state. The act allows limited selection of lands from existing national wildlife refuges and authorizes withdrawals from Bureau of Land Management lands to make up for the loss to the System.

1972

Congress establishes the Tinicum National Environmental Center for a number of purposes, including protection of "ecological features," which include plant communities. This marks the first use of the term "ecological" to define a refuge purpose.

1972

Congress establishes the San Francisco Bay National Wildlife Refuge for a number of purposes, including wildlife-oriented recreation and environmental education. This marks the first time these two activities are included as purposes, rather than permitted activities, in a refuge establishment document.

1973

Congress enacts a new Endangered Species Act to conserve "ecosystems upon which endangered species and threatened species depend." Today, 56 national wildlife refuges have been established to protect various threatened and endangered species.

1976

Congress transfers jurisdiction of "game ranges" to the Fish and Wildlife Service and requires congressional approval to dispose of any refuge units.

1980

Congress enacts the Alaska National Interest Lands Conservation Act, adding 54 million acres of land to the Refuge System, tripling its size. The act also establishes the precedent, followed in the 1997 Improvement Act, of prioritizing refuge purposes and of requiring comprehensive refuge planning.

1981

A General Accounting Office report concludes that "local pressures to use refuge lands for such benefits as grazing, timber harvesting, and public recreation prevent refuge managers from effectively managing refuges primarily for wildlife." The report also criticizes the service for failing to update the refuge *Manual,* which provides guidance and operating procedures for managers.

1986

The Service revises its *Manual* to provide compatibility determination guidelines for refuge managers; however, incompatible uses continue to cause serious problems for refuge conservation.

1989

A General Accounting Office report documents the failure of the Service to combat the proliferation of incompatible uses despite continual warnings over the previous two decades. The report states that secondary uses occur on 92 percent of the refuges and impede conservation goals on 59 percent of the refuges.

1990

Rep. Gerry Studds introduces H.R. 4948 to reform management of the Refuge System in response to the problem of incompatible uses. Similar reform bills would be introduced in every subsequent Congress until the passage of the Improvement Act in 1997.

1992

Several environmental groups sue the federal government for allowing incompatible activities on refuges that harm fish, wildlife, and habitat. The lawsuit settles the following year with an agreement by the Fish and Wildlife Service to provide written determinations of: which uses in the System are compatible with the primary purposes of the refuges on which they are occurring, and the availability of funds for managing recreational uses. The Service promises to end incompatible uses.

1993

The Canaan Valley National Wildlife Refuge in West Virginia becomes the 500th unit of the National Wildlife Refuge System.

1994

A Fish and Wildlife Service study confirms the findings of the 1989 General Accounting Office report documenting serious problems with incompatible uses in refuges.

1996

President Clinton issues an executive order reforming management of the Refuge System. The order provides an ecological conservation mission that includes plant protection and establishes a hierarchy of use preferences. Hunting, although preferred, is nonetheless subordinate to ecological conservation. The terms of the executive order are subsequently mirrored in the 1997 Improvement Act.

1997

Congress enacts the National Wildlife Refuge System Improvement Act endorsing the ecological conservation mission established in the Clinton executive order. It also establishes a hierarchy of use preferences favoring wildlife-dependent recreational uses, mandates periodic refuge planning, requires written determinations of compatibility, and imposes a number of substantive management criteria for refuges. Among the new substantive management criteria is a requirement that the Service ensure the maintenance of "biological integrity, diversity, and environmental health."

2003

The Refuge System commemorates the centennial of the establishment of the first refuge, Pelican Island.

APPENDIX B

Relevant Statutes

PUBLIC LAW 105-57—OCT. 9, 1997
111 Stat. 1252
codified at 16 U.S.C. §§ 668dd, 668ee

NATIONAL WILDLIFE REFUGE SYSTEM
IMPROVEMENT ACT OF 1997

Public Law 105–57
105th Congress

An Act

Oct. 9, 1997
[H.R. 1420]

To amend the National Wildlife Refuge System Administration Act of 1966 to improve the management of the National Wildlife Refuge System, and for other purposes.

Be it enacted by the Senate and House of Representatives of the United States of America in Congress assembled,

National Wildlife
Refuge System
Improvement Act
of 1997.
16 USC 668dd
note.

SECTION 1. SHORT TITLE; REFERENCES.

(a) SHORT TITLE.—This Act may be cited as the "National Wildlife Refuge System Improvement Act of 1997".

(b) REFERENCES.—Whenever in this Act an amendment or repeal is expressed in terms of an amendment to, or repeal of, a section or other provision, the reference shall be considered to be made to a section or provision of the National Wildlife Refuge System Administration Act of 1966 (16 U.S.C. 668dd et seq.).

16 USC 668dd
note.

SEC. 2. FINDINGS.

The Congress finds the following:

(1) The National Wildlife Refuge System is comprised of over 92,000,000 acres of Federal lands that have been incorporated within 509 individual units located in all 50 States and the territories of the United States.

(2) The System was created to conserve fish, wildlife, and plants and their habitats and this conservation mission has been facilitated by providing Americans opportunities to participate in compatible wildlife-dependent recreation, including fishing and hunting, on System lands and to better appreciate the value of and need for fish and wildlife conservation.

(3) The System serves a pivotal role in the conservation of migratory birds, anadromous and interjurisdictional fish, marine mammals, endangered and threatened species, and the habitats on which these species depend.

(4) The System assists in the fulfillment of important international treaty obligations of the United States with regard to fish, wildlife, and plants and their habitats.

(5) The System includes lands purchased not only through the use of tax dollars but also through the proceeds from sales of Duck Stamps and national wildlife refuge entrance fees. It is a System that is financially supported by those benefiting from and utilizing it.

(6) When managed in accordance with principles of sound fish and wildlife management and administration, fishing, hunting, wildlife observation, and environmental education in national wildlife refuges have been and are expected to continue to be generally compatible uses.

PUBLIC LAW 105–57—OCT. 9, 1997   111 STAT. 1253

(7) On March 25, 1996, the President issued Executive Order 12996, which recognized "compatible wildlife-dependent recreational uses involving hunting, fishing, wildlife observation and photography, and environmental education and interpretation as priority public uses of the Refuge System".

(8) Executive Order 12996 is a positive step and serves as the foundation for the permanent statutory changes made by this Act.

SEC. 3. DEFINITIONS.

(a) IN GENERAL.—Section 5 (16 U.S.C. 668ee) is amended to read as follows:

"SEC. 5. DEFINITIONS.

"For purposes of this Act:

"(1) The term 'compatible use' means a wildlife-dependent recreational use or any other use of a refuge that, in the sound professional judgment of the Director, will not materially interfere with or detract from the fulfillment of the mission of the System or the purposes of the refuge.

"(2) The terms 'wildlife-dependent recreation' and 'wildlife-dependent recreational use' mean a use of a refuge involving hunting, fishing, wildlife observation and photography, or environmental education and interpretation.

"(3) The term 'sound professional judgment' means a finding, determination, or decision that is consistent with principles of sound fish and wildlife management and administration, available science and resources, and adherence to the requirements of this Act and other applicable laws.

"(4) The terms 'conserving', 'conservation', 'manage', 'managing', and 'management', mean to sustain and, where appropriate, restore and enhance, healthy populations of fish, wildlife, and plants utilizing, in accordance with applicable Federal and State laws, methods and procedures associated with modern scientific resource programs. Such methods and procedures include, consistent with the provisions of this Act, protection, research, census, law enforcement, habitat management, propagation, live trapping and transplantation, and regulated taking.

"(5) The term 'Coordination Area' means a wildlife management area that is made available to a State—

"(A) by cooperative agreement between the United States Fish and Wildlife Service and a State agency having control over wildlife resources pursuant to section 4 of the Fish and Wildlife Coordination Act (16 U.S.C. 664); or

"(B) by long-term leases or agreements pursuant to title III of the Bankhead-Jones Farm Tenant Act (50 Stat. 525; 7 U.S.C. 1010 et seq.).

"(6) The term 'Director' means the Director of the United States Fish and Wildlife Service or a designee of that Director.

"(7) The terms 'fish', 'wildlife', and 'fish and wildlife' mean any wild member of the animal kingdom whether alive or dead, and regardless of whether the member was bred, hatched, or born in captivity, including a part, product, egg, or offspring of the member.

"(8) The term 'person' means any individual, partnership, corporation, or association.

"(9) The term 'plant' means any member of the plant kingdom in a wild, unconfined state, including any plant community, seed, root, or other part of a plant.

"(10) The terms 'purposes of the refuge' and 'purposes of each refuge' mean the purposes specified in or derived from the law, proclamation, executive order, agreement, public land order, donation document, or administrative memorandum establishing, authorizing, or expanding a refuge, refuge unit, or refuge subunit.

"(11) The term 'refuge' means a designated area of land, water, or an interest in land or water within the System, but does not include Coordination Areas.

"(12) The term 'Secretary' means the Secretary of the Interior.

"(13) The terms 'State' and 'United States' mean the several States of the United States, Puerto Rico, American Samoa, the Virgin Islands, Guam, and the territories and possessions of the United States.

"(14) The term 'System' means the National Wildlife Refuge System designated under section 4(a)(1).

"(15) The terms 'take', 'taking', and 'taken' mean to pursue, hunt, shoot, capture, collect, or kill, or to attempt to pursue, hunt, shoot, capture, collect, or kill.".

(b) CONFORMING AMENDMENT.—Section 4 (16 U.S.C. 668dd) is amended by striking "Secretary of the Interior" each place it appears and inserting "Secretary".

SEC. 4. MISSION OF THE SYSTEM.

Section 4(a) (16 U.S.C. 668dd(a)) is amended—

(1) by redesignating paragraphs (2) and (3) as paragraphs (5) and (6), respectively;

(2) in clause (i) of paragraph (6) (as so redesignated), by striking "paragraph (2)" and inserting "paragraph (5)"; and

(3) by inserting after paragraph (1) the following new paragraph:

"(2) The mission of the System is to administer a national network of lands and waters for the conservation, management, and where appropriate, restoration of the fish, wildlife, and plant resources and their habitats within the United States for the benefit of present and future generations of Americans.".

SEC. 5. ADMINISTRATION OF THE SYSTEM.

(a) ADMINISTRATION GENERALLY.—Section 4(a) (16 U.S.C. 668dd(a)), as amended by section 4 of this Act, is further amended by inserting after new paragraph (2) the following new paragraphs:

"(3) With respect to the System, it is the policy of the United States that—

"(A) each refuge shall be managed to fulfill the mission of the System, as well as the specific purposes for which that refuge was established;

"(B) compatible wildlife-dependent recreation is a legitimate and appropriate general public use of the System, directly related to the mission of the System and the purposes of many refuges, and which generally fosters refuge management and through which the American public can develop an appreciation for fish and wildlife;

"(C) compatible wildlife-dependent recreational uses are the priority general public uses of the System and shall receive priority consideration in refuge planning and management; and

"(D) when the Secretary determines that a proposed wildlife-dependent recreational use is a compatible use within a refuge, that activity should be facilitated, subject to such restrictions or regulations as may be necessary, reasonable, and appropriate.

"(4) In administering the System, the Secretary shall—

"(A) provide for the conservation of fish, wildlife, and plants, and their habitats within the System;

"(B) ensure that the biological integrity, diversity, and environmental health of the System are maintained for the benefit of present and future generations of Americans;

"(C) plan and direct the continued growth of the System in a manner that is best designed to accomplish the mission of the System, to contribute to the conservation of the ecosystems of the United States, to complement efforts of States and other Federal agencies to conserve fish and wildlife and their habitats, and to increase support for the System and participation from conservation partners and the public;

"(D) ensure that the mission of the System described in paragraph (2) and the purposes of each refuge are carried out, except that if a conflict exists between the purposes of a refuge and the mission of the System, the conflict shall be resolved in a manner that first protects the purposes of the refuge, and, to the extent practicable, that also achieves the mission of the System;

"(E) ensure effective coordination, interaction, and coopera- tion with owners of land adjoining refuges and the fish and wildlife agency of the States in which the units of the System are located;

"(F) assist in the maintenance of adequate water quantity and water quality to fulfill the mission of the System and the purposes of each refuge;

"(G) acquire, under State law, water rights that are needed for refuge purposes;

"(H) recognize compatible wildlife-dependent recreational uses as the priority general public uses of the System through which the American public can develop an appreciation for fish and wildlife;

"(I) ensure that opportunities are provided within the System for compatible wildlife-dependent recreational uses;

"(J) ensure that priority general public uses of the System receive enhanced consideration over other general public uses in planning and management within the System;

"(K) provide increased opportunities for families to experi- ence compatible wildlife-dependent recreation, particularly opportunities for parents and their children to safely engage in traditional outdoor activities, such as fishing and hunting;

"(L) continue, consistent with existing laws and interagency agreements, authorized or permitted uses of units of the System by other Federal agencies, including those necessary to facilitate military preparedness;

"(M) ensure timely and effective cooperation and collabora- tion with Federal agencies and State fish and wildlife agencies during the course of acquiring and managing refuges; and

111 STAT. 1256   PUBLIC LAW 105-57—OCT. 9, 1997

"(N) monitor the status and trends of fish, wildlife, and plants in each refuge.".

(b) POWERS.—Section 4(b) (16 U.S.C. 668dd(b)) is amended—

(1) in the matter preceding paragraph (1) by striking "authorized—" and inserting "authorized to take the following actions:";

(2) in paragraph (1) by striking "to enter" and inserting "Enter";

(3) in paragraph (2)—

(A) by striking "to accept" and inserting "Accept"; and

(B) by striking ", and" and inserting a period;

(4) in paragraph (3) by striking "to acquire" and inserting "Acquire"; and

(5) by adding at the end the following new paragraphs:

"(4) Subject to standards established by and the overall management oversight of the Director, and consistent with standards established by this Act, to enter into cooperative agreements with State fish and wildlife agencies for the management of programs on a refuge.

Regulations.

"(5) Issue regulations to carry out this Act.".

SEC. 6. COMPATIBILITY STANDARDS AND PROCEDURES.

Section 4(d) (16 U.S.C. 668dd(d)) is amended by adding at the end the following new paragraphs:

"(3)(A)(i) Except as provided in clause (iv), the Secretary shall not initiate or permit a new use of a refuge or expand, renew, or extend an existing use of a refuge, unless the Secretary has determined that the use is a compatible use and that the use is not inconsistent with public safety. The Secretary may make the determinations referred to in this paragraph for a refuge concurrently with development of a conservation plan under subsection (e).

"(ii) On lands added to the System after March 25, 1996, the Secretary shall identify, prior to acquisition, withdrawal, transfer, reclassification, or donation of any such lands, existing compatible wildlife-dependent recreational uses that the Secretary determines shall be permitted to continue on an interim basis pending completion of the comprehensive conservation plan for the refuge.

"(iii) Wildlife-dependent recreational uses may be authorized on a refuge when they are compatible and not inconsistent with public safety. Except for consideration of consistency with State laws and regulations as provided for in subsection (m), no other determinations or findings are required to be made by the refuge official under this Act or the Refuge Recreation Act for wildlife-dependent recreation to occur.

"(iv) Compatibility determinations in existence on the date of enactment of the National Wildlife Refuge System Improvement Act of 1997 shall remain in effect until and unless modified.

Regulations.

"(B) Not later than 24 months after the date of the enactment of the National Wildlife Refuge System Improvement Act of 1997, the Secretary shall issue final regulations establishing the process for determining under subparagraph (A) whether a use of a refuge is a compatible use. These regulations shall—

"(i) designate the refuge official responsible for making initial compatibility determinations;

"(ii) require an estimate of the timeframe, location, manner, and purpose of each use;

PUBLIC LAW 105–57—OCT. 9, 1997   111 STAT. 1257

"(iii) identify the effects of each use on refuge resources and purposes of each refuge;

"(iv) require that compatibility determinations be made in writing;

"(v) provide for the expedited consideration of uses that will likely have no detrimental effect on the fulfillment of the purposes of a refuge or the mission of the System;

"(vi) provide for the elimination or modification of any use as expeditiously as practicable after a determination is made that the use is not a compatible use;

"(vii) require, after an opportunity for public comment, reevaluation of each existing use, other than those uses specified in clause (viii), if conditions under which the use is permitted change significantly or if there is significant new information regarding the effects of the use, but not less frequently than once every 10 years, to ensure that the use remains a compatible use, except that, in the case of any use authorized for a period longer than 10 years (such as an electric utility right-of-way), the reevaluation required by this clause shall examine compliance with the terms and conditions of the authorization, not examine the authorization itself;

"(viii) require, after an opportunity for public comment, reevaluation of each compatible wildlife-dependent recreational use when conditions under which the use is permitted change significantly or if there is significant new information regarding the effects of the use, but not less frequently than in conjunction with each preparation or revision of a conservation plan under subsection (e) or at least every 15 years, whichever is earlier; and

"(ix) provide an opportunity for public review and comment on each evaluation of a use, unless an opportunity for public review and comment on the evaluation of the use has already been provided during the development or revision of a conservation plan for the refuge under subsection (e) or has otherwise been provided during routine, periodic determinations of compatibility for wildlife-dependent recreational uses.   Public information.

"(4) The provisions of this Act relating to determinations of the compatibility of a use shall not apply to—

"(A) overflights above a refuge; and

"(B) activities authorized, funded, or conducted by a Federal agency (other than the United States Fish and Wildlife Service) which has primary jurisdiction over a refuge or a portion of a refuge, if the management of those activities is in accordance with a memorandum of understanding between the Secretary or the Director and the head of the Federal agency with primary jurisdiction over the refuge governing the use of the refuge.".

SEC. 7. REFUGE CONSERVATION PLANNING PROGRAM.

(a) IN GENERAL.—Section 4 (16 U.S.C. 668dd) is amended—

(1) by redesignating subsections (e) through (i) as subsections (f) through (j), respectively; and

(2) by inserting after subsection (d) the following new subsection:

"(e)(1)(A) Except with respect to refuge lands in Alaska (which shall be governed by the refuge planning provisions of the Alaska National Interest Lands Conservation Act (16 U.S.C. 3101 et seq.)), the Secretary shall—

Federal Register,
publication.

"(i) propose a comprehensive conservation plan for each refuge or related complex of refuges (referred to in this subsection as a 'planning unit') in the System;

"(ii) publish a notice of opportunity for public comment in the Federal Register on each proposed conservation plan;

"(iii) issue a final conservation plan for each planning unit consistent with the provisions of this Act and, to the extent practicable, consistent with fish and wildlife conservation plans of the State in which the refuge is located; and

"(iv) not less frequently than 15 years after the date of issuance of a conservation plan under clause (iii) and every 15 years thereafter, revise the conservation plan as may be necessary.

"(B) The Secretary shall prepare a comprehensive conservation plan under this subsection for each refuge within 15 years after the date of enactment of the National Wildlife Refuge System Improvement Act of 1997.

"(C) The Secretary shall manage each refuge or planning unit under plans in effect on the date of enactment of the National Wildlife Refuge System Improvement Act of 1997, to the extent such plans are consistent with this Act, until such plans are revised or superseded by new comprehensive conservation plans issued under this subsection.

"(D) Uses or activities consistent with this Act may occur on any refuge or planning unit before existing plans are revised or new comprehensive conservation plans are issued under this subsection.

"(E) Upon completion of a comprehensive conservation plan under this subsection for a refuge or planning unit, the Secretary shall manage the refuge or planning unit in a manner consistent with the plan and shall revise the plan at any time if the Secretary determines that conditions that affect the refuge or planning unit have changed significantly.

"(2) In developing each comprehensive conservation plan under this subsection for a planning unit, the Secretary, acting through the Director, shall identify and describe—

"(A) the purposes of each refuge comprising the planning unit;

"(B) the distribution, migration patterns, and abundance of fish, wildlife, and plant populations and related habitats within the planning unit;

"(C) the archaeological and cultural values of the planning unit;

"(D) such areas within the planning unit that are suitable for use as administrative sites or visitor facilities;

"(E) significant problems that may adversely affect the populations and habitats of fish, wildlife, and plants within the planning unit and the actions necessary to correct or mitigate such problems; and

"(F) opportunities for compatible wildlife-dependent recreational uses.

"(3) In preparing each comprehensive conservation plan under this subsection, and any revision to such a plan, the Secretary, acting through the Director, shall, to the maximum extent practicable and consistent with this Act—

"(A) consult with adjoining Federal, State, local, and private landowners and affected State conservation agencies; and

"(B) coordinate the development of the conservation plan or revision with relevant State conservation plans for fish and wildlife and their habitats.

"(4)(A) In accordance with subparagraph (B), the Secretary shall develop and implement a process to ensure an opportunity for active public involvement in the preparation and revision of comprehensive conservation plans under this subsection. At a minimum, the Secretary shall require that publication of any final plan shall include a summary of the comments made by States, owners of adjacent or potentially affected land, local governments, and any other affected persons, and a statement of the disposition of concerns expressed in those comments.

"(B) Prior to the adoption of each comprehensive conservation plan under this subsection, the Secretary shall issue public notice of the draft proposed plan, make copies of the plan available at the affected field and regional offices of the United States Fish and Wildlife Service, and provide opportunity for public comment.".

SEC. 8. EMERGENCY POWER; STATE AUTHORITY; WATER RIGHTS; COORDINATION.

(a) IN GENERAL.—Section 4 (16 U.S.C. 668dd) is further amended by adding at the end the following new subsections:

"(k) Notwithstanding any other provision of this Act, the Secretary may temporarily suspend, allow, or initiate any activity in a refuge in the System if the Secretary determines it is necessary to protect the health and safety of the public or any fish or wildlife population.

"(l) Nothing in this Act shall be construed to authorize the Secretary to control or regulate hunting or fishing of fish and resident wildlife on lands or waters that are not within the System.

"(m) Nothing in this Act shall be construed as affecting the authority, jurisdiction, or responsibility of the several States to manage, control, or regulate fish and resident wildlife under State law or regulations in any area within the System. Regulations permitting hunting or fishing of fish and resident wildlife within the System shall be, to the extent practicable, consistent with State fish and wildlife laws, regulations, and management plans.

"(n)(1) Nothing in this Act shall—

"(A) create a reserved water right, express or implied, in the United States for any purpose;

"(B) affect any water right in existence on the date of enactment of the National Wildlife Refuge System Improvement Act of 1997; or

"(C) affect any Federal or State law in existence on the date of the enactment of the National Wildlife Refuge System Improvement Act of 1997 regarding water quality or water quantity.

"(2) Nothing in this Act shall diminish or affect the ability to join the United States in the adjudication of rights to the use of water pursuant to the McCarran Act (43 U.S.C. 666).

"(o) Coordination with State fish and wildlife agency personnel or with personnel of other affected State agencies pursuant to this Act shall not be subject to the Federal Advisory Committee Act (5 U.S.C. App.).".

(b) CONFORMING AMENDMENT.—Section 4(c) (16 U.S.C. 668dd(c)) is amended by striking the last sentence.

111 STAT. 1260   PUBLIC LAW 105–57—OCT. 9, 1997

16 USC 668dd
note. **SEC. 9. STATUTORY CONSTRUCTION WITH RESPECT TO ALASKA.**

(a) IN GENERAL.—Nothing in this Act is intended to affect—

(1) the provisions for subsistence uses in Alaska set forth in the Alaska National Interest Lands Conservation Act (Public Law 96–487), including those in titles III and VIII of that Act;

(2) the provisions of section 102 of the Alaska National Interest Lands Conservation Act, the jurisdiction over subsistence uses in Alaska, or any assertion of subsistence uses in Alaska in the Federal courts; and

(3) the manner in which section 810 of the Alaska National Interest Lands Conservation Act is implemented in national wildlife refuges in Alaska.

(b) CONFLICTS OF LAWS.—If any conflict arises between any provision of this Act and any provision of the Alaska National Interest Lands Conservation Act, then the provision in the Alaska National Interest Lands Conservation Act shall prevail.

Approved October 9, 1997.

PUBLIC LAW 89-669—OCT. 15, 1966
80 Stat. 926
codified at 16 U.S.C. §§ 668dd, 668ee

NATIONAL WILDLIFE REFUGE SYSTEM
ADMINISTRATION ACT OF 1966

926   PUBLIC LAW 89-669—OCT. 15, 1966   [80 STAT.

Public Law 89-669

October 15, 1966
[H.R. 9424]

AN ACT

To provide for the conservation, protection, and propagation of native species of fish and wildlife, including migratory birds, that are threatened with extinction; to consolidate the authorities relating to the administration by the Secretary of the Interior of the National Wildlife Refuge System; and for other purposes.

Be it enacted by the Senate and House of Representatives of the United States of America in Congress assembles, That (a) the Congress finds and declares that one of the unfortunate consequences of growth and development in the United States has been the extermination of some native species of fish and wildlife; that serious losses in other species of native wild animals with educational, historical, recreational, and scientific value have occurred and are occurring; and that the United States has pledged itself, pursuant to migratory bird treaties with Canada and Mexico and the Convention on Nature Protection and Wildlife Preservation in the Western Hemisphere, to conserve and protect, where practicable, the various species of native fish and wildlife, including game and nongame migratory birds, that are threatened with extinction. The purposes of this Act are to provide a program for the conservation, protection, restoration, and propagation of selected species of native fish and wildlife, including migratory birds, that are threatened with extinction, and to consolidate, restate, and modify the present authorities relating to administration by the Secretary of the Interior of the National Wildlife Refuge System.

(b) It is further declared to be the policy of Congress that the Secretary of the Interior, the Secretary of Agriculture, and the Secretary of Defense, together with the heads of bureaus, agencies, and services within their departments, shall seek to protect species of native fish and wildlife, including migratory birds, that are threatened with extinction, and, insofar as is practicable and consistent with the primary purposes of such bureaus, agencies, and services, shall preserve the habitats of such threatened species on lands under their jurisdiction.

(c) A species of native fish and wildlife shall be regarded as threatened with extinction whenever the Secretary of the Interior finds, after consultation with the affected States, that its existence is endangered because its habitat is threatened with destruction, drastic modification, or severe curtailment, or because of overexploitation, disease, predation, or because of other factors, and that its survival requires assistance. In addition to consulting with the States, the Secretary shall, from time to time, seek the advice and recommendations of interested persons and organizations including, but not limited to, ornithologists, ichthyologists, ecologists, herpetologists, and mammalogists. He shall publish in the Federal Register the names of the species of native fish and wildlife found to be threatened with extinction in accordance with this paragraph.

SEC. 2. (a) The Secretary of the Interior shall utilize the land acquisition and other authorities of the Migratory Bird Conservation Act, as amended, the Fish and Wildlife Act of 1956, as amended, and the Fish and Wildlife Coordination Act to carry out a program in the United States of conserving, protecting, restoring, and propagating selected species of native fish and wildlife that are threatened with extinction.

Fish and wildlife. Conservation and protection.

39 Stat. 1702; 50 Stat. 1311. 56 Stat. 1354.

Endangered species.

Publication in Federal Register.

45 Stat. 1222; 70 Stat. 1119; 60 Stat. 1080. 16 USC 715, 742a note, 661 note.

(b) In addition to the land acquisition authorities in such Acts, the Secretary is hereby authorized to acquire by purchase, donation, or otherwise, lands or interests therein needed to carry out the purpose of this Act relating to the conservation, protection, restoration, and propagation of selected species of native fish that are threatened With extinction.

(c) Funds made available pursuant to the Land and Water Conservation Fund Act of 1965 (78 Stat. 897) may be used for the purpose of acquiring lands, waters, or interests therein pursuant to this section that are needed for the purpose of conserving, protecting, restoring, and propagating selected species of native fish and wildlife, including migratory birds, that are threatened with extinction. Not to exceed $5,000,000 may be appropriated annually pursuant to that Act for such purpose for any fiscal year, and the total sum appropriated for such purpose shall not exceed $15,000,000: *Provided,* That the Secretary shall, to the greatest extent possible, utilize funds from the Land and Water Conservation Fund Act of 1965 for such purpose. Such sums shall remain available until expended. The Secretary shall not use more than $750,000 to acquire lands, waters, or interests therein for any one area for such purpose unless authorized by Act of Congress.

16 USC 460l-4 note.

(d) The Secretary shall review other programs administered by him and, to the extent practicable, utilize such programs in furtherance of the purpose of this Act. The Secretary shall also encourage other Federal agencies to utilize, where practicable, their authorities in furtherance of the purpose of this Act and shall consult with and assist such agencies in carrying out endangered species program.

Sec. 3.(a) In carrying out the program authorized by this Act, the Secretary shall cooperate to the maximum extent practicable with the several States. Such cooperation shall include consultation before the acquisition of any land for the purpose of conserving, protecting, restoring, or propagating any endangered species of native fish and wildlife.

Cooperation with States.

(b) The Secretary may enter into agreements with the States for the administration and management of any area established for the conservation, protection, restoration, and propagation of endangered species of native fish and wildlife. Any revenues derived from the administration of such areas under these agreements shall be subject to the provisions of section 401 of the Act of June 15, 1935 (49 Stat. 383), as amended (16 U.S.C. 715s).

Sec. 4. (a) For the purpose of consolidating the authorities relating to the various categories of areas that are administered by the Secretary of the Interior for the conservation of fish and wildlife, including species that are threatened with extinction, all lands, waters, and interests therein administered by the Secretary as wildlife refuges, areas for the protection and conservation of fish and wildlife that are threatened With extinction, wildlife ranges, game ranges, wildlife management areas, or waterfowl production areas are hereby designated as the "National Wildlife Refuge System" (referred to herein as the "System"), which shall be subject to the provisions of the section. Nothing contained in this Act shall restrict the authority of the Secretary to modify or revoke public land withdrawals affecting lands in the System as presently constituted, or as it may be constituted, whenever he determines that such action is consistent with the public interest.

78 Stat. 701. "National Wildlife Refuge System."

(b) In administering the System, the Secretary is authorized—

Administration.

    (1) to enter into contracts with any person or public or private agency through negotiation for the provision of public accommodations when, and in such locations, and to the extent that the Secretary

determines will not be inconsistent with the primary purpose for which the affected area was established.

(2) to accept donations of funds and to use such funds to acquire or manage lands or interests therein, and

(3) to acquire lands or interests therein by exchange (a) for acquired lands or public lands under his jurisdiction which he finds suitable for disposition, or (b) for the right to remove, in accordance with such terms and conditions as the Secretary may prescribe, products from the acquired or public lands within the System. The values of the properties so exchanged either shall be approximately equal, or if they are not approximately equal the values shall be equalized by the payment of cash to the grantor or to the Secretary as the circumstances require.

Prohibited activities.

(c) No person shall knowingly disturb, injure, cut, burn, remove, destroy, or possess any real or personal property of the United States, including natural growth, in any area of the System; or take or possess any fish, bird, mammal, or other wild vertebrate or invertebrate animals or part or nest or egg thereof within any such area; or enter, use, or otherwise occupy any such area for any purpose; unless such activities are performed by persons authorized to manage such area, or unless such activities are permitted either under subsection (d) of this section or by express provision of the law, proclamation, Executive order, or public land order establishing the area, or amendment thereof: *Provided,* That the United States mining and mineral leasing laws shall continue to apply to any lands within the System to the same extent they apply prior to the effective date of this Act unless subsequently withdrawn under other authority of law. Nothing in this Act shall be construed to authorize the Secretary to control or regulate hunting or fishing of resident fish and wildlife, including endangered species thereof, on lands not within the System. The regulations permitting hunting and fishing of resident fish and wildlife within the System shall be, to the extent practicable, consistent with State fish and wildlife laws and regulations. The provisions of this Act shall not be construed as affecting the authority, jurisdiction, or responsibility of the several States to manage, control, or regulate fish and resident wildlife under State law or regulations in any area within the System.

Use of areas.

(d) The Secretary is authorized, under such regulations as he may prescribe, to—

(1) permit the use of any area within the System for any purpose, including but not limited to hunting, fishing, public recreation and accommodations, and access whenever he determines that such uses are compatible with the major purposes for which such areas were areas were established: *Provided,* That not to exceed 40 per centum at any one time of any area that has been, or hereafter may be acquired, reserved, or set apart as an inviolate sanctuary for migratory birds, under any law, proclamation, Executive order, or public land order may be administered by the Secretary as an area within which the taking of migratory game birds may be permitted under such regulations as he may prescribe; and

(2) permit the use of, or grant easements in, over, across, upon, through, or under any areas within the System for purposes such as but not necessarily limited to, powerlines, telephone lines, canals, ditches, pipelines, and roads, including the construction, operation, and maintenance thereof, whenever he determines that such uses are compatible with the purposes for which these areas are established.

Penalties.

(e) Any person who violates or fails to comply with any of the provisions of this Act or any regulations issued thereunder shall be fined not more than

$500 or be imprisoned not more than six months, or both.

(f) Any person authorized by the Secretary of the Interior to enforce the provisions of this Act or any regulations issued thereunder, may, without a warrant, arrest any person violating this Act or regulations in his presence or view, and may execute any warrant or other process issued by an officer or court of competent jurisdiction to enforce the provisions of this Act or regulations, and may with a search warrant search for any seize any property, fish, bird, mammal, or other wild vertebrate or invertebrate animals or part or nest or egg thereof, taken or possessed in violation of this Act or the regulations issued thereunder. Any property, fish, bird, mammal, or other wild vertebrate or invertebrate animals or part or egg thereof seized with or without a search warrant shall be held by such person or by a United States marshal, and upon conviction, shall be forfeited to the United States and disposed of by the court. Enforcement.

(g) Regulations applicable to areas of the System that are in effect on the date of enactment of this Act shall continue in effect until modified or rescinded.

(h) Nothing in this section shall be construed to amend, repeal, or otherwise modify the provision of the Act of September 28, 1962 (76 Stat. 653; 16 U.S.C. 460K—460K—4) which authorizes the Secretary of the Interior to administer the areas within the System for public recreation. The provisions of this section relating to recreation shall be administered in accordance with the provisions of said Act.

(i) Nothing in this Act shall constitute an express or implied claim or denial on the part of the Federal Government as to exemption from State water laws.

SEC. 5. (a) The term "person" as used in this Act means any individual, partnership, corporation, or association. Definitions.

(b) The terms "take" or "taking" or "taken" as used in this Act mean to pursue, hunt, shoot, capture, collect, kill, or attempt to pursue, hunt, shoot, capture, collect, or kill.

(c) The terms "State" and the "United States" as used in this Act mean the several States of the United States, the Commonwealth of Puerto Rico, American Samoa, the Virgin Islands, and Guam.

SEC. 6. Section 4 (b) of the Act of March 16, 1934 (45 Stat. 451), as amended (16 U.S.C. 718d (b)), is further amended by changing the colon after the word "areas" to a period and striking the provisos, which relate to hunting at certain wildlife refuges and which are now covered by section 4 of this Act. 72 Stat. 486.

SEC. 7. (a) Sections 4 and 12 of the Migratory Bird Conservation Act (45 Stat. 1222), as amended (16 U.S.C. 715c and 715k), are further amended by deleting the word "game" wherever it appears.

(b) Section 10 of the Migratory Bird Conservation Act (45 Stat. 1224), as amended (16 U.S.C. 715l), which relates to the administration of certain wildlife refuges, is amended to read as follows:

"SEC. 10. (a) Areas of lands, waters, or interests therein acquired or reserved pursuant to this Act shall, unless otherwise provided by law, be administered by the Secretary of the Interior under rules and regulations prescribed by him to conserve and protect migratory birds in accordance with treaty obligations with Mexico and Canada, and other species of wildlife found thereon, including species that are threatened with extinction, and to restore or develop adequate wildlife habitat.

"(b) In administering such areas, the Secretary is authorized to manage timber, range, and agricultural crops; to manage other species of animals, including but not limited to fenced range animals, with the objectives of perpetuating, distributing, and utilizing the resources; And to enter into agreements with public and private agencies."

45 Stat. 1224.

(c) Section 11 of the Migratory Bird Conservation Act (45 Stat. 1224) (16 U.S.C. 715j) is amended by striking the period at the end thereof and adding the following: "(39 Stat. 1702) and the treaty between the United States and the United Mexican States for the protection of Migratory birds and game mammals concluded February 7, 1936 (50 Stat. 1311)."

Repeal.

(d) Sections 13 and 14 of the Migratory Bird Conservation Act (45 Stat. 1225), as amended (16 U.S.C. 715] and 715m), which provide for the enforcement of said Act and for penalties for violations thereof and which are covered by section 4 of this Act, are repealed.

Repeal.

SEC. 8. (a) Sections 302 and 303 of title III of the Act of June 15, 1935 (49 Stat. 382), as amended (16 U.S.C. 715d-1 and 715d-2), which authorize exchanges at wildlife refuges and which are covered by section 4 of this Act, are repealed.

78 Stat. 701.

(b) The last sentence of section 401(a) of the Act of June 15, 1935 (49 Stat. 383), as amended (16 U.S.C. 715s), is amended by inserting after the term "wildlife refuges", the following: "lands acquired or reserved for the protection and conservation of fish and wildlife that are threatened with extinction,".

16 USC 460k.

SEC. 9. The first clause in section 1 of the Act of September 28, 1962 (76 Stat. 653), is amended by deleting the words "national wildlife refuges, games ranges," and inserting therein "areas within the National Wildlife Refuge System,".

Key deer and other wildlife, preservation.

SEC. 10. (a) The first sentence in section 1 of the Act of August 22, 1957 (71 Stat. 412; 16 U.S.C. 696), is amended to read as follows:

"SEC. 1. In order to protect and preserve in the national interest the key deer and other wildlife resources in the Florida Keys, the Secretary of the Interior is authorized to acquire by purchase, lease, exchange, and donations, including the use of donated funds, such lands or interests therein in townships 65 and 66 south, ranges 28, 29, and 30 east, Monroe County, Florida, as he shall find to be suitable for the conservation and management of the said key deer and other wildlife: *Provided,* That no lands within a one thousand-foot zone adjacent to either side of United States Highway Numbered 1 in Monroe County shall be acquired for the Key Deer National Wildlife Refuge by condemnation. The Secretary, in the exercise of his exchange authority, may accept title to any non-Federal property in townships 65 and 66 south, ranges 28, 29, and 30 east, Monroe County, Florida, and in exchange therefor convey to the grantor of such property any federally owned property in the State of Florida under his jurisdiction which he classifies as suitable for exchange or other disposal. The values of the properties so exchanged either shall be approximately equal, or if they are not approximately equal the values shall be equalized by the payment of cash to the grantor or to the Secretary as the circumstances require."

71 Stat. 413.

(b) Section 3 of such Act of August 22, 1957 (16 U.S.C. 696b), is amended by striking out the second and third sentences and inserting in lieu thereof the following: "The Secretary shall not utilize more than $2,035,000 from appropriated funds for the acquisition of land and interests in land for the purposes of this Act."

Approved October 15, 1966.

PUBLIC LAW 87-714—SEPT. 28, 1962
76 Stat. 653
codified at 16 U.S.C. §§ 460k - k-4

NATIONAL WILDLIFE REFUGE
RECREATION ACT OF 1962

Public Law 87-714

An Act

To assure continued fish and wildlife benefits from the national fish and wildlife
conservation areas by authorizing their appropriate incidental or secondary
use for public recreation to the extent that such use is compatible with the
primary purposes of such areas, and for other purposes.

September 28, 1962
[H.R. 1171]

*Be it enacted by the Senate and House of Representatives of the United
States of America in Congress assembled,* That in recognition of
mounting public demands for recreational opportunities on national
wildlife refuges, games ranges, national fish hatcheries, and other
conservation areas administered by the Secretary of the Interior for
fish and wildlife purposes; and in recognition also of the resulting
imperative need, if such recreational opportunities are provided, to
assure that any present or future recreational use will be compatible
with, and will not prevent accomplishment of, the primary purposes
for which the said conservation areas were acquired or established, the
Secretary of the Interior is authorized, as an appropriate incidental
or secondary use, to administer such areas or parts thereof for public
recreation when in his judgment public recreation can be an appropriate incidental or secondary use: *Provided,* That such public recreation use shall be permitted only to the extent that is practicable and
not inconsistent with other previously authorized Federal operations
or with the primary objectives for which each particular area is
established: *Provided further,* That in order to insure accomplishment
of such primary objectives, the Secretary, after consideration of all
authorized uses, purposes, and other pertinent factors relating to individual areas, shall curtail public recreation use generally or certain
types of public recreation use within individual areas or in portions
thereof whenever he considers such action to be necessary: *And provided further,* That none of the aforesaid refuges, hatcheries, game
ranges, and other conservation areas shall be used during any fiscal
year for those forms of recreation that are not directly related to the
primary purposes and functions of the individual areas until the Secretary shall have determined—

> (a) that such recreational use will not interfere with the
> primary purposes for which the areas were established, and
> (b) that funds are available for the development, operation,
> and maintenance of these permitted forms of recreation.
> This section shall not be construed to repeal or amend
> previous enactments relating to particular areas.

Interior Dept.
National fish
and wildlife
areas, public
recreational use.

SEC. 2. In order to avoid adverse effects upon fish and wildlife
populations and management operations of the said areas that might
otherwise result from public recreation or visitation to such areas,
the Secretary is authorized to acquire limited areas of land for recreational development adjacent to the said conservation areas in existence
or approved by the Migratory Bird Conservation Commission as of the
date of enactment of this Act: *Provided,* That the acquisition of any
land or interest therein pursuant to this section shall be accomplished
only with such funds as may be appropriated therefore by the Congress
or donated for such purposes, but such property shall not be acquired
with funds obtained from the sale of Federal migratory bird hunting
stamps. Lands acquired pursuant to this section shall become a part
of the particular conservation area to which they are adjacent.

Land acquisi-
tion.

SEC. 3. In furtherance of the purposes of this Act, the Secretary is
authorized to cooperate with public and private agencies, organizations, and individuals, and he may accept and use, without further

Acceptance of
funds, etc.

authorization, donations of funds and real and personal property. Such acceptance may be accomplished under the terms and conditions of restrictive covenants imposed by donors when such covenants are deemed by the Secretary to be compatible with the purposes of the wildlife refuges, games ranges, fish hatcheries, and other fish and wildlife conservation areas.

SEC. 4. The Secretary may establish reasonable charges and fees and issue permits for public use of national wildlife refuges, game ranges, national fish hatcheries, and other conservation areas administered by the Department of the Interior for fish and wildlife purposes.

Regulations
Penalties.
62 Stat. 684.

The Secretary may issue regulations to carry out the purposes of this Act. A violation of such regulations shall be a petty offense (18 U.S.C. 1) with maximum penalties of imprisonment for not more than six months, or a fine of not more than $500, or both.

Appropriation.

SEC. 5. There is authorized to be appropriated such funds as may be necessary to carry out the purposes of this Act, including the construction and maintenance of public recreational facilities.

Approved September 28, 1962.

APPENDIX C

The National Wildlife Refuge Units

Refuge Name[1]	Location[2]	Establishment Date[3]	Size[4] (in acres)
Ace Basin NWR	S.C.	21 Sept. 1990	11,815
Agassiz NWR	Minn.	23 Mar. 1937	61,501
Alamosa NWR	Colo.	25 July 1963	11,169
Alaska Maritime NWR	Alaska	3 Mar. 1869	3,465,247
Alaska Penninsula NWR	Alaska	2 Dec. 1980	3,534,410
Alligator River NWR	N.C.	14 Mar. 1984	152,195
Amagansett NWR	N.Y.	16 Dec. 1968	36
Anaho Island NWR	Nev.	4 Sept. 1913	248
Anahuac NWR	Tex.	27 Feb. 1963	34,296
Ankeny NWR	Oreg.	18 Jan. 1965	2,796
Antioch Dunes NWR	Calif.	4 Mar. 1980	55
Appert Lake NWR	N.Dak.	10 May 1939	908
Aransas NWR	Tex.	18 Nov. 1937	114,412
Arapaho NWR	Colo.	26 Sept. 1967	23,246

1. This chart lists all 540 named national wildlife refuges in existence as of Sept. 30, 2002. "NWR" is an abbreviation for "National Wildlife Refuge."

2. "Pac. Terr." indicates that the refuge is a Pacific Ocean territory of the United States.

3. These are the establishment dates assigned by the officials of the Fish and Wildlife Service concerned with realty. The realty establishment date is the time when the federal government first reserved or acquired land for conservation purposes in the area that is now a refuge. Several refuges, such as the Alaska Maritime NWR and the Kodiak NWR, have realty dates that precede the official establishment of the refuge unit. This is because the federal government reserved land for some form of conservation in the Pribilof and Afognak islands before they were subsumed into the Alaska Maritime and Kodiak refuges. Other refuges have realty establishment dates later than the date of the actual document authorizing the refuge and setting out establishment purposes. Refuges do not receive a realty establishment date until the federal government acquires the first property interest in the authorized area.

4. Rounded to the nearest acre. The size includes all property interests held by the United States, including leases and easements. This column shows the refuge size as of Sept. 30, 2002. The total acreage of these named national wildlife refuges is 92,104,081.

Archie Carr NWR	Fla.	25 June 1991	234
Arctic NWR	Alaska	2 Dec. 1980	19,285,922
Ardoch NWR	N.Dak.	25 Aug. 1936	2,696
Aroostook NWR	Me.	1 Oct. 1998	4,655
Arrowwood NWR	N.Dak.	11 Mar. 1935	15,943
Arthur R. Marshall Loxahatchee NWR	Fla.	8 June 1951	145,787
Ash Meadows NWR	Nev.	13 June 1984	13,741
Assabet River NWR	Mass.	8 July 2001	2,229
Atchafalaya NWR	La.	8 Aug. 1986	15,255
Attwater Prairie Chicken NWR	Tex.	1 July 1972	10,821
Audubon NWR	N.Dak.	25 May 1956	14,739
Back Bay NWR	Va.	25 Feb. 1938	8,603
Baker Island NWR	Pac. Terr.	27 June 1974	31,737
Balcones Canyonlands NWR	Tex.	25 Feb. 1992	19,463
Bald Knob NWR	Ark.	22 Sept. 1993	14,760
Bamforth NWR	Wyo.	29 Jan. 1932	1,166
Bandon Marsh NWR	Oreg.	14 Feb. 1983	716
Banks Lake NWR	Ga.	16 Apr. 1980	3,559
Baskett Slough NWR	Oreg.	22 Oct. 1965	2,492
Bayou Cocodrie NWR	La.	11 Feb. 1992	13,169
Bayou Sauvage NWR	La.	25 Apr. 1990	22,263
Bayou Teche NWR	La.	31 Oct. 2001	9,074
Bear Butte NWR	S.Dak.	25 May 1937	374
Bear Lake NWR	Idaho	9 May 1968	18,086
Bear River Migratory Bird Refuge	Utah	14 May 1929	73,645
Bear Valley NWR	Oreg.	31 May 1978	4,200
Becharof NWR	Alaska	1 Dec. 1978	1,200,018
Benton Lake NWR	Mont.	21 Nov. 1929	12,459
Big Boggy NWR	Tex.	8 July 1983	4,526
Big Branch Marsh NWR	La.	13 Oct. 1994	16,004
Big Lake NWR	Ark.	2 Aug. 1915	11,036
Big Muddy National Fish and Wildlife Refuge	Mo.	9 Sept. 1994	8,147
Big Oaks NWR	Ind.	30 June 2000	51,000
Big Stone NWR	Minn.	21 May 1975	11,520
Bill Williams River NWR	Ariz.	17 June 1993	6,055
Bitter Creek NWR	Calif.	1 July 1985	14,097
Bitter Lake NWR	N.Mex.	19 May 1936	24,609
Black Bayou Lake NWR	La.	16 June 1997	3,892
Black Coulee NWR	Mont.	28 Jan. 1938	1,309
Blackbeard Island NWR	Ga.	15 Feb. 1924	5,618
Blackfoot Valley Wildlife Management Area	Mont.	3 Feb. 1997	8,164
Blackwater NWR	Md.	23 Jan. 1933	24,990
Block Island NWR	R.I.	1 Nov. 1973	129
Blue Ridge NWR	Calif.	30 Dec. 1982	897
Bogue Chitto NWR	La., Miss.	4 Mar. 1981	36,502

Bombay Hook NWR	Del.	16 Mar. 1937	16,058
Bon Secour NWR	Ala.	23 Feb. 1979	6,798
Bond Swamp NWR	Ga.	16 Oct. 1989	5,490
Bone Hill NWR	N.Dak.	10 May 1939	640
Bosque Del Apache NWR`	N.Mex.	18 Dec. 1936	57,191
Bowdoin NWR	Mont.	14 Feb. 1936	15,552
Boyer Chute NWR	Nebr.	30 Sept. 1997	3,300
Brazoria NWR	Tex.	17 Oct. 1966	44,414
Breton NWR	La.	4 Oct. 1904	9,047
Browns Park NWR	Colo.	13 July 1965	13,455
Brumba NWR	N.Dak.	12 June 1939	1,977
Buck Island NWR	V.I.	8 Jan. 1969	45
Buenos Aires NWR	Ariz.	27 Feb. 1985	117,776
Buffalo Lake NWR	N.Dak.	10 May 1939	1,564
Buffalo Lake NWR	Tex.	6 Nov. 1958	7,664
Butte Sink Wildlife Management Area	Calif.	4 Mar. 1980	11,044
Cabeza Prieta NWR	Ariz.	18 Nov. 1940	860,041
Cabo Rojo NWR	P.R.	20 May 1974	1,857
Cache River NWR	Ark.	16 June 1986	56,959
Caddo Lake NWR	Tex.	21 Oct. 2000	8,492
Cahaba River NWR	Ala.	25 Sept. 2002	1,120
Caloosahatchee NWR	Fla.	1 Jan. 1921	40
Camas NWR	Idaho	16 Oct. 1936	10,579
Cameron Prairie NWR	La.	29 Dec. 1988	9,621
Camp Lake NWR	N.Dak.	10 May 1939	585
Canaan Valley NWR	W.Va.	11 Aug. 1994	15,254
Canfield Lake NWR	N.Dak.	10 May 1939	313
Cape May NWR	N.J.	27 June 1989	10,910
Cape Meares NWR	Oreg.	19 Aug. 1938	139
Cape Romain NWR	S.C.	3 Apr. 1930	65,225
Carolina Sandhills NWR	S.C.	20 Mar. 1939	45,548
Castle Rock NWR	Calif.	20 Nov. 1980	16
Cat Island NWR	La.	30 May 2000	2,355
Catahoula NWR	La.	28 Oct. 1958	14,910
Cedar Island NWR	N.C.	18 Aug. 1964	14,482
Cedar Keys NWR	Fla.	16 July 1929	891
Cedar Point NWR	Ohio	18 Dec. 1964	2,450
Charles M. Russell NWR	Mont.	11 Dec. 1936	912,349
Chase Lake NWR	N.Dak.	28 Aug. 1908	4,449
Chassahowitzka NWR	Fla.	22 Dec. 1941	30,843
Chautauqua NWR	Ill.	3 Apr. 1935	6,446
Chickasaw NWR	Tenn.	5 Aug. 1985	23,540
Chincoteague NWR	Md., Va.	13 May 1943	14,032
Choctaw NWR	Ala.	27 Jan. 1964	4,218
Cibola NWR	Ariz., Calif.	21 Aug. 1964	12,853
Clarence Cannon NWR	Mo.	11 Aug. 1964	3,750
Clarks River NWR	Ky.	19 Aug. 1998	6,614

Clear Lake NWR	Calif.	11 Apr. 1911	46,460
Coachella Valley NWR	Calif.	28 Aug. 1985	3,578
Cokeville Meadows NWR	Wyo.	12 Oct. 1993	8,587
Cold Springs NWR	Oreg.	25 Feb. 1909	3,117
Coldwater River NWR	Miss.	30 Jan. 2001	2,468
Colorado River Wildlife Management Area	Colo., Utah	1 Oct. 1998	732
Columbia NWR	Wash.	13 June 1944	29,596
Colusa NWR	Calif.	15 Mar. 1944	4,040
Conboy Lake NWR	Wash.	14 Apr. 1965	6,905
Conscience Point NWR	N.Y.	20 July 1971	60
Copalis NWR	Wash.	23 Oct. 1907	61
Cottonwood Lake NWR	N.Dak.	12 June 1939	1,013
Crab Orchard NWR	Ill.	5 Aug. 1947	43,889
Crane Meadows NWR	Minn.	10 Sept. 1993	1,688
Creedman Coulee NWR	Mont.	25 Oct. 1941	2,728
Crescent Lake NWR	Nebr.	16 Mar. 1931	45,995
Crocodile Lake NWR	Fla.	22 May 1979	6,688
Cross Creeks NWR	Tenn.	9 Nov. 1962	8,861
Cross Island NWR	Me.	3 July 1980	1,703
Crystal River NWR	Fla.	17 Aug. 1983	80
Culebra NWR	P.R.	27 Feb. 1909	1,561
Currituck NWR	N.C.	29 Aug. 1984	8,030
Cypress Creek NWR	Ill.	27 July 1990	15,099
D'Arbonne NWR	La.	19 May 1975	17,420
Dahomey NWR	Miss.	11 Feb. 1991	9,167
Dakota Lake NWR	N.Dak.	10 May 1939	2,800
Dakota Tallgrass Prairie Wildlife Management Area	N.Dak., S.Dak.	19 Dec. 2000	27,444
Deep Fork NWR	Okla.	30 June 1993	8,387
Deer Flat NWR	Idaho, Oreg.	25 Feb. 1909	11,428
Delevan NWR	Calif.	12 Sept. 1962	5,797
Delta NWR	La.	19 Nov. 1935	48,799
Des Lacs NWR	N.Dak.	5 Mar. 1935	19,547
Desecheo NWR	P.R.	22 Dec. 1976	360
Desert NWR	Nev.	20 May 1936	1,588,819
Desoto NWF	Iowa, Nebr.	13 Dec. 1958	7,827
Detroit River International Wildlife Refuge	Mich.	21 Dec. 2001	325
Don Edwards San Francisco Bay NWR	Calif.	8 Oct. 1974	22,390
Driftless Area NWR	Iowa	16 Oct. 1989	777
Dungeness NWR	Wash.	20 Jan. 1915	773
Eastern Neck NWR	Md.	27 Dec. 1962	2,286
Eastern Shore of Virginia NWR	Va.	6 Aug. 1984	1,123
Edwin B. Forsythe NWR	N.J.	5 Oct. 1939	45,191
Egmont Key NWR	Fla.	10 July 1974	328
Elizabeth Alexandra			

Morton NWR	N.Y.	27 Dec. 1954	187
Ellicott Slouth NWR	Calif.	21 Nov. 1975	200
Emiquon NWR	Ill.	29 Dec. 1993	2,155
Erie NWR	Pa.	22 May 1959	8,777
Eufaula NWR	Ala., Ga.	1 Sept. 1964	11,184
Fallon NWR	Nev.	22 Apr. 1931	17,902
Farallon NWR	Calif.	27 Feb. 1909	211
Featherstone NWR	Va.	29 Dec. 1978	326
Felsenthal NWR	Ark.	19 May 1975	64,902
Fern Cave NWR	Ala.	28 Oct. 1981	199
Fish Springs NWR	Utah	10 Mar. 1959	17,992
Fisherman Island NWR	Va.	17 Jan. 1969	1,950
Flattery Rocks NWR	Wash.	23 Oct. 1907	125
Flint Hills NWR	Kans.	1 Sept. 1966	18,463
Florence Lake NWR	N.Dak.	10 May 1939	1,888
Florida Panther NWR	Fla.	1 June 1989	26,529
Fort Niobrara NWR	Nebr.	11 Jan. 1912	19,133
Fox River NWR	Wis.	19 Apr. 1979	925
Franklin Island NWR	Me.	19 Sept. 1973	12
Franz Lake NWR	Wash.	22 May 1990	552
Grand Bay NWR	Ala., Miss.	22 Sept. 1989	9,831
Grand Cote NWR	La.	6 Mar. 1992	6,077
Grasslands Wildlife Management Area	Calif.	27 July 1979	80,544
Gravel Island NWR	Wis.	9 Jan. 1913	27
Grays Harbor NWR	Wash.	29 Aug. 1990	1,471
Grays Lake NWR	Idaho	17 June 1965	19,565
Great Bay NWR	N.H.	11 Aug. 1992	1,083
Great Dismal Swamp NWR	N.C., Va.	22 Feb. 1973	111,203
Great Meadows NWR	Mass.	3 May 1944	3,712
Great River NWR	Ill., Mo.	2 July 1947	9,219
Great Swamp NWR	N.J.	3 Nov. 1960	7,531
Great White Heron NWR	Fla.	27 Oct. 1938	192,788
Green Bay NWR	Wis.	21 Feb. 1912	2
Green Cay NWR	V.I.	19 Dec. 1977	14
Grulla NWR	N.Mex., Tex.	7 Nov. 1968	3,236
Guadalupe–Nipomo Dunes NWR	Calif.	1 Aug. 2000	2,553
Guam NWR	Guam	1 Oct. 1993	23,228
Hagerman NWR	Tex.	9 Feb. 1946	11,320
Hailstone NWR	Mont.	31 Dec. 1942	920
Hakalau Forest NWR	Hawaii	29 Oct. 1985	38,050
Halfbreed Lake NWR	Mont.	19 May 1942	4,318
Half-Way Lake NWR	N.Dak.	10 May 1939	160
Hamden Slough NWR	Minn.	5 Jan. 1989	3,194
Hanalei NWR	Hawaii	30 Nov. 1972	917
Handy Brake NWR	La.	25 Nov. 1992	501
Harbor Island NWR	Mich.	8 Dec. 1983	695
Harris Neck NWR	Ga.	25 May 1962	2,824

Hart Mountain National Antelope Refuge	Oreg.	6 Sept. 1935	269,924
Hatchie NWR	Tenn.	16 Nov. 1964	11,556
Havasu NWR	Ariz., Calif.	22 Jan. 1941	37,515
Hawaiian Islands NWR	Hawaii	3 Feb. 1909	254,418
Hewitt Lake NWR	Mont.	7 Mar. 1938	1,361
Hiddenwood NWR	N.Dak.	12 June 1939	568
Hillside NWR	Miss.	14 Apr. 1975	19,051
Hobart Lake NWR	N.Dak.	15 June 1939	2,077
Hobe Sound NWR	Fla.	23 Sept. 1968	1,034
Holla Bend NWR	Ark.	30 Aug. 1957	6,299
Hopper Mountain NWR	Calif.	18 Dec. 1974	2,471
Horicon NWR	Wis.	24 Jan. 1941	21,182
Howland Island NWR	Pac. Terr.	27 June 1974	32,550
Huleia NWR	Hawaii	24 Apr. 1973	241
Humboldt Bay NWR	Calif.	4 Apr. 1973	2,912
Huron NWR	Mich.	10 Oct. 1905	147
Hutchinson Lake NWR	N.Dak.	10 May 1939	479
Hutton Lake NWR	Wyo.	28 Jan. 1932	1,968
Imperial NWR	Ariz., Calif.	14 Feb. 1941	25,768
Innoko NWR	Alaska	12 Feb. 1980	3,850,321
Iroquois NWR	N.Y.	19 May 1958	10,828
Island Bay NWR	Fla.	23 Oct. 1908	20
Izembek NWR	Alaska	6 Dec. 1960	311,076
J. Clark Salyer NWR	N.Dak.	5 Mar. 1935	59,375
J. N. "Ding" Darling NWR	Fla.	1 Dec. 1945	6,388
James Campbell NWR	Hawaii	17 Dec. 1976	166
James River NWR	Va.	27 Mar. 1991	4,200
Jarvis Island NWR	Pac. Terr.	27 June 1974	37,519
John H. Chafee NWR	R.I.	26 June 1989	332
John Hay NWR	N.H.	19 Mar. 1987	165
John Heinz NWR at Tinicum	Pa.	18 Mar. 1963	993
John W. and Louise Seier NWR	Nebr.	26 Oct. 2000	2,400
Johnson Lake NWR	N.Dak.	10 May 1939	2,008
Johnston Island NWR	Pac. Terr.	29 June 1926	100
Julia Butler Hansen Refuge for the Columbian White-Tailed Deer	Oreg., Wash.	17 Dec. 1971	5,798
Kakahaia NWR	Hawaii	15 Mar. 1976	45
Kanuti NWR	Alaska	12 Feb. 1980	1,430,160
Karl E. Mundt NWR	Nebr., S.Dak.	17 Apr. 1975	1,063
Kealia Pond NWR	Hawaii	8 Dec. 1992	692
Kellys Slough NWR	N.Dak.	19 Mar. 1936	1,270
Kenai NWR	Alaska	16 Dec. 1941	1,908,178
Kern NWR	Calif.	16 Sept. 1960	10,618
Key Cave NWR	Ala.	3 Jan. 1997	1,060
Key West NWR	Fla.	8 Aug. 1908	208,308
Kilauea Point NWR	Hawaii	19 Dec. 1984	199

Kingman Reef NWR	Pac. Terr.	18 Jan. 2001	426,392
Kirtlands Warbler Wildlife Management Area	Mich.	3 Sept. 1980	6,684
Kirwin NWR	Kans.	17 June 1954	10,778
Klamath Marsh NWR	Oreg.	12 June 1958	40,885
Kodiak NWR	Alaska	1 Feb. 1898	1,933,392
Kofa NWR	Ariz.	25 Jan. 1939	666,480
Kootenai NWR	Idaho	31 Aug. 1964	2,774
Koyukuk NWR	Alaska	2 Dec. 1980	3,550,000
Lacassine NWR	La.	26 Oct. 1937	34,379
Lacreek NWR	S.Dak.	26 Mar. 1935	16,855
Laguna Atascosa NWR	Tex.	29 Mar. 1946	65,096
Laguna Cartegena NWR	P.R.	8 Aug. 1989	1,036
Lake Alice NWR	N.Dak.	14 Mar. 1940	12,096
Lake Andes NWR	S.Dak.	1 Apr. 1935	5,639
Lake George NWR	N.Dak.	12 June 1939	3,119
Lake Ilo NWR	N.Dak.	12 June 1939	4,033
Lake Isom NWR	Tenn.	10 May 1935	1,846
Lake Mason NWR	Mont.	3 June 1941	16,815
Lake Nettie NWR	N.Dak.	12 June 1939	3,055
Lake Ophelia NWR	La.	30 June 1988	17,555
Lake Otis NWR	N.Dak.	6 Mar. 1935	320
Lake Patricia NWR	N.Dak.	12 June 1939	800
Lake Thibadeau NWR	Mont.	23 Sept. 1937	3,868
Lake Umbagog NWR	Me., N.H.	17 Nov. 1992	16,550
Lake Wales Ridge NWR	Fla.	22 Apr. 1994	1,840
Lake Woodruff NWR	Fla.	18 Nov. 1963	21,559
Lake Zahl NWR	N.Dak.	12 June 1939	3,823
Lambs Lake NWR	N.Dak.	12 June 1939	1,207
Lamsteer NWR	Mont.	19 May 1942	800
Las Vegas NWR	N.Mex.	25 Apr. 1966	8,672
Lee Metcalf NWR	Mont.	10 Apr. 1964	2,793
Leslie Canyon NWR	Ariz.	17 June 1993	9,795
Lewis and Clark NWR	Oreg.	19 Apr. 1972	7,632
Little Goose NWR	N.Dak.	10 May 1939	288
Little Pend Oreille NWR	Wash.	2 May 1939	42,594
Little River NWR	Okla.	10 Feb. 1987	13,600
Little Sandy NWR	Tex.	18 Dec. 1986	3,802
Logan Cave NWR	Ark.	14 Mar. 1989	124
Long Lake NWR	N.Dak.	25 Feb. 1932	22,499
Lords Lake NWR	N.Dak.	10 May 1939	1,915
Lost Lake NWR	N.Dak.	10 May 1939	960
Lost Trail NWR	Mont.	24 Aug. 1999	8,834
Lostwood NWR	N.Dak.	26 Mar. 1935	26,904
Lower Hatchie NWR	Tenn.	19 June 1980	10,836
Lower Klamath NWR	Calif., Oreg.	8 Aug. 1908	50,912
Lower Rio Grande Valley NWR	Tex.	12 Feb. 1979	84,613
Lower Suwannee NWR	Fla.	5 May 1979	51,031

Mackay Island NWR	N.C., Va.	30 Dec. 1960	8,138
Malheur NWR	Oreg.	18 Aug. 1908	187,053
Mandalay NWR	La.	2 May 1996	4,619
Maple River NWR	N.Dak.	12 June 1939	712
Marais Des Cygnes NWR	Kans.	7 Aug. 1992	7,303
Marin Islands NWR	Calif.	16 Apr. 1992	131
Martin NWR	Md., Va.	20 Dec. 1954	4,569
Mashpee NWR	Mass.	28 Sept. 1995	342
Mason Neck NWR	Va.	1 Feb. 1969	2,277
Massasoit NWR	Mass.	21 Sept. 1983	198
Mathews Brake NWR	Miss.	3 Sept. 1980	2,419
Matlacha Pass NWR	Fla.	26 Sept. 1908	393
Mattamuskeet NWR	N.C.	18 Dec. 1934	50,180
Maxwell NWR	N.Mex.	26 Apr. 1966	3,699
McFaddin NWR	Tex.	2 Jan. 1980	56,181
McKay Creek NWR	Oreg.	7 June 1927	1,837
McLean NWR	N.Dak.	12 June 1939	760
McNary NWR	Wash.	29 Dec. 1955	15,526
Medicine Lake NWR	Mont.	29 Mar. 1935	31,484
Merced NWR	Calif.	30 July 1951	3,806
Meredosia NWR	Ill.	25 Oct. 1972	3,401
Merritt Island NWR	Fla.	28 Aug. 1963	139,189
Michigan Islands NWR	Mich.	10 Apr. 1947	597
Middle Mississippi River NWR	Ill., Mo.	2 July 1947	3,942
Midway Atoll NWR	Pac. Terr.	22 Apr. 1988	298,362
Mille Lacs NWR	Minn.	14 May 1915	1
Mingo NWR	Mo.	7 June 1944	21,746
Minidoka NWR	Idaho	25 Feb. 1909	20,702
Minnesota Valley NWR	Minn.	8 Oct. 1976	10,684
Missisquoi NWR	Vt.	4 Feb. 1943	6,521
Mississippi Sandhill Crane NWR	Miss.	25 Nov. 1975	19,716
Moapa Valley NWR	Nev.	10 Sept. 1979	104
Modoc NWR	Calif.	5 Nov. 1960	7,021
Monomoy NWR	Mass.	1 June 1944	2,702
Monte Vista NWR	Colo.	3 Sept. 1952	14,834
Montezuma NWR	N.Y.	21 July 1937	8,457
Moody NWR	Tex.	9 Nov. 1961	3,517
Moosehorn NWR	Me.	13 Jan. 1937	27,680
Morgan Brake NWR	Miss.	29 Sept. 1977	7,373
Mortenson Lake NWR	Wyo.	20 May 1992	1,776
Muleshoe NWR	Tex.	24 Oct. 1935	5,809
Muscatatuck NWR	Ind.	6 Oct. 1966	7,802
Nansemond NWR	Va.	20 Dec. 1973	423
Nantucket NWR	Mass.	1 May 1973	24
National Bison Range	Mont.	15 June 1909	18,800
National Elk Refuge	Wyo.	16 Mar. 1914	24,778
National Key Deer Refuge	Fla.	1 Feb. 1954	8,952
Navassa Island NWR	Caribbean	30 Sept. 1999	364,950

Neal Smith NWR	Iowa	16 Apr. 1991	5,366
Necedah NWR	Wis.	19 Mar. 1939	43,696
Nestucca Bay NWR	Oreg.	21 Mar. 1991	651
Nine-Pipe NWR	Mont.	25 June 1921	4,028
Ninigret NWR	R.I.	12 Aug. 1970	699
Nisqually NWR	Wash.	21 Feb. 1974	3,720
Nomans Land Island NWR	Mass.	29 Apr. 1970	628
North Central Valley Wildlife Management Area	Calif.	23 Oct. 1991	7,130
North Dakota Wildlife Management Area	N.Dak.	25 Feb. 2000	32,839
North Platte NWR	Nebr.	21 Aug. 1916	3,473
Northern Tallgrass Prairie NWR	Iowa, Minn.	15 Sept. 2000	820
Nowitna NWR	Alaska	2 Dec. 1980	1,560,000
Noxubee NWR	Miss.	14 June 1940	47,049
Oahu Forest NWR	Hawaii	21 Dec. 2000	4,570
Occoquan Bay NWR	Va.	29 June 1973	662
Ohio River Islands NWR	Ky., Pa., W. Va.	13 Nov. 1990	2,903
Okefenokee NWR	Fla., Ga.	24 Nov. 1936	395,126
Optima NWR	Okla.	24 Mar. 1975	4,333
Oregon Islands NWR	Oreg.	6 May 1935	1,080
Ottawa NWR	Ohio	28 July 1961	6,345
Ouray NWR	Utah	22 Nov. 1960	12,258
Overflow NWR	Ark.	25 Nov. 1980	12,963
Oxbow NWR	Mass.	24 May 1974	1,677
Oyster Bay NWR	N.Y.	18 Dec. 1968	3,204
Ozark Cavefish NWR	Mo.	22 Oct. 1991	42
Ozark Plateau NWR	Okla.	26 Sept. 1985	3,637
Pablo NWR	Mont.	25 June 1921	2,542
Pahranagat NWR	Nev.	6 Aug. 1963	5,383
Palmyra Atoll NWR	Pac. Terr.	18 Jan. 2001	504,576
Panther Swamp NWR	Miss.	11 Jan. 1978	35,272
Parker River NWR	Mass.	26 Dec. 1941	4,653
Passage Key NWR	Fla.	10 Oct. 1905	64
Pathfinder NWR	Wyo.	19 Apr. 1928	16,807
Patoka River NWR	Ind.	8 Sept. 1994	5,592
Patuxent Research Refuge	Md.	16 Dec. 1936	12,841
Pea Island NWR	N.C.	17 May 1937	5,834
Pearl Harbor NWR	Hawaii	17 Oct. 1972	99
Pee Dee NWR	N.C.	13 May 1964	8,439
Pelican Island NWR	Fla.	14 Mar. 1903	5,376
Petit Manan NWR	Me.	9 July 1974	5,657
Piedmont NWR	Ga.	18 Jan. 1939	34,967
Pierce NWR	Wash.	31 Dec. 1983	329
Pilot Knob NWR	Mo.	17 July 1987	90
Pinckney Island NWR	S.C.	3 Dec. 1975	4,053
Pine Island NWR	Fla.	15 Sept. 1908	602

Pinellas NWR	Fla.	1 Apr. 1951	394
Pixley NWR	Calif.	6 Nov. 1958	6,389
Pleasant Lake NWR	N.Dak.	12 June 1939	897
Plum Tree Island NWR	Va.	24 Apr. 1972	3,502
Pocosin Lakes NWR	N.C.	26 June 1990	110,107
Pond Creek NWR	Ark.	12 Aug. 1994	26,816
Pond Island NWR	Me.	9 Mar. 1973	10
Port Louisa NWR	Ill., Iowa	2 July 1947	24,094
Presquile NWR	Va.	11 Mar. 1953	1,329
Pretty Rock NWR	N.Dak.	3 Feb. 1941	800
Prime Hook NWR	Del.	8 Aug. 1963	10,066
Protection Island NWR	Wash.	22 Dec. 1982	659
Quillayute Needles NWR	Wash.	23 Oct. 1907	300
Quivira NWR	Kans.	8 Oct. 1955	22,019
Rabb Lake NWR	N.Dak.	23 Sept. 1937	261
Rachel Carson NWR	Me.	21 Dec. 1966	5,088
Rappahannock River Valley NWR	Va.	28 May 1996	4,736
Red River NWR	La.	22 Aug. 2002	3,857
Red Rock Lakes NWR	Mont.	22 Apr. 1935	51,744
Reelfoot NWR	Ky., Tenn.	28 Aug. 1941	10,450
Rice Lake NWR	Minn.	31 Oct. 1935	16,472
Ridgefield NWR	Wash.	27 Jan. 1966	5,218
Roanoke River NWR	N.C.	27 Sept. 1990	17,977
Rock Lake NWR	N.Dak.	12 June 1939	5,506
Rocky Mountain Arsenal NWR	Colo.	9 Oct. 1992	17,000
Rose Atoll NWR	Am. Sam.	24 Aug. 1973	39,066
Rose Lake NWR	N.Dak.	9 Sept. 1935	836
Ruby Lake NWR	Nev.	5 Nov. 1937	39,286
Rydell NWR	Minn.	31 Jan. 1992	2,070
Sabine NWR	La.	6 Dec. 1937	140,717
Sachuest Point NWR	R.I.	3 Nov. 1970	242
Sacramento NWR	Calif.	18 Jan. 1937	10,783
Sacramento River NWR	Calif.	21 Sept. 1989	17,530
Saddle Mountain NWR	Wash.	11 Mar. 1953	161,486
Salinas River NWR	Calif.	27 June 1973	367
Salt Plains NWR	Okla.	26 Mar. 1930	32,057
San Andres NWR	N.Mex.	22 Jan. 1941	57,215
San Bernard NWR	Tex.	7 Nov. 1968	33,657
San Bernardino NWR	Ariz.	1 Apr. 1982	2,369
San Diego NWR	Calif.	10 Apr. 1996	10,012
San Joaquin River NWR	Calif.	2 Dec. 1987	9,723
San Juan Islands NWR	Wash.	24 Dec. 1960	449
San Luis NWR	Calif.	2 Feb. 1967	22,893
San Pablo Bay NWR	Calif.	6 Feb. 1974	13,190
Sand Lake NWR	S.Dak.	23 Mar. 1935	21,820
Sandy Point NWR	V.I.	30 Aug. 1984	512
Santa Ana NWR	Tex.	1 Sept. 1943	2,088

Santee NWR	S.C.	1 Jan. 1942	12,483
Sauta Cave NWR	Ala.	15 Sept. 1978	264
Savannah NWR	Ga., S.C.	6 Apr. 1927	28,196
School Section Lake NWR	N.Dak.	11 Sept. 1935	297
Seal Beach NWR	Calif.	5 July 1974	911
Seal Island NWR	Me.	24 July 1972	65
Seatuck NWR	N.Y.	26 Sept. 1968	209
Seedskadee NWR	Wyo.	30 Nov. 1965	27,230
Selawik NWR	Alaska	2 Dec. 1980	2,150,002
Seney NWR	Mich.	22 May 1935	95,245
Sequoyah NWR	Okla.	11 Dec. 1970	20,800
Sevilleta NWR	N.Mex.	28 Dec. 1973	229,674
Shawangunk Grasslands NWR	N.Y.	27 July 1999	567
Sheldon NWR	Nev., Oreg.	3 May 1978	573,504
Shell Keys NWR	La.	17 Aug. 1907	8
Shell Lake NWR	N.Dak.	12 June 1939	1,910
Sherburne NWR	Minn.	8 Sept. 1965	29,607
Sheyenne Lake NWR	N.Dak.	8 Mar. 1935	797
Shiawassee NWR	Mich.	21 Oct. 1953	9,363
Sibley Lake NWR	N.Dak.	12 June 1939	1,077
Siletz Bay NWR	Oreg.	23 Oct. 1991	513
Silver Lake NWR	N.Dak.	9 Apr. 1937	3,348
Silvio O. Conte National Fish and Wildlife Refuge	Mass., N.H., Vt.	3 Oct. 1997	27,391
Slade NWR	N.Dak.	10 Oct. 1944	3,000
Snyder Lake NWR	N.Dak.	3 Feb. 1941	1,550
Sonny Bono Salton Sea NWR	Calif.	25 Nov. 1930	37,659
Springwater NWR	N.Dak.	3 Feb. 1941	640
Squaw Creek NWR	Mo.	2 Apr. 1935	7,415
St. Catherine Creek NWR	Miss.	16 Jan. 1990	24,931
St. Johns NWR	Fla.	16 Aug. 1971	6,257
St. Marks NWR	Fla.	9 Mar. 1931	67,623
St. Vincent NWR	Fla.	12 Feb. 1968	12,490
Steigerwald Lake NWR	Wash.	27 Mar. 1986	1,046
Stewart B. McKinney NWR	Conn.	25 Feb. 1985	872
Stewart Lake NWR	N.Dak.	27 Oct. 1939	2,230
Stillwater NWR	Nev.	26 Nov. 1948	86,895
Stone Lakes NWR	Calif.	12 Oct. 1994	2,844
Stoney Slough NWR	N.Dak.	3 Feb. 1941	880
Storm Lake NWR	N.Dak.	4 Aug. 1936	686
Stump Lake NWR	N.Dak.	9 Mar. 1905	27
Sullys Hill National Game Preserve	N.Dak.	22 Dec. 1921	1,675
Sunburst Lake NWR	N.Dak.	3 Feb. 1941	328
Sunkhaze Meadows NWR	Me.	22 Oct. 1988	10,190
Supawna Meadows NWR	N.J.	23 Sept. 1973	2,895
Susquehanna NWR	Md.	24 Aug. 1939	4
Sutter NWR	Calif.	30 Mar. 1945	2,590

Swan Lake NWR	Mo.	3 Aug. 1936	11,493
Swan River NWR	Mont.	14 May 1973	1,569
Swanquarter NWR	N.C.	23 June 1932	16,411
Sweetwater Marsh NWR	Calif.	12 Aug. 1988	316
Tallahatchie NWR	Miss.	5 Mar. 1991	2,677
Tamarac NWR	Minn.	28 Jan. 1936	35,191
Target Rock NWR	N.Y.	15 Dec. 1967	80
Ten Thousand Islands NWR	Fla.	18 Dec. 1996	35,034
Tennessee	Tenn.	28 Dec. 1945	51,359
Tensas River NWR	La.	5 Feb. 1985	66,395
Tetlin NWR	Alaska	2 Dec. 1980	700,059
Tewaukon NWR	N.Dak.	4 Aug. 1936	8,364
Texas Point NWR	Tex.	21 Dec. 1978	8,952
Thacher Island NWR	Mass.	25 July 1972	22
Three Arch Rocks NWR	Oreg.	14 Oct. 1907	15
Tijuana Slough NWR	Calif.	24 Dec. 1980	1,023
Tishomingo NWR	Okla.	24 Jan. 1946	16,464
Togiak NWR	Alaska	2 Dec. 1980	4,098,741
Tomahawk	N.Dak.	3 Feb. 1941	440
Toppenish NWR	Wash.	27 Apr. 1964	1,979
Trempealeau NWR	Wis.	18 Feb. 1935	6,199
Trinity River NWR	Tex.	4 Jan. 1994	12,920
Trustom Pond NWR	R.I.	15 Aug. 1974	777
Tualatin River NWR	Oreg.	31 Dec. 1992	1,198
Tule Lake NWR	Calif.	4 Oct. 1928	39,117
Turnbull NWR	Wash.	15 Sept. 1936	17,812
Two Ponds NWR	Colo.	26 May 1992	72
Two Rivers NWR	Ill., Mo.	2 July 1947	8,265
Tybee NWR	S.C.	9 May 1938	100
Ul Bend NWR	Mont.	30 Oct. 1967	56,050
Umatilla NWR	Oreg., Wash.	3 July 1969	23,781
Union Slough NWR	Iowa	20 Feb. 1937	2,916
Upper Klamath NWR	Oreg.	3 Apr. 1928	14,966
Upper Mississippi River National Wildlife and Fish Refuge	Ill., Iowa, Minn., Wis.	7 Aug. 1925	197,496
Upper Ouachita NWR	La.	9 Nov. 1978	45,861
Upper Souris NWR	N.Dak.	27 Aug. 1935	32,302
Valentine NWR	Nebr.	14 Aug. 1935	73,038
Vieques NWR	P.R.	1 May 2001	3,100
Waccamaw NWR	S.C.	1 Dec. 1997	7,369
Wallkill River NWR	N.J., N.Y.	16 Feb. 1992	4,817
Wallops Island NWR	Va.	11 Mar. 1971	3,373
Wapack NWR	N.H.	17 May 1972	1,672
Wapanocca NWR	Ark.	1 Feb. 1961	5,484
War Horse NWR	Mont.	6 Nov. 1958	3,192
Washita NWR	Okla.	15 Apr. 1961	8,075
Wassaw NWR	Ga.	20 Oct. 1969	10,070

Watercress Darter NWR	Ala.	1 Oct. 1980	25
Waubay NWR	S.Dak.	19 Apr. 1935	4,740
Wertheim NWR	N.Y.	7 June 1947	2,569
West Sister Island NWR	Ohio	2 Aug. 1938	80
Wheeler NWR	Ala.	7 July 1938	34,431
White Lake NWR	N.Dak.	3 Feb. 1941	1,040
White River NWR	Ark.	4 Sept. 1935	158,415
Whittlesey Creek NWR	Wis.	30 Sept. 1999	118
Wichita Mountains Wildlife Refuge	Okla.	2 June 1905	59,020
Wild Rice Lake NWR	N.Dak.	20 Sept. 1936	779
Willapa NWR	Wash.	14 Oct. 1936	15,514
William L. Finley NWR	Oreg.	17 June 1964	5,673
Willow Creek–Lurline Wildlife Management Area	Calif.	7 Aug. 1985	5,468
Willow Lake NWR	N.Dak.	3 Feb. 1941	2,620
Wintering River NWR	N.Dak.	3 Feb. 1941	239
Wolf Island NWR	Ga.	3 Apr. 1930	5,126
Wood Lake NWR	N.Dak.	20 Apr. 1936	280
Yazoo NWR	Miss.	7 Dec. 1936	13,023
Yukon Delta NWR	Alaska	2 Dec. 1980	19,166,094
Yukon Flats NWR	Alaska	2 Dec. 1980	8,630,400

APPENDIX D

Acronyms and Abbreviations

aff'd	affirmed
ANCSA	Alaska Native Claims Settlement Act
ANILCA	Alaska National Interest Lands Conservation Act
APA	Administrative Procedure Act
art.	article
BLM	Bureau of Land Management
BNA	Bureau of National Affairs
BRD	Biological Resources Division
CCP	comprehensive conservation plan
c.e.	common era
cert.	certiorari
C.F.R.	Code of Federal Regulations
ch.	chapter
Cir.	circuit
CIRI	Cook Inlet Region, Inc.
CMP	conceptual management plan
Comm'n	commission
Cong.	Congress
Cong. Rec.	Congressional Record
Ct. Cl.	Court of Claims
CWA	Clean Water Act
EA	environmental assessment
EIS	environmental impact statement
Env.	environment
EPA	Environmental Protection Agency
ESA	Endangered Species Act
FACA	Federal Advisory Committee Act
Fed. Reg.	Federal Register
FEIS	final environmental impact statement
FLPMA	Federal Land Policy and Management Act
FSA	Farm Service Agency
FW	United States Fish and Wildlife Service Manual
FWCA	Fish and Wildlife Coordination Act
FWS	United States Fish and Wildlife Service

FY	fiscal year
GAO	United States General Accounting Office
GPRA	Government Performance and Results Act
KIC	Kaktovik Inupiat Corporation
LPP	land protection plan
MBCA	Migratory Bird Conservation Act
NBS	National Biological Survey
NEPA	National Environmental Policy Act
NFMA	National Forest Management Act
NPS	National Park Service
NSO	no surface occupancy
NWR	national wildlife refuge
NWRS	National Wildlife Refuge System
NWRSAA	National Wildlife Refuge System Administration Act
OTA	Office of Technology Assessment
PLLRC	Public Land Law Review Commission
Pub. L. No.	public law number
RCRA	Resource Conservation and Recovery Act
RPA	Forest and Rangeland Renewable Resources Planning Act (the "Resources Planning Act")
SDMP	step-down management plan
Stat.	Statutes at Large
UNESCO	United Nations Educational, Scientific and Cultural Organization
U.S.	United States
U.S.C.	United States Code
U.S. Const.	United States Constitution
USFWS	United States Fish and Wildlife Service
WMA	wildlife management area
WPA	waterfowl production area

REFERENCES

Adams, J. 2002. "Controversy on Alaska's Coastal Plain," *National Wetlands Newsletter* (Jan./Feb.) 24:1, 15–17.

Albright, H. M., and R. Cahn. 1985. *The Birth of the National Park Service.* Salt Lake City: Howe Bros.

Albright, H. M., and M. A. Shenck. 1999. *Creating the National Park Service.* Norman: University of Oklahoma Press.

Aman, A. C., Jr., and W. T. Mayton. 2001. *Administrative Law.* 2d ed. St. Paul, Minn.: West.

Arizona v. California, 373 U.S. 546 (1963).

Ashmore, A. R. 1981. *Presidential Proclamations Concerning Public Lands, January 24, 1791–March 19, 1936.* Washington, D.C.: Library of Congress.

Babbitt v. Sweet Home Chapter of Communities for a Great Oregon, 515 U.S. 687 (1995).

Baldwin, P. 2002. *Legal Issues Related to Proposed Drilling for Oil and Gas in the Arctic National Wildlife Refuge.* Report for Congress (RL31115). Washington, D.C.: Congressional Research Service, Library of Congress.

Bean, M. J., and M. J. Rowland. 1997. *The Evolution of National Wildlife Law.* 3d ed. Westport, Conn.: Praeger.

Berman, D. 2002. "Mellon Donation Adds 34K Acres to Alaska Refuge," *Land Letter,* 10 October, 9.

Black's Law Dictionary. 1910. St. Paul, Minn.: West.

Blumm, M. C. 2002. "Reversing the Winters Doctrine? Denying Reserved Water Rights for Idaho Wilderness and Its Implications," *University of Colorado Law Review* 73:173–226.

Bobertz, B., and R. L. Fischman. 1993. "Administrative Appeal Reform: The Case of the Forest Service," *University of Colorado Law Review* 64:371–456.

Caire v. Fulton, No. 84-3184 (W.D. La. Feb 10, 1986).

California Coastal Comm'n v. Granite Rock Co., 480 U.S. 572 (1987).

Campbell, F. 1988. "Legal Protection of Plants in the United States," *Pace Environmental Law Review* 6:1–22.

Cappaert v. United States, 426 U.S. 128 (1976).

Cheever, F. 1999. "Four Failed Forest Standards: What We Can Learn from the History of the National Forest Management Act's Sustainable Timber Management Provisions," *Oregon Law Review* 77:601–706.

Citizens to Preserve Overton Park v. Volpe, 401 U.S. 402 (1971).

Clark, T. W. 2000. "Wildlife Resources: The Elk of Jackson Hole, Wyoming." In *Developing Sustainable Management Policy for the National Elk Refuge, Wyoming.* Yale Sch. of Forestry and Envtl. Stud. Bull. Series No. 104. New Haven: Yale University.

Clark, T. W., and G. D. Brewer. 2000. "Introduction." In *Developing Sustainable Management Policy for the National Elk Refuge, Wyoming*. Yale Sch. of Forestry and Envtl. Stud. Bull. Series No. 104. New Haven: Yale University.

Clarke, J. N., and D. C. McCool. 1996. *Staking Out the Terrain*. Albany: State University of New York Press.

Clarren, R. 2001. "An Agency in Need of Refuge?" *High Country News*, 26 February, 5.

Clawson, M., and B. Held. 1957. *The Federal Lands*. Lincoln: University of Nebraska Press.

Clinton, W. J. 1997. "Statement by President William J. Clinton Upon Signing H.R. 1420," *Weekly Compilation of Presidential Documents* 33:1535.

Coggins, G. C., and R. L. Glicksman. 2002. *Public Natural Resources Law*. St. Paul, Minn.: West.

Congressional Research Service. 2002. *Appropriations for FY2003: Interior and Related Agencies*. Washington, D.C.: Congressional Research Service.

Corbisier, R. W. 2002. "The Arctic National Wildlife Refuge, Correlative Rights, and Sourdough: Not Just for Bread Anymore," *Alaska Law Review* 19:393–430.

Corn, L. M., B. A. Gelb, and P. Baldwin. 2002. *Arctic National Wildlife Refuge*. Issue Brief for Congress (IB10094). Washington, D.C.: Congressional Research Service, Library of Congress.

Covell, C. F. 1998. "A Survey of State Instream Flow Programs in the Western United States," *Water Law Review* 1:177–205.

Criss, A. 1999. "Refuges at Risk," *National Wetlands Newsletter* (July/Aug.) 21:1, 12–17.

Cutright, P. R. 1985. *Theodore Roosevelt, the Making of a Conservationist*. Urbana: University of Illinois Press.

Daily, G. C., ed. 1997. *Nature's Services*. Washington, D.C.: Island Press.

Dana, S. T. 1956. *Forest and Rangeland Policy, Its Development in the United States*. New York: McGraw-Hill.

Davies, J. C., and J. Mazurek. 1998. *Pollution Control in the United States*. Washington, D.C.: Resources for the Future.

Decisions Relating to the Public Lands. June 17, 1890. "Opinion of Assistant Attorney General Shields to Secretary of the Interior," 426–429.

Defenders of Wildlife v. Andrus, 11 Env't Rep. Cas. (Bureau of National Affairs) 2098 (D.D.C. 1978); 455 F. Supp. 446 (D.D.C. 1978).

Denver University Law Review. 1997. Symposium. "The National Park System." 74: 567–874.

Dilsaver, L. M. 1994. *America's National Park System*. Lanham, Md.: Rowman & Littlefield.

Donahue, D. L. 1999. *The Western Range Revisited*. Norman: University of Oklahoma Press.

Doremus, H. 2001. "Adaptive Management, the Endangered Species Act, and the Institutional Challenges of 'New Age' Environmental Protection," *Washburn Law Journal* 41:50–89.

Dower, R. C., D. Ditz, and P. Faeth. 1997. *Frontiers of Sustainability*. Washington, D.C.: Island Press.

Eckl, E. 1999. "New Policies Revolutionize Refuges: Relationship with the Public," *Fish and Wildlife News* (Nov./Dec.):3.

Environmental Law. 1992. Symposium. "Integrated Pollution Control." 22:1–348.

Fairfax, S. K. 2000. "State Trust Lands Management." In *A Vision for the U.S. Forest Service,* ed. R. A. Sedjo. Washington, D.C.: Resources for the Future.

Farber, D. A. 1999. *Eco Pragmatism.* Chicago: University of Chicago Press.

Fink, R. J. 1994. "The National Wildlife Refuges: Theory, Practice, and Prospect," *Harvard Environmental Law Review* 18:1–135.

Firestone, D. 2003. "Republicans Resigning Themselves to Defeat on Drilling Plan for Alaska Wildlife Refuge," *New York Times,* 18 March, A24.

Fischman, R. L. 1992. "Endangered Species Conservation: What Should We Expect of Federal Agencies?" *Public Land Law Review* 13:1–23.

———. 1997. "The Problem of Statutory Detail in National Park Establishment Legislation and Its Relationship to Pollution Control Law," *Denver University Law Review* 74:779–814.

———. 2001. "The EPA's NEPA Duties and Ecosystem Services," *Stanford Environmental Law Journal* 20:497–536.

———. 2002. "The National Wildlife Refuge System and the Hallmarks of Modern Organic Legislation," *Ecology Law Quarterly* 29:457–622.

Fischman, R. L., and J. Hall-Rivera. 2002. "A Lesson for Conservation from Pollution Control Law: Cooperative Federalism for Recovery under the Endangered Species Act," *Columbia Journal of Environmental Law* 27:45–172.

Fischman, R. L., and V. J. Meretsky. 2001. "Endangered Species Information: Access and Control," *Washburn Law Journal* 41:90–113.

Fischman, R. L., and M. S. Squillace. 2000. *Environmental Decisionmaking.* 3d ed. Cincinnati, Ohio: Anderson.

Franklin, J. 1989. "Toward a New Forestry," *American Forests* (Nov./Dec.) 95:37–44.

Friends of Animals v. Hodel, 1988 WL 236545 (D.D.C. 1988).

Friends of the Earth v. Laidlaw, 528 U.S. 167 (2000).

Fund for Animals v. Clark, 27 F. Supp. 2d 8 (D.D.C. 1998).

Gates, P. W. 1978. *History of Public Land Law Development.* Washington, D.C.: U.S. Government Printing Office, 1968. Reprint, Washington, D.C.: Zenger.

Gergely, K., J. M. Scott, and D. Goble. 2000. "A New Direction for the U.S. National Wildlife Refuges: The National Wildlife Refuge System Improvement Act of 1997," *Natural Areas Journal* 20:107–118.

Getches, D. 1982. "Managing the Public Lands: The Authority of the Executive to Withdraw Lands," *Natural Resources Journal* 22:279–335.

———. 2001. "The Metamorphosis of Western Water Policy: Have Federal Laws and Local Decisions Eclipsed the States' Roles?" *Stanford Environmental Law Journal* 20:3–72.

Gillis, A. M. 1990. "The New Forestry: An Ecosystem Approach to Land Management," *Bioscience* 40:558–562.

Grumbine, R. E. 1997. "Reflections on 'What Is Ecosystem Management?'" *Conservation Biology* 11:41–47.

Halverson A. 2000. "The National Elk Refuge and the Jackson Hole Elk Herd: Management Appraisal and Recommendations." In *Developing Sustainable Management Policy for the National Elk Refuge, Wyoming.* Yale Sch. of Forestry and Envtl. Stud. Bull. Series No. 104. New Haven: Yale University.

Haycox, S. 2002. *Frigid Embrace: Politics, Economics, and Environment in Alaska.* Corvallis: Oregon State University Press.

Hays, S. P. 1959. *Conservation and the Gospel of Efficiency.* Cambridge: Harvard University Press.

Heinzerling, L. 1999. "Discounting Life," *Yale Law Journal* 108:1,911–1,915.

Henry, N. 2002. "Dry Year May Mean Less Water Than Ever for Refuges," *Land Letter,* 17 April, 10:9.

Hohovek, S. H. 2000. "Refuge Inside Arctic Circle Is Also in the Middle of U.S. Energy Debate," *New York Times,* 8 October, A14.

Houck, O. 1994. "Of BATs, Birds, B-A-T: The Convergent Evolution of Environmental Law," *Mississippi Law Journal* 63:403–471.

Huffman, J. L. 1978. "A History of Forest Policy in the United States," *Environmental Law* 8:239–280.

———. 1986. "Trusting the Public Interest to Judges: A Comment on the Public Trust Writings of Professors Sax, Wilkinson, Dunning and Johnson," *Denver University Law Review* 63:565–585.

———. 1989. "A Fish Out of Water: The Public Trust Doctrine in a Constitutional Democracy," *Environmental Law* 19:527–572.

Humane Society v. Hodel, 840 F.2d 45 (D.C. Cir. 1988).

In re: Water Right Claim No. 1927-2, 524 N.W.2d 855 (S.D. 1994).

Ise, J. 1920. *The United States Forest Policy.* New Haven: Yale University Press.

———. 1979. *Our National Park Policy.* Baltimore: Johns Hopkins University Press, 1961. Reprint, New York: Arno.

Karkkainen, B. C. 1997. "Biodiversity and Land," *Cornell Law Review* 83:1–104.

Kaufman, H. 1960. *The Forest Ranger.* Baltimore: Johns Hopkins University Press.

Keiter, R. B. 1985. "On Protecting the National Parks from the External Threats Dilemma," *Land and Water Law Review* 20:355–420.

———. 1994. "Beyond the Boundary Line: Constructing a Law of Ecosystem Management," *University of Colorado Law Review* 65:293–333.

Klamath Forest Alliance v. Babbitt, CIV S-97-2274 GEB GGH (Order Dec. 24, 1998).

Kleppe v. New Mexico, 426 U.S. 529 (1976).

Knapp, D. 1997. "The Relationship between Environmental Interpretation and Environmental Education," *Legacy: Magazine of the National Association of Interpretation* 8(3):10–13.

Laitos, J. G., and T. A. Carr. 1999. "The Transformation on Public Lands," *Ecology Law Quarterly* 26:140–242.

Larsen, A. 1975. "National Game Ranges: The Orphans of the National Wildlife Refuge System," *Environmental Law* 6:515–541.

Lazarus, R. J. 1986. "Changing Conceptions of Property and Sovereignty in Natural Resources: Questioning the Public Trust Doctrine," *Iowa Law Review* 71:631–716.

Leopold, A. S., S. A. Cain, C. M. Cottam, I. N. Gabrielson, and T. L. Kimball. 1963. *Wildlife Management in the National Parks.* Washington, D.C.: U.S. Department of the Interior, National Park Service.

Leopold, A. S., C. Cottam, I. Cowan, I. N. Gabrielson, and T. L. Kimball. 1968. "The National Wildlife Refuge System, Report of the Advisory Committee on Wildlife Management." In *Final Environmental Statement, Operation of the National Wildlife Refuge System.* Washington, D.C.: U.S. Department of the Interior, U.S. Fish and Wildlife Service: W-1.

Leshy, J. D. 1987. *The Mining Law.* Washington, D.C.: Resources for the Future.

Loomis, J. B. 1993. *Integrated Public Lands Management*. New York: Columbia University Press.

Louter, D. 1998. *Contested Terrain*. Seattle: U.S. Department of the Interior, National Park Service.

Lujan v. Defenders of Wildlife, 504 U.S. 555 (1992).

Maley, T. S. 1996. *Mineral Law*. 6th ed. Boise: Mineral Lands Publications.

Matson, N. P. 2000. "Biodiversity and Its Management on the National Elk Refuge, Wyoming." In *Developing Sustainable Management Policy for the National Elk Refuge, Wyoming*. Yale Sch. of Forestry and Envtl. Stud. Bull. Series No. 104. New Haven: Yale University.

McCloskey, J. M. 1961. "The Multiple Use–Sustained Yield Act of 1960," *Oregon Law Review* 41:49–78.

———. 1966. "The Wilderness Act of 1964: Its Background and Meaning," *Oregon Law Review* 45:288–321.

McDowell v. Alaska, 785 P.2d 1 (Alaska 1989).

McGrail and Rowley v. Babbitt, 986 F. Supp. 1386 (S.D. Fla. 1997).

Meier, B. 1991. "Refuges Feel Strain as Wildlife and Commerce Collide," *New York Times*, 1 December, 38.

Morris, E. 2001. *Theodore Rex*. New York: Random House.

Mullin, E. D. 2000. *The Art of Commenting*. Washington, D.C.: Environmental Law Institute.

National Academy of Public Administration (NAPA). 1995. *Setting Priorities, Getting Results*. Report to Congress. Washington, D.C.: National Academy of Public Administration.

National Audubon Society. (undated a). "Refuges in Crisis." Available at: http://www.audubon.org/campaign/refuge_report/index.html. [last accessed June 16, 2003]

———. (undated b). "America's Hidden Lands: A Proposal to Discover Our National Wildlife Refuge System." Available at: http://www.audubon.org/campaign/refuge_report/index.html. [last accessed June 16, 2003]

National Audubon Society v. Davis, 307 F.3d 835 (9th Cir. 2002).

National Audubon Society v. Hodel, 606 F. Supp. 825 (D. Alaska 1984).

National Research Council. 1995. *Science and the Endangered Species Act*. Washington, D.C.: National Academy Press.

———. 2003. *Cumulative Environmental Effects of Oil and Gas Activities on Alaska's North Slope*. Washington, D.C.: National Academy Press.

Natural Resources Journal. 1967. Symposium. "Administration of Public Lands." 7:149–265.

North Dakota v. United States, 460 U.S. 300 (1983).

Noss, R. F. 1994. "Some Principles of *Conservation Biology* as They Apply to Environmental Law," *Chicago-Kent Law Review* 69:893–909.

Noss, R. F., and A. Y. Cooperrider. 1994. *Saving Nature's Legacy*. Washington, D.C.: Island Press.

Noss, R. F., M. A. O'Connell, and D. D. Murphy. 1997. *The Science of Conservation Planning*. Washington, D.C.: Island Press.

Office of Technology Assessment. 1987. *Technologies to Maintain Biological Diversity*. Washington, D.C.: U.S. Congress.

Ohio Forestry Association v. Sierra Club, 523 U.S. 726 (1998).

Oklahoma v. Texas, 258 U.S. 574 (1922).

Olinger, T. M. 1998. "Comment, Public Rangeland Reform: New Prospects for Collaboration and Local Control Using the Resource Advisory Councils," *University of Colorado Law Review* 69:633–692.

Olsen, D. 1989. "Human Activity Is Found to Harm Wildlife Areas," *New York Times,* 13 September, A21.

Oregon Natural Resources Council v. U.S. Forest Service, 59 F. Supp. 2d 1,085 (W.D. Wash. 1999).

Parfit, D. 1976. "On Doing the Best for Our Children." In *Ethics and Population,* ed. Michael D. Bayles. Cambridge: Schenkman.

Pathfinder Mines v. Hodel, 811 F.2d 1,288 (9th Cir. 1987.).

Peterson, R. M. 2000. "Discussion: Does the Forest Service Have a Future?" In *A Vision for the U.S. Forest Service,* ed. Roger A. Sedjo. Washington, D.C.: Resources for the Future.

Pinchot, Gifford. 1972. *Breaking New Ground.* New York: Harcourt, Brace, 1947. Reprint, Seattle: University of Washington Press.

Popper, F. 1988. "A Nest Egg Approach to the Public Lands." In *Managing Public Lands in the Public Interest,* ed. Benjamin C. Dysart and Marion Clawson. New York: Praeger, p. 81.

Potlatch Corp. v. United States, 12 P.3d 1,260 (Idaho 2000).

Public Employees for Environmental Responsibility. 1999. *Survey of Refuge Managers of the National Wildlife Refuge System.* Available at: http://www.peer.org /refuge/survey.html. [last accessed June 16, 2003]

Public Land Law Review Commission (PLLRC). 1968. *Digest of Public Land Laws.* Washington, D.C.: U.S. Government Printing Office.

———. 1970. *One Third of the Nation's Land.* Washington, D.C.: U.S. Government Printing Office.

Public Land News. 2000. "DOI Cool to Complaints about Refuge Management," *Public Land News* 25(2), 21 January.

Rasband, J. R. 2001. "Moving Forward: The Future of the Antiquities Act," *Journal of Land Resources and Environmental Law* 21:619–634.

Redford, K. H., and B. D. Richter. 1999. "Conservation of Biodiversity in a World of Use," *Conservation Biology* 13:1,246–1,256.

Reed, N. P., and D. Drabelle. 1984. *The United States Fish and Wildlife Service.* Boulder: Westview Press.

Rodgers, W., Jr. 1993. "Where Environmental Law and Biology Meet: Of Pandas. Thumbs, Statutory Sleepers, and Effective Law," *University of Colorado Law Review* 65:25–75.

Rosen, J. 2001. "The Ghost Bird," *New Yorker,* 14 May, 61–67.

Ross, K. 2000. *Environmental Conflict in Alaska.* Boulder: University Press of Colorado.

Ruhl, J. B. 1995. "Section 7(a)(1) of the 'New' Endangered Species Act: Rediscovering and Redefining the Untapped Power of Federal Agencies' Duty to Conserve Species," *Environmental Law* 25:1,107–1,163.

Runte, A. 1987. *National Parks.* 2d ed. Lincoln: University of Nebraska Press.

Safire, W. 2001. "On Language: Fulminations," *New York Times Magazine,* 6 May, 22.

Sagoff, M. 1988. *The Economy of the Earth.* Cambridge [England]; New York: Cambridge University Press.

Samson, F. B., and F. L. Knopf. 2001. "Archaic Agencies, Muddled Missions, and Conservation in the 21st Century," *Bioscience* 51:869–873.

Sax, J. L. 1993. "Property Rights and the Economy of Nature: Understanding *Lucas v. South Carolina Coastal Council,*" *Stanford Law Review* 45:1,433–1,455.

Sax, J. L., and R. B. Keiter. 1987. "Glacier National Park and Its Neighbors: A Study of Federal Inter-agency Cooperation," *Ecology Law Quarterly* 14:207–263.

Schwenke v. Secretary of the Interior, 720 F.2d 571 (9th Cir. 1983).

Seattle Audubon Society v. Moseley, 798 F. Supp. 1473 (W.D. Wash. 1992), aff'd *Seattle Audubon Society v. Espy,* 998 F.2d 699 (9th Cir. 1993).

Sierra Club v. Department of the Interior, 376 F. Supp. 90 (N.D. Cal. 1974).

Sierra Club v. Department of the Interior, 398 F. Supp. 284 (N.D. Cal. 1975), *modified* 424 F. Supp. 172 (N.D. Cal. 1976).

Sierra Club v. Glickman, 156 F.3d 606 (5th Cir. 1998).

Sierra Club v. Hickel, 433 F.2d 24 (9th Cir. 1970), aff'd as *Sierra Club v. Morton,* 405 U.S. 727 (1970).

Sierra Club v. Lujan, 36 Env't. Rep. Cas. (Bureau of National Affairs) 1533 (W.D. Tex. 1993), *appeal dismissed,* 995 F.2d 571 (5th Cir. 1993).

Sierra Club v. Marita, 46 F.3d 606 (7th Cir. 1995).

Sierra Club v. Martin, 168 F.3d 1 (11th Cir. 1999).

Sierra Club v. U.S. Forest Service, 259 F.3d 1,281 (10th Cir. 2001).

Simon, D. J., ed. 1988. *Our Common Lands.* Washington, D.C.: Island Press.

Smith, D. H. 1930. *The Forest Service.* Washington, D.C.: Brookings Institution.

Southern Utah Wilderness Alliance v. Dabney, 222 F.3d 819 (10th Cir. 2000).

Squillace, M. 2003. "The Monumental Legacy of the Antiquities Act of 1906," *Georgia Law Review* 37:473–610.

Stephens, R. 2002. "Innovation Is Needed but It's Performance That Counts," *Environmental Forum* (Mar./Apr.):24.

Stewart, R. B. 1975. "The Reformation of American Administrative Law," *Harvard Law Review* 88:1,669–1,813.

Strickland v. Morton, 519 F.2d 467 (9th Cir. 1975).

Sussman, R. 1996. "An 'Integrating' Statute," *Environmental Forum* (Mar./Apr.): 16–25.

Tarlock, A. D. 2002. *Law of Water Rights and Resources.* St. Paul, Minn.: West.

Thomas, J. W. 1995. "Making Forests Work Better," *American Forests* (Mar.–Apr.) 101:7.

Tredennick, C. 2000. "The National Wildlife System Improvement Act of 1997: Defining the National Wildlife Refuge System for the Twenty-first Century," *Fordham Environmental Law Journal* 12:41–109.

Udall v. Tallman, 380 U.S. 1 (1965).

United States v. Alaska, 521 U.S. 1 (1997).

United States v. Grimaud, 220 U.S. 506 (1911).

United States v. Mead Corp., 533 U.S. 218 (2001).

United States v. Midwest Oil, 236 U.S. 459 (1915).

United States v. New Mexico, 438 U.S. 696 (1978).

United States v. Perko, 108 F. Supp. 315 (D. Minn. 1952), *aff'd* 204 F.2d 446 (8th Cir. 1953), *cert. denied* 346 U.S. 832 (1953).

United States v. State of Idaho, 23 P.3d 117 (Idaho 2001).

U.S. Attorney General. 1941. "Authority to Protect Oil Deposits against Drainage," *Opinions of Atty. Gen.* 40:41.

————. 1964 "Rights-of-Way across National Forests," *Opinions of Atty. Gen.* 40:127.

U.S. Department of the Interior. 1987. *Arctic National Wildlife Refuge, Alaska: Coastal Plain Resource Assessment.* Report and Recommendation to the Congress of the United States and Final Legislative Environmental Impact Statement.

————. 2002. *Fiscal Year 2003 Interior Budget in Brief.*

U.S. Department of Justice. Office of Legal Counsel. 1982. "Federal Non-reserved Water Rights." *Opinions of the Off. Legal Counsel* 6:328.

U.S. Fish and Wildlife Service (FWS). 1959. *Annual Report of Lands under Control of the U.S. Fish and Wildlife Service as of June 30, 1959.*

————. 1976. *Operation of the National Wildlife Refuge System: Final Environmental Impact Statement.*

————. 1983. *Report on Resource Problems on National Wildlife Refuges, National Fish Hatcheries, Research Centers.*

————. 1992. *Upper Ouachita National Wildlife Refuge Contaminants Study* (Conzelmann & Schultz).

————. 1999. *Director's Order No. 110.*

————. 2000a. *Annual Performance Plan FY 2001/Annual Performance Report FY 1999.*

————. 2000b. *Refuge Compatibility: How to Prepare a Compatibility Determination* (training guidance).

————. 2000–2005. *Strategic Plan FY 2000–2005.*

————. 2001a. *A How-to Handbook to Support the National Wildlife Refuge System's Centennial.*

————. 2001b. *Director's Order No. 132.*

————. 2002a. *Annual Report of Lands under Control of the U.S. Fish and Wildlife Service as of September 30, 2002.*

————. 2002b. *Waterfowl Production Areas.*

————. 2002c. *Director's Order No. 148.*

————. 2002d. Div. of Envtl. Contaminants. *Consumption Advisory Details—Wildlife.*

————. 2002e. *An Ecosystem Approach to Fish and Wildlife Conservation.*

————. 2002f. *Official Arctic National Wildlife Refuge Site.* Updated 30 August. Available at: http://www.r7.fws.gov/nwr/arctic/index.html. [last accessed 16 June 2003].

————. (undated). *Manual.* Continually updated at: http://policy.fws.gov/series.html.

U.S. General Accounting Office (GAO). 1981. *National Direction Required for Effective Management of America's Fish and Wildlife.* CED-81-107.

————. 1984. *Economic Uses of the National Wildlife Refuge System: Unlikely to Increase Significantly.* RCED-84-108.

————. 1989. *National Wildlife Refuges: Continuing Problems with Incompatible Uses Call for Bold Action.* RCED-89.196.

————. 1994. *National Wildlife Refuge System: Contributions Being Made to Endangered Species Recovery.* RCED-95-7.

————. 2000. *Fish and Wildlife Service: Agency Needs to Inform Congress of Future Costs Associated with Land Acquisitions.* RCED-00-52.

————. 2001. *U.S. Fish and Wildlife Service: Information on Oil and Gas Activities in the National Wildlife Refuge System.* GAO-02-64R.

U.S. House. 1953. House Committee on Agriculture. *Re: Conservation.* 83rd Cong. 7 May.

———. 1961. Subcommittee on Fisheries and Wildlife Conservation of the Committee on Merchant Marine and Fisheries. *Hearings on H.R. 1171.* 87th Cong. 1st sess. *Statement of Daniel Janzen, Director, Bureau of Sport Fisheries and Wildlife.*

———. 1975. Subcommittee on Fisheries and Wildlife Conservation and the Environment of the House Committee on Merchant Marine and Fisheries. *Hearings on H.R. 2329, Wildlife Refuges and Organic Act.* 94th Cong. 1st sess.

———. 1989. Environment, Energy and Natural Resources Subcommittee of the Committee on Government Operations and the Subcommittee on Fisheries and Wildlife Conservation and the Environment of the Committee on Merchant Marine and Fisheries. *Joint Hearing on the Review of the Management of the National Wildlife Refuge System.* 101st Cong. 1st sess. 12 September.

———. 1992. H.R. 2881 (Studds). 102d Cong.

———. 1993. H.R. 833 (Gibbons). 103d Cong.

———. 1995a. H.R. 1675 (Young). 104th Cong.

———. 1995b. H.R. 2491 (Kasich). 104th Cong.

———. 1996. Subcommittee on Fisheries, Wildlife, and Oceans of the Committee on Resources. *Hearing on Operation and Maintenance Backlog in the National Wildlife Refuge System.* 104th Cong. 2d sess. 19 September.

———. 1997a. *Report on the National Wildlife Refuge System Improvement Act of 1997.* Rep. No. 105-106. 105th Cong. 1st sess.

———. 1997b. *National Wildlife Refuge System Volunteer and Community Partnership Act of 1997.* Rep. No. 105-329. 105th Cong. 1st sess.

———. 1997c. H.R. 511 (Young). 105th Cong.

———. 1997d. H.R. 1420 (Young). 105th Cong.

———. 1997e. Subcommittee on Fisheries, Wildlife, and Oceans of the Committee on Resources, *Hearing on H.R. 511 and H.R. 512.* 105th Cong. 1st sess. 6 March.

———. 2001. Committee on Resources. *Oversight Field Hearing: Water Management and Endangered Species Issues in the Klamath Basin.* 107th Cong. 1st sess. 6 June. Statement of Sue Ellen Woolridge, Deputy Chief of Staff, Dept. of the Interior.

U.S. National Park Service (NPS). 1998. *Director's Order #2: Park Planning.*

———. 2001. *Management Policies.*

U.S. Senate. 1958. *Fish and Wildlife Conservation and Water-Resource Developments—Coordination.* Rep. No. 1981. 85th Cong. 2d sess.

———. 1962. *Fish and Wildlife Conservation Areas.* Rep. No. 1858. 87th Cong. 2d sess.

———. 1966. *Fish and Wildlife—Conservation.* Rep. No. 1463. 89th Cong. 2d sess. Reprinted in 1966 *U.S. Code Congressional and Administrative News* 3342, 3355.

———. 1975. Subcommittee on Environment of the Senate Committee on Commerce, Science, and Transportation. *National Wildlife Refuge System.* 94th Cong. 1st sess.

———. 1992a. Subcommittee on Environmental Protection of the Committee on Environment and Public Works. *Hearing on S. 1862.* Hrg. 102-595. 102d Cong. 2d sess. 19 June. *Statement of William C. Reffalt, The Wilderness Society.*

———. 1992b. S. 1862 (Graham). 102d Cong.

———. 1993. S. 823 (Graham). 103d Cong.

———. 1994. *Report on the National Wildlife Refuge System Management and Policy Act of 1994.* Rep. No. 103-324. 103d Cong. 2d sess.

———. 1997. Committee on Environment and Public Works, *Hearing on 1059.* Hrg. 105-286. 105th Cong. 1st sess. 30 July.

Utah Environmental Congress v. Zieroth, 190 F. Supp. 2d 1,265 (D. Utah 2002).

Wagner, F. H. 1999. "Whatever Happened to the National Biological Survey?" *Bioscience* 49:219–222.

Walsh, J. F. 1985. "Settling the Alaska Native Claims Settlement Act," *Stanford Law Review* 38:227–263.

Western Water Policy Review Advisory Commission. 1998. *Water in the West: Challenge for the Next Century.* Report of the Western Water Policy Review Advisory Commission. Washington, D.C.: U.S. Bureau of Reclamation (CD-ROM).

Wilcove, D. S. 1999. *The Condor's Shadow.* New York: W. H. Freeman.

Wilkinson, C. 1996. "Clinton Learns the Art of Audacity," *High Country News,* 30 September. http://www.hcn.org/servlets/hcn.article?article_id=2799.

Williams, M. E., and J. Z. Cannon. 1991. "Rethinking the Resource Conservation and Recovery Act," *Environmental Law Reporter* (Envtl. Law Inst.) 21:10,063–10,075.

Wilson, E. O., ed. 1988. *Biodiversity.* Washington, D.C.: National Academy Press.

Wilson, J. Q. 1989. *Bureaucracy.* New York: Basic Books.

Words and Phrases. 1972. "Organic." Permanent ed. Vol. 30, 477. St. Paul, Minn.: West.

World Commission on Environment and Development. 1987. *Our Common Future.* Oxford: Oxford University Press.

Worster, D. 1994. *Nature's Economy: A History of Ecological Ideas.* 2d ed. Cambridge [England]; New York: Cambridge University Press.

Yaffee, S. L. 1982. *Prohibitive Policy.* Cambridge: MIT Press.

———. 1999. "Three Faces of Ecosystem Management," *Conservation Biology* 13: 713–725.

About the Author

Robert L. Fischman is professor of law and Louis F. Niezer Faculty Fellow at Indiana University School of Law–Bloomington. He has published widely on issues related to public land management, endangered species recovery, biological diversity protection, environmental impact analysis, and sustainable forestry. He holds an A.B. degree from Princeton University, and M.S. and J.D. degrees from the University of Michigan. Before entering teaching in 1991, he served as director of the Natural Resources Program at the Environmental Law Institute.

INDEX